The Romantic Tradition in American Literature

The Romantic Tradition in American Literature

Advisory Editor

HAROLD BLOOM
Professor of English, Yale University

THE

POETICAL WORKS

OF

JOHN TOWNSEND TROWBRIDGE

ARNO PRESS

A NEW YORK TIMES COMPANY
New York • 1972

Reprint Edition 1972 by Arno Press Inc.

Reprinted from a copy in The Newark Public Library

The Romantic Traditions in American Literature
ISBN for complete set: 0-405-04620-0
See last pages of this volume for titles.

Manufactured in the United States of America

ช∙ෑ೨ೞ∙ෑ೨ೞ∙ෑ೨ೞ∙ෑ೨ೞ∙ෑ೨ೞ∙ෑ೨ೞ

Library of Congress Cataloging in Publication Data

Trowbridge, John Townsend, 1827-1916.
    The poetical works of John Townsend Trowbridge.

    (The Romantic tradition in American literature)
    I. Series.
PS3095.A2 1972   811'.4   72-4978
ISBN 0-405-04647-2

THE POETICAL WORKS OF
JOHN TOWNSEND TROWBRIDGE

John Townsend Trowbridge

THE

POETICAL WORKS

OF

JOHN TOWNSEND TROWBRIDGE

BOSTON AND NEW YORK
HOUGHTON, MIFFLIN AND COMPANY
The Riverside Press, Cambridge
MDCCCCIII

CONTENTS

BOOK I

BOOK III

THE BOOK OF GOLD AND OTHER POEMS.

BOOK IV

A HOME IDYL AND OTHER POEMS.

BOOK V

CONTENTS

BOOK I

THE VAGABONDS AND OTHER POEMS

Seize traits of the living and human, — no copy of copy and cast !
Nor swaddle the theme of the Present in fable and lore of the Past ;
Find love in hearts that are nighest, contentment in common things,
And give to the creeping moment the lightness and glimmer of wings.

THE VAGABONDS AND OTHER POEMS

THE VAGABONDS

WE are two travellers, Roger and I.
　Roger's my dog. — Come here, you scamp!
Jump for the gentlemen, — mind your eye!
　Over the table, — look out for the lamp! —
The rogue is growing a little old;
　Five years we've tramped through wind and weather,
And slept out-doors when nights were cold,
　And eaten and drank — and starved — together.

We've learned what comfort is, I tell you!
　A bed on the floor, a bit of rosin,
A fire to thaw our thumbs (poor fellow!
　The paw he holds up there's been frozen),
Plenty of catgut for my fiddle
　(This out-door business is bad for strings),
Then a few nice buckwheats hot from the griddle,
　And Roger and I set up for kings!

No, thank ye, Sir, — I never drink;
　Roger and I are exceedingly moral, —
Are n't we, Roger? — See him wink! —
　Well, something hot, then, — we won't quarrel.
He's thirsty, too, — see him nod his head?
　What a pity, Sir, that dogs can't talk!
He understands every word that's said, —
　And he knows good milk from water-and-chalk.

The truth is, Sir, now I reflect,
　I've been so sadly given to grog,
I wonder I've not lost the respect
　(Here's to you, Sir!) even of my dog.

But he sticks by, through thick and thin;
  And this old coat, with its empty pockets,
And rags that smell of tobacco and gin,
  He 'll follow while he has eyes in his sockets.

There is n't another creature living
  Would do it, and prove, through every disaster,
So fond, so faithful, and so forgiving,
  To such a miserable, thankless master!
No, Sir! — see him wag his tail and grin!
  By George! it makes my old eyes water!
That is, there 's something in this gin
  That chokes a fellow.   But no matter!

We 'll have some music, if you 're willing,
  And Roger here (what a plague a cough is, Sir!)
Shall march a little — Start, you villain!
  Paws up! Eyes front! Salute your officer!
'Bout face! Attention! Take your rifle!
  (Some dogs have arms, you see!)   Now hold your
Cap while the gentlemen give a trifle,
  To aid a poor old patriot soldier!

March! Halt! Now show how the rebel shakes
  When he stands up to hear his sentence.
Now tell us how many drams it takes
  To honor a jolly new acquaintance.
Five yelps, — that 's five; he 's mighty knowing!
  The night 's before us, fill the glasses! —
Quick, Sir! I 'm ill, — my brain is going! —
  Some brandy, — thank you, — there! — it passes!

Why not reform?   That 's easily said;
  But I 've gone through such wretched treatment,
Sometimes forgetting the taste of bread,
  And scarce remembering what meat meant,
That my poor stomach 's past reform;
  And there are times when, mad with thinking,
I 'd sell out heaven for something warm
  To prop a horrible inward sinking.

Is there a way to forget to think?
　　At your age, Sir, home, fortune, friends,
A dear girl's love, — but I took to drink; —
　　The same old story; you know how it ends.
If you could have seen these classic features, —
　　You need n't laugh, Sir; they were not then
Such a burning libel on God's creatures:
　　I was one of your handsome men!

If you had seen HER, so fair and young,
　　Whose head was happy on this breast!
If you could have heard the songs I sung
　　When the wine went round, you would n't have guessed
That ever I, Sir, should be straying
　　From door to door, with fiddle and dog,
Ragged and penniless, and playing
　　To you to-night for a glass of grog!

She 's married since, — a parson's wife:
　　'T was better for her that we should part, —
Better the soberest, prosiest life
　　Than a blasted home and a broken heart.
I have seen her? Once: I was weak and spent
　　On the dusty road: a carriage stopped:
But little she dreamed, as on she went,
　　Who kissed the coin that her fingers dropped!

You 've set me talking, Sir; I 'm sorry;
　　It makes me wild to think of the change!
What do you care for a beggar's story?
　　Is it amusing? you find it strange?
I had a mother so proud of me!
　　'T was well she died before — Do you know
If the happy spirits in heaven can see
　　The ruin and wretchedness here below?

Another glass, and strong, to deaden
　　This pain; then Roger and I will start.
I wonder, has he such a lumpish, leaden,
　　Aching thing in place of a heart?

He is sad sometimes, and would weep, if he could,
  No doubt, remembering things that were, —
A virtuous kennel, with plenty of food,
  And himself a sober, respectable cur.

I 'm better now ; that glass was warming. —
  You rascal ! limber your lazy feet !
We must be fiddling and performing
  For supper and bed, or starve in the street. —
Not a very gay life to lead, you think ?
  But soon we shall go where lodgings are free,
And the sleepers need neither victuals nor drink ; —
  The sooner, the better for Roger and me !

THE FROZEN HARBOR

WHEN Winter encamps on our borders,
  And dips his white beard in the rills,
And lays his broad shield over highway and field,
  And pitches his tents on the hills, —
In the wan light I wake, and see on the lake,
  Like a glove by the night-winds blown,
With fingers that crook up creek and brook,
  His shining gauntlet thrown.

Then over the lonely harbor,
  In the quiet and deadly cold
Of a single night, when only the bright,
  Cold constellations behold,
Without trestle or beam, without mortise or seam,
  Is swiftly and silently spread
A bridge as of steel, which a Titan's heel
  In the early light might tread.

Where Morning over the waters
  Her net of splendor spun,
Till the web, all a-twinkle with ripple and wrinkle,
  Hung shimmering in the sun, —

Where the liquid lip at the breast of the ship
 Whispered and laughed and kissed,
And the long, dark streamer of smoke from the steamer
 Trailed off in the rose-tinted mist, —

Now all is gray desolation,
 As up from the hoary coast,
Over snow-fields and islands her white arms in silence
 Outspreading like a ghost,
Her feet in shroud, her forehead in cloud,
 Pale walks the sheeted Dawn:
The sea's blue rim lies shorn and dim,
 In the purple East withdrawn.

Where floated the fleets of traffic,
 With proud breasts cleaving the tide, —
Like emmet or bug with its burden, the tug
 Hither and thither plied, —
Where the quick paddles flashed, where the dropped anchor plashed,
 And rattled the running chain,
Where the merchantman swung in the current, where sung
 The sailors their wild refrain ; —

Where, aloft in the sunlit cordage,
 I watched the climbing tar,
With his shadow beside on the sail white and wide,
 Climbing a shadow spar ;
While, weaving the union of cities,
 With hoar wakes belting the blue,
From slip to slip, past schooner and ship,
 The ferry's shuttles flew ; —

Now the hulls at their anchors are frozen,
 From rudder to sloping chain :
Rock-like they rise : the low sloop lies
 An oasis in the plain ;
Loosed from its stall, on the yielding wall
 The ferry-boat paws and rears ;
Citizens pass on a pavement of glass,
 And climb the frosted piers.

With the ebb and the flow, strange moanings
　　Come up from the burdened bay :
As a camel that kneels for his burden, reels,
　　And cannot bear it away,
The mighty load is slowly
　　Upheaved with struggle and pain
From centre to side, then the groaning tide
　　Sinks heavily down again.

Flown are the flocks of commerce,
　　Like wild swans hurrying south ;
The coaster, belated, is frozen, full-freighted,
　　Within the harbor's mouth ;
The brigantine, homeward bringing
　　Sweet spices from afar,
All night must wait with its fragrant freight
　　Below the lighthouse star.

Where, in the November gloaming,
　　To the ribs of the skeleton bark
That stranded lay in the bend of the bay,
　　Motionless, low, and dark,
Came ever three shags, like three lone hags,
　　And sat o'er the desolate water,
Each nursing apart her shrivelled heart,
　　With her mantle wrapped about her, —

Now over the ancient timbers
　　Is built a magic deck ;
Children run out with laughter and shout
　　And dance around the wreck ;
The fisherman near his long eel-spear
　　Thrusts in through the ice, or stands
With fingers on lips, and now and then whips
　　His sides with mittened hands.

Far out from the wharves I wander,
　　By the ships in their frozen chains,
To the buoy below in its cap of snow,
　　While the wintry daylight wanes ;

And I think of the hopes belated,
  Like fleets in their leaguer of ice,
Of lives that wait for Love's sweet freight
  And the spices of Paradise! —

I linger and muse till, at twilight,
  The town-roofs, towering high,
Uprear in the dimness their tall, dark chimneys,
  Indenting the sunset sky,
And the pendent spear on the icicled pier
  Signals my homeward way,
As it gleams through the dusk like a walrus's tusk
  On the floes of a polar bay.

OUR LADY

OUR lady lives on the hillside here,
  Amid shady avenues, terraced lawns,
And fountains that leap like snow-white deer,
  With flashing antlers, and silver fawns;
And the twinkling wheels of the rich and great
Hum in and out of the high-arched gate;
And willing worshippers throng and wait,
  Where she wearily sits and yawns.

I remember her pretty and poor, —
  Now she has servants, jewels, and land:
She gave her heart to a poet-wooer, —
  To a wealthy suitor she bartered her hand.
A very desirable mate to choose, —
Believing in viands, in good port-juice,
In solid comfort and solid use, —
  Things simple to understand.

She loves poetry, music, and art, —
  He dines, and races, and smokes, and shoots;
She walks in an ideal realm apart, —
  He treads firm ground, in his prosperous boots:

A wise design; for you see, 't is clear,
Their paths do not lie so unsuitably near
As that ever either should interfere
    With the other's chosen pursuits.

By night, as you roam through the rich saloons,
    When music's purple and crimson tones
Float, in invisibly fine festoons,
    Over the hum of these human drones,
You are ready to swear that no happier pair
Have lived than your latter-day Adam there,
And our sweet, pale Eve, of the dark-furrowed hair,
    Thick sown with glittering stones.

But I see, in the midst of the music and talk,
    A shape steal forth from the glowing room,
And pass, by a lonely cypress walk,
    Far down through the ghostly midnight gloom,
Sighing and sorrowful, wringing its hands,
And bruising its feet on the pointed sands,
Till, white, despairing, and dumb it stands,
    In the shadowy damp of a tomb.

The husband sprawls in his easy-chair,
    And smirks, and smacks, and tells his jest,
And strokes his chin with a satisfied air,
    And hooks his thumbs in his filagreed vest;
And the laugh rings round, and still she seems
To sit smiling there, and nobody deems
That her soul has gone down to that region of dreams,
    A weary, disconsolate guest.

Dim ghosts of happiness haunt the grot,
    Phantoms of buried hopes untold,
And ashen memories strew the spot
    Where her young heart's love lies coffined and cold.
With her burden of sin she kneels within,
And kisses, and presses, with fingers thin,
Brow, mouth, and bosom, and beautiful chin
    Of the dead that grows not old.

He is ever there, with his dark wavy hair,
 Unchanged through years of anguish and tears;
His hands are pressed on his passionate breast,
 His eyes still plead with foreboding and fears.
O, she dwells not at all in that stately hall!
But, day and night, by the cypresses tall,
She opens the coffin, uplifts the pall,
 And the living dead appears!

THE MILL–POND

THE linden, maple, and birch-tree bless,
With cooling shades, the banks I press
In the midsummer sultriness;
And under the thickest shade of all
Singeth a musical waterfall.

The burnished breast of a silver pond
In the sunlight lieth beyond, —
Clear, and calm, and still as death,
Save where the south-wind's blurring breath,
Like an angel's pinion, fluttereth.

The south-wind moveth, but maketh no noise,
Nor ever disturbeth the delicate poise
Of the little fishing floats the boys
Sit idly watching on log and ledge:
It toucheth but softly the languid sedge,
Drooping all day by the water's edge.

In the thickets shady and cool
The white sheep tear their tender wool;
Shaking and clashing the heavy boughs,
The limber colts and the sober cows
Down from the woody hillside come,
To stand in the shallows, and hark to the hum
Of the waterfall beating its airy drum.

Deep in the shadowy dell at noon
I lie, and list to the drowsy tune,

Fanned by the sweet south-wind ;
And I think how like to the poet's mind
Are the skyey depths of the silver pond,
That in the sunlight lieth beyond
These lindens tall, and the slimy wall
Over which poureth the waterfall.

When the angry March winds blow,
And rains descend, and freshets flow
In torrent and rill from mountain and hill,
And the ponderous wheels of the sunken mill
Go round and round, with a sullen sound,
Rumbling, mumbling, half under ground, —
Hoarsely the waterfall singeth all day,
And the waters are streaked with marl and clay.

But when these shaded banks I press,
In the midsummer sultriness,
Standeth all still the mumbling mill ;
The quiet pond doth seem to thrill
With joys which all its windings fill ;
And in its depths the eye may view
A world of soft and dreamy hue, —
Banks, and trees, and a sky of blue.

Willow and sedge, by the water's edge,
And children fishing from log and ledge ;
Flags and cresses and wild swamp grasses,
And every butterfly that passes,
The lakelet's placid bosom glasses.

THE RESTORED PICTURE

In later years, veiling its unblest face
    In a most loathsome place,
The cheap adornment of a house of shame,
    It hung, till, gnawed away
    By teeth of slow decay,
It fell, and parted from its mouldering **frame**.

The rotted canvas, faintly smiling still,
From worldly puff and frill,
Its ghastly smile of coquetry and pride,
    Crumpling its faded charms
    And yellow jewelled arms,
Mere rubbish now, was rudely cast aside.

The shadow of a Genius crossed the gate:
    He, skilled to re-create
In old and ruined paintings their lost soul
    And beauty, — one who knew
    The Master's touch by true,
Swift instinct, as the needle knows the pole, —

Looked on it, and straightway his searching eyes
    Saw, through its coarse disguise
Of vulgar paint and grime and varnish stain,
    The Art that slept beneath, —
    A chrysalis in its sheath,
That waited to be waked to life again.

Upon enduring canvas to renew
    Each wondrous trait and hue, —
This is the miracle, his chosen task!
    He bears it to his house,
    And there from lips and brows
With loving touch removes their alien mask.

For so on its perfection time had laid
    An early mellowing shade;
Then hands unskilled, each seeking to impart
    Fresh tints to form and face,
    With some more modern grace,
Had buried quite the mighty Master's Art.

First, razed from the divine original,
    Brow, cheek, and lid, went all
That outer shape of worldliness; when, lo!
    Beneath the varnished crust
    Of long imbedded dust
A fairer face appears, emerging slow, —

The features of a simple shepherdess !
　　Pure eyes, and golden tress,
And, lastly, crook in hand.　But deeper still
　　The Master's work lies hid ;
　　And still through lip and lid
Works the Restorer with unsparing skill.

Behold at length, in tender light revealed,
　　The soul so long concealed !
All heavenly faint at first, then softly bright,
　　As smiles the young-eyed Dawn
　　When darkness is withdrawn,
A shining angel breaks upon the sight !

Restored, perfected, after the divine
　　Imperishable design,
Lo now ! that once despised and outcast thing
　　Holds its true place among
　　The fairest pictures hung
In the high palace of our Lord the King !

THE PEWEE

THE listening Dryads hushed the woods ;
　　The boughs were thick, and thin and few
　　The golden ribbons fluttering through ;
Their sun-embroidered, leafy hoods
　　The lindens lifted to the blue :
Only a little forest-brook
The farthest hem of silence shook :
When in the hollow shades I heard, —
Was it a spirit, or a bird ?
Or, strayed from Eden, desolate,
Some Peri calling to her mate,
　　Whom nevermore her mate would cheer ?
　　　" Pe-ri ! pe-ri ! peer ! "

Through rocky clefts the brooklet fell
　　With plashy pour, that scarce was sound,

But only quiet less profound,
A stillness fresh and audible:
A yellow leaflet to the ground
Whirled noiselessly: with wing of gloss
A hovering sunbeam brushed the moss,
And, wavering brightly over it,
Sat like a butterfly alit:
The owlet in his open door
Stared roundly: while the breezes bore
The plaint to far-off places drear, —
    "Pe-ree! pe-ree! peer!"

To trace it in its green retreat
  I sought among the boughs in vain;
  And followed still the wandering strain,
So melancholy and so sweet
  The dim-eyed violets yearned with pain.
'T was now a sorrow in the air,
Some nymph's immortalized despair
Haunting the woods and waterfalls;
And now, at long, sad intervals,
Sitting unseen in dusky shade,
His plaintive pipe some fairy played,
    With long-drawn cadence thin and clear, —
    "Pe-wee! pe-wee! peer!"

Long-drawn and clear its closes were, —
  As if the hand of Music through
  The sombre robe of Silence drew
A thread of golden gossamer:
  So pure a flute the fairy blew.
Like beggared princes of the wood,
In silver rags the birches stood;
The hemlocks, lordly counsellors,
Were dumb; the sturdy servitors,
In beechen jackets patched and gray,
Seemed waiting spellbound all the day
    That low, entrancing note to hear, —
    "Pe-wee! pe-wee! peer!"

I quit the search, and sat me down
　　Beside the brook, irresolute,
　　And watched a little bird in suit
Of sober olive, soft and brown,
　　Perched in the maple-branches, mute:
With greenish gold its vest was fringed,
Its tiny cap was ebon-tinged,
With ivory pale its wings were barred,
And its dark eyes were tender-starred.
" Dear bird," I said, " what is thy name ? "
And thrice the mournful answer came,
　　So faint and far, and yet so near, —
　　　" Pe-wee ! pe-wee ! peer ! "

For so I found my forest bird, —
　　The pewee of the loneliest woods,
　　Sole singer in these solitudes,
Which never robin's whistle stirred,
　　Where never bluebird's plume intrudes.
Quick darting through the dewy morn,
The redstart trilled his twittering horn,
And vanished in thick boughs : at even,
Like liquid pearls fresh showered from heaven,
The high notes of the lone wood-thrush
Fall on the forest's holy hush:
　　But thou all day complainest here, —
　　　" Pe-wee ! pe-wee ! peer ! "

Hast thou, too, in thy little breast,
　　Strange longings for a happier lot, —
　　For love, for life, thou know'st not what, —
A yearning, and a vague unrest,
　　For something still which thou hast not ? —
Thou soul of some benighted child
That perished, crying in the wild !
Or lost, forlorn, and wandering maid,
By love allured, by love betrayed,
Whose spirit with her latest sigh
Arose, a little wingéd cry,
　　Above her chill and mossy bier !
　　　" Dear me ! dear me ! dear ! "

Ah, no such piercing sorrow mars
  The pewee's life of cheerful ease!
  He sings, or leaves his song to seize
An insect sporting in the bars
  Of mild bright light that gild the trees.
A very poet he! For him
All pleasant places still and dim:
His heart, a spark of heavenly fire,
Burns with undying, sweet desire:
And so he sings; and so his song,
Though heard not by the hurrying throng,
  Is solace to the pensive ear:
    " Pewee! pewee! peer! "

MIDSUMMER

AROUND this lovely valley rise
The purple hills of Paradise.

O softly on yon banks of haze
Her rosy face the Summer lays!

Becalmed along the azure sky,
The argosies of cloudland lie,
Whose shores, with many a shining rift,
Far off their pearl-white peaks uplift.

Through all the long midsummer-day
The meadow-sides are sweet with hay.
I seek the coolest sheltered seat,
Just where the field and forest meet, —
Where grow the pine-trees tall and bland,
The ancient oaks austere and grand,
And fringy roots and pebbles fret
The ripples of the rivulet.

I watch the mowers, as they go
Through the tall grass, a white-sleeved row.
With even stroke their scythes they swing,
In tune their merry whetstones ring.

Behind the nimble youngsters run,
And toss the thick swaths in the sun.
The cattle graze, while, warm and still,
Slopes the broad pasture, basks the hill,
And bright, where summer breezes break,
The green wheat crinkles like a lake.

The butterfly and humble-bee
Come to the pleasant woods with me;
Quickly before me runs the quail,
Her chickens skulk behind the rail;
High up the lonely wood dove sits,
And the woodpecker pecks and flits.
Sweet woodland music sinks and swells,
The brooklet rings its tinkling bells,
The swarming insects drone and hum,
The partridge beats his throbbing drum.
The squirrel leaps among the boughs,
And chatters in his leafy house.
The oriole flashes by; and, look!
Into the mirror of the brook,
Where the vain bluebird trims his coat,
Two tiny feathers fall and float.

As silently, as tenderly,
The down of peace descends on me.
O, this is peace!   I have no need
Of friend to talk, of book to read:
A dear Companion here abides;
Close to my thrilling heart He hides;
The holy silence is His Voice:
I lie and listen, and rejoice.

MY COMRADE AND I

WE two have grown up so divinely together,
  Flower within flower from seed within seed,
The sagest astrologer cannot say whether
  His being or mine was first called and decreed.

In the life before birth, by inscrutable ties,
　　We were linked each to each; I am bound up in him;
He sickens, I languish; without me he dies;
　　I am life of his life, he is limb of my limb.

Twin babes from one cradle, I tottered about with him,
　　Chased the bright butterflies, singing, a boy with him;
Still as a man I am borne in and out with him,
　　Sup with him, sleep with him, suffer, enjoy with him.
Faithful companion, me long he has carried
　　Unseen in his bosom, a lamp to his feet;
More near than a bridegroom, to him I am married,
　　As light in the sunbeam is wedded to heat.

If my beam be withdrawn he is senseless and blind;
　　I am sight to his vision, I hear with his ears;
His the marvellous brain, I the masterful mind;
　　I laugh with his laughter and weep with his tears
So well that the ignorant deem us but one:
　　They see but one shape and they name us one name.
O pliant accomplice! what deeds we have done,
　　Thus banded together for glory or shame!

When evil waylays us, and passion surprises,
　　And we are too feeble to strive or to fly,
When hunger compels or when pleasure entices,
　　Which most is the sinner, my comrade or I?
And when over perils and pains and temptations
　　I triumph, where still I should falter and faint,
But for him, iron-nerved for heroical patience,
　　Whose then is the virtue, and which is the saint?

Am I the one sinner? of honors sole claimant
　　For actions which only we two can perform?
Am I the true creature, and thou but the raiment?
　　Thou magical mantle, all vital and warm,
Wrapped about me, a screen from the rough winds of Time,
　　Of texture so flexile to feature and gesture!
Can ever I part from thee? Is there a clime
　　Where Life needs no more this terrestrial vesture?

When comes the sad summons to sever the sweet
    Subtle tie that unites us, and tremulous, fearful,
I feel thy loosed fetters depart from my feet;
    When friends gathered round us, pale-visaged and tearful,
Beweep and bewail thee, thou fair earthly prison!
And kiss thy cold doors, for thy inmate mistaken;
    Their eyes seeing not the freed captive, arisen
From thy trammels unclasped and thy shackles downshaken;

O, then shall I linger, reluctant to break
    The dear sensitive chains that about me have grown?
And all this bright world, can I bear to forsake
    Its embosoming beauty and love, and alone
Journey on to I know not what regions untried?
    Exists there, beyond the dim cloud-rack of death,
Such life as enchants us?   O skies arched and wide!
    O delicate senses!   O exquisite breath!

Ah, tenderly, tenderly over thee hovering,
    I shall look down on thee empty and cloven,
Pale mould of my being! — thou visible covering
    Wherefrom my invisible raiment is woven.
Though sad be the passage, nor pain shall appall me,
    Nor parting, assured, wheresoever I range
The glad fields of existence, that naught can befall me
    That is not still beautiful, blessed, and strange.

LA CANTATRICE

By day, at a high oak desk I stand,
    And trace in a ledger line by line;
But at five o'clock yon dial's hand
    Opens the cage wherein I pine;
And as faintly the stroke from the belfry peals
Down through the thunder of hoofs and wheels,
I wonder if ever a monarch feels
    Such royal joy as mine!

Beatrice, with her little banquet, waits;
    I know she has heard that signal-chime;

And my strong heart leaps and palpitates,
  As lightly the winding stair I climb
To her fragrant room, where the winter's gloom
Is changed by the heliotrope's perfume,
And the shaded lamp's soft crimson bloom,
  To love's own summer prime.

She meets me there, so strangely fair
  That my soul aches with a happy pain. —
And now — a touch of her true lips, such
  As a seraph might give and take again;
A lingering pressure : " Adieu ! adieu !
They wait for me while I stay for you ! "
And a parting smile of her dark eyes through
  The glimmering carriage-pane.

O, not as we parted once, we part!
  Then, years of waiting and sacrifice ;
Exile for her, while her glorious art
  Unfolded and flowered in sunnier skies :
The slow, laborious, lonely years,
The nights of longing, of doubts and fears, —
Her heart's sweet debt, and the long arrears
  Of love in those dear dark eyes !

O night ! be friendly to her and me ! —
  To floor and aisle and balcony swarm
The expectant throngs ; — I am there to see ; —
  And now she is bending her radiant form
To the clapping crowd ; — I am thrilled and proud ;
My dim eyes look through a misty cloud,
And my joy mounts up on the plaudits loud,
  As a sea-bird·on a storm !

A murmur and ripple of strings, as the rush
  Of applause sinks down : then silverly
Her voice glides forth on the quivering hush,
  As the white-robed moon on a tremulous sea !
And wherever her shining influence calls,
I swing on the billow that swells and falls, —

I know no more, — till the very walls
Seem joining the jubilee!

Little she cares for the fop who airs
His glove and glass, or the gay array
Of fans and perfumes, of jewels and plumes,
Where wealth and pleasure have met to pay
Their nightly homage to her sweet song;
But over the bravas clear and strong,
Over all the flaunting and fluttering throng,
She smiles my soul away.

Why am I happy? why am I proud?
Can it be true she is all my own? —
I make my way through the ignorant crowd;
I know, I know where my love has flown.
Again we meet; I am here at her feet,
And with kindling kisses and promises sweet,
Her glowing, victorious lips repeat
That they sing for me alone!

BEAUTY

Fond lover of the Ideal Fair,
My soul, eluded everywhere,
Is lapsed into a sweet despair.

Perpetual pilgrim, seeking ever,
Baffled, enamored, finding never;
Each morn the cheerful chase renewing,
Misled, bewildered, still pursuing;
Not all my lavished years have bought
One steadfast smile from her I sought,
But sidelong glances, glimpsing light,
A something far too fine for sight,
Veiled voices, far-off thridding strains,
And precious agonies and pains:
Not love, but only love's dear wound
And exquisite unrest I found.

At early morn I saw her pass
The lone lake's blurred and quivering glass ;
Her trailing veil of amber mist
The unbending beaded clover kissed ;
And straight I hasted to waylay
Her coming by the willowy way ; —
But, swift companion of the Dawn,
She left her footprints on the lawn,
And, in arriving, she was gone.

Alert I ranged the winding shore ;
Her luminous presence flashed before ;
The wild-rose and the daisies wet
From her light touch were trembling yet ;
Faint smiled the conscious violet.
Each bush and brier and rock betrayed
Some tender sign her parting made ;
And when far on her flight I tracked
To where the thunderous cataract
O'er walls of foamy ledges broke,
She vanished in the vapory smoke.

To-night I pace this pallid floor,
The sparkling waves curl up the shore,
The August moon is flushed and full ;
The soft, low winds, the liquid lull,
The whited, silent, misty realm,
The wan-blue heaven, each ghostly elm,
All these, her ministers, conspire
To fill my bosom with the fire
And sweet delirium of desire.
Enchantress ! leave thy sheeny height,
Descend, be all mine own this night,
Transfuse, enfold, entrance me quite !
Or break thy spell, my heart restore,
And disenchant me evermore !

SERVICE

WHEN I beheld a lover woo
    A maid unwilling,
And saw what lavish deeds men do,
    Hope's flagon filling, —
What vines are tilled, what wines are spilled,
    And madly wasted,
To fill the flask that 's never filled,
    And rarely tasted:

Devouring all life's heritage,
    And inly starving;
Dulling the spirit's mystic edge,
    The banquet carving;
Feasting with Pride, that Barmecide
    Of unreal dishes;
And wandering ever in a wide,
    Wide world of wishes:

For gain or glory, lands and seas
    Endlessly ranging,
Safety and years and health and ease
    Freely exchanging : —
When, ever as I moved, I saw
    Pride and privation,
Then turned, O Love! to thy sweet law
    And compensation, —

Well might red shame my cheek consume!
    O service slighted!
O Bride of Paradise, to whom
    I long was plighted!
Do I with burning lips profess
    To serve thee wholly,
Yet labor less for blessedness
    Than fools for folly?

The wary worldling spread his toils
    Whilst I was sleeping;

The wakeful miser locked his spoils,
    Keen vigils keeping:
I loosed the latches of my soul
    To pleading Pleasure,
Who stayed one little hour, and stole
    My heavenly treasure.

A friend for friend's sake will endure
    Sharp provocations;
And knaves are cunning to secure,
    By cringing patience,
And smiles upon a smarting cheek,
    Some dear advantage, —
Swathing their grievances in meek
    Submission's bandage.

Yet for thy sake I will not take
    One drop of trial,
But raise rebellious hands to break
    The bitter vial.
At hardship's surly-visaged churl
    My spirit sallies;
And melts, O Peace! thy priceless pearl
    In passion's chalice.

Yet never quite, in darkest night,
    Was I forsaken:
Down trickles still some starry rill
    My heart to waken.
O Love Divine! could I resign
    This changeful spirit
To walk thy ways, what wealth of grace
    Might I inherit!

If one poor flower of thanks to thee
    Be truly given,
All night thou snowest down to me
    Lilies of heaven!
One task of human love fulfilled,
    Thy glimpses tender

My days of lonely labor gild
  With gleams of splendor!

One prayer, — " Thy will, not mine ! " — and bright,
  O'er all my being,
Breaks blissful light, that gives to sight
  A subtler seeing ;
Straightway mine ear is tuned to hear
  Ethereal numbers,
Whose secret symphonies insphere
  The dull earth's slumbers.

" Thy will ! " — and I am armed to meet
  Misfortune's volleys ;
For every sorrow I have sweet,
  O, sweetest solace !
For me the diamond dawns are set
  In rings of beauty,
And all my paths are dewy wet
  With pleasant duty.

AT SEA

THE night is made for cooling shade,
  For silence, and for sleep ;
And when I was a child, I laid
My hands upon my breast and prayed,
  And sank to slumbers deep :
Childlike as then, I lie to-night,
And watch my lonely cabin light.

Each movement of the swaying lamp
  Shows how the vessel reels :
As o'er her deck the billows tramp,
And all her timbers strain and cramp,
  With every shock she feels,
It starts and shudders, while it burns,
And in its hingéd socket turns.

Now swinging slow, and slanting low,
  It almost level lies ;
And yet I know, while to and fro
I watch the seeming pendule go
  With restless fall and rise,
The steady shaft is still upright,
Poising its little globe of light.

O hand of God! O lamp of peace!
  O promise of my soul! —
Though weak, and tossed, and ill at ease,
Amid the roar of smiting seas,
  The ship's convulsive roll,
I own, with love and tender awe,
Yon perfect type of faith and law!

A heavenly trust my spirit calms,
  My soul is filled with light :
The ocean sings his solemn psalms,
The wild winds chant : I cross my palms,
  Happy as if, to-night,
Under the cottage-roof, again
I heard the soothing summer-rain.

REAL ESTATE

THE pleasant grounds are greenly turfed and graded ;
  A sturdy porter waits beside the gate ;
The graceful avenues, serenely shaded,
And curving paths, are interlaced and braided
  In many a maze around my fair estate.

Here blooms the early hyacinth, and clover
  And amaranth and myrtle wreathe the ground ;
The pensive lily leans her pale cheek over ;
And hither comes the bee, light-hearted rover,
  Wooing the sweet-breathed flowers with soothing sound.

Intwining, in their manifold digressions,
  Lands of my neighbors, wind these peaceful ways.

The masters, coming to their calm possessions,
Followed in solemn state by long processions,
  Make quiet journeys these still summer days.

This is my freehold! Elms and fringy larches,
  Maples and pines, and stately firs of Norway,
Build round me their green pyramids and arches;
Sweetly the robin sings, while slowly marches
  The stately pageant past my verdant doorway.

O, sweetly sing the robin and the sparrow!
  But the pale tenant very silent rides.
A low green roof bends over him; — so narrow
His hollowed tenement, a schoolboy's arrow
  Might span the space betwixt its grassy sides.

The flowers around him ring their wind-swung chalices,
  A great bell tolls the pageant's slow advance.
The poor alike, and lords of parks and palaces,
From all their busy schemes, their fears and fallacies,
  Find here their rest and sure inheritance.

No more had Cæsar or Sardanapalus!
  Of all our wide dominions, soon or late,
Only a fathom's space can aught avail us;
This is the heritage that shall not fail us:
  Here man at last comes to his Real Estate.

BY THE RIVER

I

In the beautiful greenwood's charméd light,
And down through the meadows wide and bright,
Deep in the silence, and smooth in the gleam,
For ever and ever flows the stream.

Where the mandrakes grow, and the pale, thin grass
The airy scarf of the woodland weaves,
By dim, enchanted paths I pass,
Crushing the twigs and the last year's leaves.

Over the wave, by the crystal brink,
A kingfisher sits on a low, dead limb :
He is always sitting there, I think, —
And another, within the crystal brink,
Is always pendent under him.

I know where an old tree leans across
From bank to bank, an ancient tree,
Quaintly cushioned with curious moss,
A bridge for the cool wood-nymphs and me :
Half seen they flit, while here I sit
By the magical water, watching it.

In its bosom swims the fair phantasm
Of a subterraneous azure chasm,
So soft and clear, you would say the stream
Was dreaming of heaven a visible dream.

Where the noontide basks, and its warm rays tint
The nettles and clover and scented mint,
And the crinkled airs, that curl and quiver,
Drop their wreaths in the mirroring river,
Along its sinuous shining bed
In sheets of splendor it lies outspread.

In the twilight stillness and solitude
Of green caves roofed by the brooding wood,
Where the woodbine swings, and beneath the trailing
Sprays of the queenly elm-tree sailing, —
By ribbed and wave-worn ledges shimmering,
Gilding the rocks with a rippled glimmering,
All pictured over in shade and sun,
The wavering silken waters run.

Upon this mossy trunk I sit,
Over the river, watching it.
A shadowed face peers up at me ;
And another tree in the chasm I see,
Clinging above the abyss it spans ;
The broad boughs curve their spreading fans,

From side to side, in the nether air;
And phantom birds in the phantom branches
Mimic the birds above; and there,
Oh! far below, solemn and slow,
The white clouds roll the crumbling snow
Of ever-pendulous avalanches,
Till the brain grows giddy, gazing through
Their wild, wide rifts of bottomless blue.

II

Through the river, and through the rifts
Of the sundered earth I gaze,
While Thought on dreamy pinion drifts,
Over cerulean bays,
Into the deep ethereal sea
Of her own serene eternity.

Transfigured by my trancéd eye,
Wood and meadow, and stream and sky,
Like vistas of a vision lie :
THE WORLD is the River that flickers by.

Its skies are the blue-arched centuries;
And its forms are the transient images
Flung on the flowing film of Time
By the steadfast shores of a fadeless clime.

My Soul leans over the murmuring flow,
And I am the image it sees below.

THE NAME IN THE BARK

THE self of so long ago,
And the self I struggle to know,
I sometimes think we are two, — or are we shadows of one?
To-day the shadow I am
Returns in the sweet summer calm
To trace where the earlier shadow flitted awhile in the sun.

Once more in the dewy morn
I came through the whispering corn ;
Cool to my fevered cheek soft breezy kisses were blown ;
The ribboned and tasselled grass
Leaned over the flattering glass,
And the sunny waters trilled the same low musical tone.

To the gray old birch I came,
Where I whittled my schoolboy name :
The nimble squirrel once more ran skippingly over the rail,
The blackbirds down among
The alders noisily sung,
And under the blackberry-brier whistled the serious quail.

I came, remembering well
How my little shadow fell,
As I painfully reached and wrote to leave to the future a sign :
There, stooping a little, I found
A half-healed, curious wound,
An ancient scar in the bark, but no initial of mine !

Then the wise old boughs overhead
Took counsel together, and said, —
And the buzz of their leafy lips like a murmur of prophecy passed, —
" He is busily carving a name
In the tough old wrinkles of fame ;
But, cut he as deep as he may, the lines will close over at last ! "

Sadly I pondered awhile,
Then I lifted my soul with a smile,
And I said, " Not cheerful men, but anxious children are we,
Still hurting ourselves with the knife,
As we toil at the letters of life,
Just marring a little the rind, never piercing the heart of the tree."

And now by the rivulet's brink
I leisurely saunter, and think
How idle this strife will appear when circling ages have run,
If then the real I am
Descend from the heavenly calm,
To trace where the shadow I seem once flitted awhile in the sun.

THE SWORD OF BOLIVAR [1]

WITH the steadfast stars above us,
  And the molten stars below,
We sailed through the Southern midnight,
  By the coast of Mexico.

Alone, on the desolate, dark-ringed,
  Rolling and flashing sea,
A grim old Venezuelan
  Kept the deck with me,

And talked to me of his country,
  And the long Spanish war,
And told how a young Republic
  Forged the sword of Bolivar.

That it might shine the symbol
  Of law and light in the land,
Dropped down as a star from heaven,
  To flame in a hero's hand,

And be to the world a token
  Of eternal might and right,
For the chaste, bright steel was chosen
  A sky-born aerolite.

For the fair states, New Granada
  And Venezuela, they pour

[1] The Republic of Colombia, comprising New Granada and Venezuela, was proclaimed by Bolivar in 1819 and dismembered, soon after his death, in 1831. The story of the sword forged from meteoric ore has a foundation in fact; and the character of the so-called Liberator — who has been likened to our Washington, and who is honored with a monument in his native city of Caracas — is, I believe, not unfairly sketched in the lines, allowance being made for some political bias on the part of the "grim old Venezuelan." Still larger allowance must be craved for the too pointed application of the fable to Lincoln's unfortunate successor in the Presidency, disappointment and indignation at whose weak, undignified, reactionary conduct in office formed the shaping motive of the poem, — feelings long since softened by time and a juster perspective. The poem, first printed in the *Atlantic Monthly* for November, 1866, was written in the August or September of that year, now almost thirty-seven years ago.
ARLINGTON, August, 1903.

From twin crucibles the dazzling
  White meteoric ore.

In two ingots it is moulded,
  And welded into one,
For an emblem of Colombia,
  Proud daughter of the sun!

In the din of the forge it is fashioned,
  It is heated and hammered and rolled,
It is tempered and edged and burnished,
  And set in a hilt of gold;

For thus by the fire and the hammer
  Of war a nation is built,
And ever the sword of its power
  Is swayed by a golden hilt.

Then with pomp and oratory
  The mustachioed señores brought
To the house of the Liberator
  The weapon they had wrought;

And they said, in their stately phrases,
  "O mighty in peace and war!
No mortal blade we bring you,
  But a flaming meteor.

"The sword of the Spaniard is broken,
  And to you in its stead is given,
To lead and redeem a nation,
  This ray of light from heaven."

The gaunt-faced Liberator
  From their hands the symbol took,
And waved it aloft in the sunlight,
  With a high, heroic look;

And he called the saints to witness:
  "May these lips turn into dust,

And this right hand fail, if ever
  It prove recreant to its trust!

"Never the sigh of a bondman
  Shall cloud this gleaming steel,
But only the foe and the traitor
  Its vengeful edge shall feel.

"Never a tear of my country
  Its purity shall stain,
Till into your hands, who gave it,
  I render it again."

Now if ever a chief was chosen
  To cover a cause with shame,
And if ever there breathed a caitiff,
  Bolivar was his name.

From his place among the people
  To the highest seat he went,
By the winding paths of party
  And the stair of accident.

A restless, weak usurper,
  Striving to rear a throne,
Filling his fame with counsels
  And conquests not his own ; —

Now seeming to put from him
  The sceptre of command,
Only that he might grasp it
  With yet a firmer hand ; —

His country's trusted leader,
  In league with his country's foes,
Stabbing the cause that nursed him,
  And openly serving those ; —

The chief of a great republic
  Plotting rebellion still, —

An apostate faithful only
To his own ambitious will.

Drunk with a vain ambition,
In his feeble, reckless hand,
The sword of Eternal Justice
Became but a brawler's brand.

And Colombia was dissevered,
Rent by factions, till at last
Her place among the nations
Is a memory of the past.

Here the grim old Venezuelan
Puffed fiercely his red cigar
A brief moment, then in the ocean
It vanished like a star:

And he slumbered in his hammock;
And only the ceaseless rush
Of the reeling and sparkling waters
Filled the solemn midnight hush,

As I leaned by the swinging gunwale
Of the good ship, sailing slow,
With the steadfast heavens above her,
And the molten heavens below.

Then I thought with sorrow and yearning
Of my own distracted land,
And the sword let down from heaven
To flame in her ruler's hand, —

The sword of Freedom, resplendent
As a beam of the morning star,
Received, reviled, and dishonored
By another than Bolivar!

LYRICS OF THE WAR

THE LAST RALLY

[NOVEMBER, 1864.]

RALLY! rally! rally!
  Arouse the slumbering land!
Rally! rally! from mountain and valley,
  From city and ocean-strand!
Ye sons of the West, America's best!
  New Hampshire's men of might!
From prairie and crag unfurl the flag,
  And rally to the fight!

Armies of untried heroes,
  Disguised in craftsman and clerk!
Ye men of the coast, invincible host!
  Come, every one, to the work, —
From the fisherman gray as the salt-sea spray
  That on Long Island breaks,
To the youth who tills the uttermost hills
  By the blue northwestern lakes!

Old men shall fight with the ballot,
  Weapon the last and best, —
And the bayonet, with blood red-wet,
  Shall write the will of the rest;
And the boys shall fill men's places,
  And the little maid shall rock
Her doll as she sits with her grandam and knits
  An unknown hero's sock.

And the hearts of heroic mothers,
  And the deeds of noble wives,
With their power to bless shall aid no less
  Than the brave who give their lives.
The rich their gold shall bring, and the old
  Shall help us with their prayers;
While hovering hosts of pallid ghosts
  Attend us unawares.

From the ghastly fields of Shiloh
   Muster the phantom bands,
From Virginia's swamps, and Death's white camps
   On Carolina sands;
From Fredericksburg, and Gettysburg,
   I see them gathering fast;
And up from Manassas, what is it that passes
   Like thin clouds in the blast?

From the Wilderness, where blanches
   The nameless skeleton;
From Vicksburg's slaughter and red-streaked water,
   And the trenches of Donelson;
From the cruel, cruel prisons,
   Where their bodies pined away,
From groaning decks, from sunken wrecks,
   They gather with us to-day.

And they say to us, " Rally! rally!
   The work is almost done!
Ye harvesters, sally from mountain and valley,
   And reap the fields we won!
We sowed for endless years of peace,
   We harrowed and watered well;
Our dying deeds were the scattered seeds:
   Shall they perish where they fell? "

And their brothers, left behind them
   In the deadly roar and clash
Of cannon and sword, by fort and ford,
   And the carbine's quivering flash, —
Before the Rebel citadel
   Just trembling to its fall,
From Georgia's glens, from Florida's fens,
   For us they call, they call!

One more sublime endeavor
   And behold the dawn of peace!
One more endeavor, and war forever
   Throughout the land shall cease!

For ever and ever the vanquished power
Of slavery shall be slain,
And freedom's stained and trampled flower
Shall blossom white again!

THE COLOR-BEARER

'T WAS a fortress to be stormed:
Boldly right in view they formed,
All as quiet as a regiment parading:
Then in front a line of flame!
Then at left and right the same!
Two platoons received a furious enfilading.
To their places still they filed,
And they smiled at the wild
Cannonading.

" 'T will be over in an hour!
'T will not be much of a shower!
Never mind, my boys," said he, " a little drizzling!"
Then to cross that fatal plain,
Through the whirring, hurtling rain
Of the grape-shot and the minie-bullets' whistling!
But he nothing heeds nor shuns,
As he runs with the guns
Brightly bristling!

Leaving trails of dead and dying
In their track, yet forward flying
Like a breaker where the gale of conflict rolled them,
With a foam of flashing light
Borne before them on their bright
Burnished barrels, — O, 't was fearful to behold them!
While from ramparts roaring loud
Swept a cloud like a shroud
To enfold them!

O, his color was the first!
Through the burying cloud he burst,

With the standard to the battle forward slanted!
  Through the belching, blinding breath
  Of the flaming jaws of Death,
With the banner on the bastion to be planted!
  By the screaming shot that fell,
  And the yell of the shell,
    Nothing daunted.

  Right against the bulwark dashing,
  Over tangled branches crashing,
'Mid the plunging volleys thundering ever louder,
  There he clambers, there he stands,
  With the ensign in his hands, —
O, was ever hero handsomer or prouder?
  Streaked with battle-sweat and slime
  And sublime in the grime
    Of the powder!

  'T was six minutes, at the least,
  Ere the closing combat ceased, —
Near as we the mighty moments then could measure, —
  And we held our souls with awe,
  Till his haughty flag we saw
On the lifting vapors drifting o'er the embrasure,
  Saw it glimmer in our tears,
  While our ears heard the cheers
    Rend the azure!

THE JAGUAR HUNT

[MAY, 1865]

THE dark jaguar was abroad in the land;
His strength and his fierceness what foe could withstand?
The breath of his anger was hot on the air,
And the white lamb of Peace he had dragged to his lair.

Then up rose the Farmer; he summoned his sons:
"Now saddle your horses, now look to your guns!"

And he called to his hound, as he sprang from the ground
To the back of his black pawing steed with a bound.

O, their hearts, at the word, how they tingled and stirred!
They followed, all belted and booted and spurred.
" Buckle tight, boys!" said he, "for who gallops with me,
Such a hunt as was never before he shall see!

" This traitor, we know him! for when he was younger,
We flattered him, patted him, fed his fierce hunger:
But now far too long we have borne with the wrong,
For each morsel we tossed makes him savage and strong."

Then said one, " He must die!" And they took up the cry,
" For this last crime of his he must die! he must die!"
But the slow eldest-born sauntered sad and forlorn,
For his heart was at home on that fair hunting-morn.

" I remember," he said, " how this fine cub we track
Has carried me many a time on his back!"
And he called to his brothers, " Fight gently! be kind!"
And he kept the dread hound, Retribution, behind.

The dark jaguar on a bough in the brake
Crouched, silent and wily, and lithe as a snake:
They spied not their game, but, as onward they came,
Through the dense leafage gleamed two red eyeballs of flame.

Black-spotted, and mottled, and whiskered, and grim,
White-bellied, and yellow, he lay on the limb,
All so still that you saw but just one tawny paw
Lightly reach through the leaves and as softly withdraw.

Then shrilled his fierce cry, as the riders drew nigh,
And he shot from the bough like a bolt from the sky:
In the foremost he fastened his fangs as he fell,
While all the black jungle reëchoed his yell.

O, then there was carnage by field and by flood!
The green sod was crimsoned, the rivers ran blood,

The cornfields were trampled, and all in their track
The beautiful valley lay blasted and black.

Now the din of the conflict swells deadly and loud,
And the dust of the tumult rolls up like a cloud:
Then afar down the slope of the Southland recedes
The wild rapid clatter of galloping steeds.

With wide nostrils smoking, and flanks dripping gore,
The black stallion bore his bold rider before,
As onward they thundered through forest and glen,
A-hunting the dark jaguar to his den.

In April, sweet April, the chase was begun;
It was April again, when the hunting was done:
The snows of four winters and four summers green
Lay red-streaked and trodden and blighted between.

Then the monster stretched all his grim length on the ground;
His life-blood was wasting from many a wound;
Ferocious and gory and dying he lay,
Amid heaps of the whitening bones of his prey.

" So rapine and treason forever shall cease ! "
The slain lamb is raised, a white angel of Peace !
Now Freedom may walk where the black jungle grew,
And all the glad valley shall blossom anew.

LIGHTER PIECES

DARIUS GREEN AND HIS FLYING-MACHINE

IF ever there lived a Yankee lad,
Wise or otherwise, good or bad,
Who, seeing the birds fly, did n't jump
With flapping arms from stake or stump,
    Or, spreading the tail
    Of his coat for a sail,

Take a soaring leap from post or rail,
 And wonder why
 He could n't fly,
And flap and flutter and wish and try, —
If ever you knew a country dunce
Who did n't try that as often as once,
All I can say is, that 's a sign
He never would do for a hero of mine.

An aspiring genius was D. Green:
The son of a farmer, — age fourteen ;
His body was long and lank and lean, —
Just right for flying, as will be seen ;
He had two eyes, each bright as a bean,
And a freckled nose that grew between,
A little awry, — for I must mention
That he had riveted his attention
Upon his wonderful invention,
Twisting his tongue as he twisted the strings,
Working his face as he worked the wings,
And with every turn of gimlet and screw
Turning and screwing his mouth round too.
 Till his nose seemed bent
 To catch the scent,
Around some corner, of new-baked pies,
And his wrinkled cheeks and his squinting eyes
Grew puckered into a queer grimace,
That made him look very droll in the face,
 And also very wise.

And wise he must have been, to do more
Than ever a genius did before,
Excepting Dædalus of yore
And his son Icarus, who wore
 Upon their backs
 Those wings of wax
He had read of in the old almanacs.
Darius was clearly of the opinion,
That the air is also man's dominion,
And that, with paddle or fin or pinion,

We soon or late
Shall navigate
The azure as now we sail the sea.
The thing looks simple enough to me ;
And if you doubt it,
Hear how Darius reasoned about it.

" Birds can fly,
An' why can't I ?
Must we give in,"
Says he with a grin,
" 'T the bluebird an' phœbe
Are smarter 'n we be ?
Jest fold our hands an' see the swaller
An' blackbird an' catbird beat us holler ?
Doos the leetle chatterin', sassy wren,
No bigger 'n my thumb, know more than men ?
Jest show me that !
Er prove 't the bat
Hez got more brains than 's in my hat,
An' I 'll back down, an' not till then ! "

He argued further : " Ner I can't see
What 's th' use o' wings to a bumble-bee,
Fer to git a livin' with, more 'n to me ; —
Ain't my business
Important 's his'n is ?

" That Icarus
Was a silly cuss, —
Him an' his daddy Dædalus.
They might 'a' knowed wings made o' wax
Would n't stan' sun-heat an' hard whacks.
I 'll make mine o' luther,
Er suthin' er other."

And he said to himself, as he tinkered and planned :
" But I ain't goin' to show my hand
To nummies that never can understand
The fust idee that 's big an' grand.

They 'd 'a' laft an' made fun
O' Creation itself afore 't was done ! "
So he kept his secret from all the rest,
Safely buttoned within his vest ;
And in the loft above the shed
Himself he locks, with thimble and thread
And wax and hammer and buckles and screws,
And all such things as geniuses use ; —
Two bats for patterns, curious fellows !
A charcoal-pot and a pair of bellows ;
An old hoop-skirt or two, as well as
Some wire, and several old umbrellas ;
A carriage-cover, for tail and wings ;
A piece of harness ; and straps and strings ;
  And a big strong box,
   In which he locks
These and a hundred other things.

His grinning brothers, Reuben and Burke
And Nathan and Jotham and Solomon, lurk
Around the corner to see him work, —
Sitting cross-leggéd, like a Turk,
Drawing the waxed end through with a jerk,
And boring the holes with a comical quirk
Of his wise old head, and a knowing smirk.
But vainly they mounted each other's backs,
And poked through knot-holes and pried through cracks ;
With wood from the pile and straw from the stacks
He plugged the knot-holes and calked the cracks ;
And a bucket of water, which one would think
He had brought up into the loft to drink
  When he chanced to be dry,
   Stood always nigh,
   For Darius was sly !
And whenever at work he happened to spy
At chink or crevice a blinking eye,
He let a dipper of water fly.
" Take that ! an' ef ever ye git a peep,
Guess ye 'll ketch a weasel asleep ! "
  And he sings as he locks
   His big strong box : —

SONG

"The weasel's head is small an' trim,
An' he is leetle an' long an' slim,
An' quick of motion an' nimble of limb,
    An' ef yeou 'll be
    Advised by me,
Keep wide awake when ye 're ketchin' him ! "

    So day after day
He stitched and tinkered and hammered away,
    Till at last 't was done, —
The greatest invention under the sun !
"An' now," says Darius, " hooray fer some fun ! "

    'T was the Fourth of July,
    And the weather was dry,
And not a cloud was on all the sky,
Save a few light fleeces, which here and there,
    Half mist, half air,
Like foam on the ocean went floating by :
Just as lovely a morning as ever was seen
For a nice little trip in a flying-machine.

Thought cunning Darius : " Now I shan't go
Along 'ith the fellers to see the show.
I 'll say I 've got sich a terrible cough !
An' then, when the folks 'ave all gone off,
    I 'll hev full swing
    Fer to try the thing,
An' practyse a leetle on the wing."

"Ain't goin' to see the celebration ? "
Says Brother Nate.   " No ; botheration !
I 've got sich a cold — a toothache — I —
My gracious ! — feel's though I should fly ! "

    Said Jotham, " 'Sho !
    Guess ye better go."
    But Darius said, " No !
Should n't wonder 'f yeou might see me, though,

'Long 'bout noon, ef I git red
O' this jumpin', thumpin' pain 'n my head."
For all the while to himself he said : —

    " I tell ye what !
I 'll fly a few times around the lot,
To see how 't seems, then soon 's I 've got
The hang o' the thing, ez likely 's not,
        I 'll astonish the nation,
        An' all creation,
By flyin' over the celebration !
Over their heads I 'll sail like an eagle ;
I 'll balance myself on my wings like a sea-gull ;
I 'll dance on the chimbleys ; I 'll stan' on the steeple ;
I 'll flop up to winders an' scare the people !
I 'll light on the libbe'ty-pole, an' crow ;
An' I 'll say to the gawpin' fools below,
        ' What world 's this 'ere
        That I 've come near ? '
Fer I 'll make 'em b'lieve I 'm a chap f'm the moon !
An' I 'll try a race 'ith their ol' bulloon."

        He crept from his bed ;
And, seeing the others were gone, he said,
" I 'm a gittin' over the cold 'n my head."
        And away he sped,
To open the wonderful box in the shed.

His brothers had walked but a little way
When Jotham to Nathan chanced to say,
" What on airth is he up to, hey ? "
" Don'o', — the' 's suthin' er other to pay,
Er he would n't 'a' stayed to hum to-day."
Says Burke, " His toothache 's all 'n his eye !
He never 'd miss a Fo'th-o'-July,
Ef he hed n't got some machine to try."
Then Sol, the little one, spoke : " By darn !
Le 's hurry back an' hide 'n the barn,
An' pay him fer tellin' us that yarn ! "
" Agreed ! "   Through the orchard they creep back,

Along by the fences, behind the stack,
And one by one, through a hole in the wall,
In under the dusty barn they crawl,
Dressed in their Sunday garments all;
And a very astonishing sight was that,
When each in his cobwebbed coat and hat
Came up through the floor like an ancient rat.
And there they hid;
And Reuben slid
The fastenings back, and the door undid.
"Keep dark!" said he,
"While I squint an' see what the' is to see."

As knights of old put on their mail, —
From head to foot
An iron suit,
Iron jacket and iron boot,
Iron breeches, and on the head
No hat, but an iron pot instead,
And under the chin the bail, —
I believe they called the thing a helm;
And the lid they carried they called a shield;
And, thus accoutred, they took the field,
Sallying forth to overwhelm
The dragons and pagans that plagued the realm: —
So this modern knight
Prepared for flight,
Put on his wings and strapped them tight;
Jointed and jaunty, strong and light;
Buckled them fast to shoulder and hip, —
Ten feet they measured from tip to tip!
And a helm had he, but that he wore,
Not on his head like those of yore,
But more like the helm of a ship.

"Hush!" Reuben said,
"He's up in the shed!
He's opened the winder, — I see his head!
He stretches it out,
An' pokes it about,

Lookin' to see 'f the coast is clear,
        An' nobody near ; —
Guess he don'o' who 's hid in here !
He 's riggin' a spring-board over the sill !
Stop laffin', Solomon ! Burke, keep still !
He 's a climbin' out now —   Of all the things !
What 's he got on ?   I van, it 's wings !
An' that 't other thing ?   I vum, it 's a tail !
An' there he sets like a hawk on a rail !
Steppin' careful, he travels the length
Of his spring-board, and teeters to try its strength.
Now he stretches his wings, like a monstrous bat ;
Peeks over his shoulder, this way an' that,
Fer to see 'f the' 's any one passin' by ;
But the' 's on'y a ca'f an' a goslin' nigh.
They turn up at him a wonderin' eye,
To see —   The dragon ! he 's goin' to fly !
Away he goes !   Jimminy ! what a jump !
        Flop — flop — an' plump
        To the ground with a thump !
Flutt'rin' an' flound'rin', all 'n a lump ! "

As a demon is hurled by an angel's spear,
Heels over head, to his proper sphere, —
Heels over head, and head over heels,
Dizzily down the abyss he wheels, —
So fell Darius. Upon his crown,
In the midst of the barnyard, he came down,
In a wonderful whirl of tangled strings,
Broken braces and broken springs,
Broken tail and broken wings,
Shooting-stars, and various things !
Away with a bellow fled the calf,
And what was that ?   Did the gosling laugh ?
        'T is a merry roar
        From the old barn-door,
And he hears the voice of Jotham crying,
" Say, D'rius ! how de yeou like flyin' ? "

Slowly, ruefully, where he lay,
Darius just turned and looked that way,

As he stanched his sorrowful nose with his cuff.
" Wal, I like flyin' well enough,"
He said ; " but the' ain't sich a thunderin' sight
O' fun in 't when ye come to light."

MORAL

I just have room for the moral here :
And this is the moral, — Stick to your sphere.
Or if you insist, as you have the right,
On spreading your wings for a loftier flight,
The moral is, — Take care how you light.

WATCHING THE CROWS

" *CAW, caw !* " — You don't say so ! — " *Caw, caw !* " — What, once
  more ?
Seems to me I 've heard *that* observation before,
And I wish you would *some* time begin to talk sense.
Come, I 've sat here about long enough on the fence,
And I 'd like you to tell me in confidence what
Are your present intentions regarding this lot ?
Why don't you do something ? or else go away ?
" *Caw, caw !* " — Does that mean that they 'll go or they 'll stay ?
While I 'm watching to learn what they 're up to, I see
That for similar reasons they 're just watching me !

That 's right !   Now be brave, and I 'll show you some fun !
Just light within twenty-nine yards of my gun !
I 've hunted and hunted you all round the lot,
Now *you* must come *here*, if you want to be shot !
" *Caw, caw !* " — There they go again !   Is n't it strange
How they always contrive to keep just out of range ?
The scamps have been shot at so often, they know
To a rod just how far the old shot-gun will throw.

Now I 've thought how I 'll serve 'em to-morrow : I 'll play
The game old Jack Haskell played with 'em one day.
His snares would n't catch 'em, his traps would n't spring,
And, in spite of the very best guns he could bring

To bear on the subject, the powder he spent,
And the terriblest scarecrows his wits could invent —
Loud-clattering windmills and fluttering flags,
Straw-stuffed old codgers rigged out in his rags,
And looking quite lifelike in tail-coat and cap,
Twine stretched round the cornfield, suggesting a trap, —
Spite of all, — and he did all that ever a man did, —
They pulled his corn almost before it was planted!

Then he built him an ambush right out in the field,
Where a man could lie down at his ease, quite concealed;
But though he kept watch in it, day after day,
And the thieves would light on it when he was away,
And tear up the corn all around it, not once
Did a crow, young or old, show himself such a dunce
As to come within hail while the old man was there;
For they are the cunningest fools, I declare!
And, seeing him enter, they reasoned, no doubt,
That he must be in there until he came out!

Then, one morning, says he to young Jack, "Now I bet
I 've got an idee that 'll do for 'em yet!
Go with me down into the corn-lot to-day;
Then, when I 'm well placed in the ambush, I 'll stay,
While you shoulder your gun and march back to the barn;
For there 's this leetle notion crows never could larn:
They can't count, as I 'll show ye!" And show him he did!
Young Haskell went home while old Haskell lay hid.

And the crows' education had been so neglected, —
They were so poor in figures, — they never suspected,
If two had come down, and one only went back,
Then one must remain! So, no sooner was Jack
Out of sight, than again to the field they came flocking
As thick as three rats in a little boy's stocking.
They darkened the air, and they blackened the ground;
They came in a cloud to the windmill, and drowned
Its loudest *clack-clack* with a louder *caw-caw!*
They lit on the tail-coat, and laughed at the straw.
"By time!" says old Jack, "now I 've got ye!" *Bang! bang!*
Blazed his short double-shooter right into the gang!

Then, picking the dead crows up out of the dirt, he
Was pleased to perceive that he 'd killed about thirty !

Now that 's just the way I 'll astonish the rascals !
I 'll set up an ambush, like old Mr. Haskell's —
" *Caw, caw !* " — You 're as knowing a bird as I know ;
But there *are* things a little too deep for a crow !
Just add one to one now, and what 's the amount ?
You 're mighty 'cute creeturs, but, then, you can't count !
You 'll see if I don't get a shot ! Yes, I 'll borrow
Another boy somewhere and try ye to-morrow !

EVENING AT THE FARM

OVER the hill the farm-boy goes.
His shadow lengthens along the land,
A giant staff in a giant hand ;
In the poplar-tree, above the spring,
The katydid begins to sing ;
The early dews are falling ; —
Into the stone-heap darts the mink ;
The swallows skim the river's brink ;
And home to the woodland fly the crows,
When over the hill the farm-boy goes,
    Cheerily calling,
  " Co', boss ! co', boss ! co' ! co' ! co' ! "
Farther, farther, over the hill,
Faintly calling, calling still,
  " Co', boss ! co', boss ! co' ! co' ! "

Into the yard the farmer goes,
With grateful heart, at the close of day :
Harness and chain are hung away ;
In the wagon-shed stand yoke and plough,
The straw 's in the stack, the hay in the mow,
    The cooling dews are falling ; —
The friendly sheep his welcome bleat,
The pigs come grunting to his feet,

And the whinnying mare her master knows,
When into the yard the farmer goes,
    His cattle calling, —
     "Co', boss! co', boss! co'! co'! co'!"
While still the cow-boy, far away,
Goes seeking those that have gone astray, —
     "Co', boss! co', boss! co'! co'!"

Now to her task the milkmaid goes.
The cattle come crowding through the gate,
Looing, pushing, little and great;
About the trough, by the farmyard pump,
The frolicsome yearlings frisk and jump,
    While the pleasant dews are falling; —
The new milch heifer is quick and shy,
But the old cow waits with tranquil eye,
And the white stream into the bright pail flows,
When to her task the milkmaid goes,
    Soothingly calling,
     "So, boss! so, boss! so! so! so!"
The cheerful milkmaid takes her stool,
And sits and milks in the twilight cool,
    Saying "So! so, boss! so! so!"

To supper at last the farmer goes.
The apples are pared, the paper read,
The stories are told, then all to bed.
Without, the crickets' ceaseless song
Makes shrill the silence all night long;
    The heavy dews are falling.
The housewife's hand has turned the lock;
Drowsily ticks the kitchen clock;
The household sinks to deep repose,
But still in sleep the farm-boy goes
    Singing, calling, —
     "Co', boss! co', boss! co'! co'! co'!"
And oft the milkmaid, in her dreams,
Drums in the pail with the flashing streams,
    Murmuring "So, boss! so!"

THE WILD GOOSE

WHEN gruff winter goes, and from under his snows
    Peeps the infantine clover,
And little lambs shrink on the bleak hills of March,
And April comes smiling beneath the blue arch,
Then the forester sees from his door the wild geese
    Flying over.

Some to Winnipeg's shore; those to cold Labrador;
    Upon dark Memphremagog,
Swift flying, loud crying, these soon shall alight,
And station their sentries to guard them by night,
Or marshal their ranks to the thick-wooded banks
    Of Umbagog.

Now high in the sky, scarcely seen as they fly,
    Like the head of an arrow
Shot free from its shaft; then a dark-wingéd chain;
Or at eventide wearily over the plain,
Flying low, flying slow, sagging, lagging they go,
    Like a harrow.

Soon all have departed, save one regal-hearted
    Sad prisoner only.
No more shall he breast the blue ether, or rest
In the reeds with his mate, keeping guard by her nest, —
Never glide by her side down the green-fringéd tide
    Fair and lonely.

With clipped pinions, fast in a farmyard, at last
    They have caged the sky-ranger,
'Mid the bustle and clucking and cackle of flocks,
The gossip of geese, and the crowing of cocks;
But apart from the rest, with his proud-curving breast,
    Walks the stranger.

He refuses, with scorn braving hunger, the corn
    From the hands of the givers,
Like a prince in captivity pacing his path;

Little pleasure he hath in his low, stagnant bath;
In that green, standing pool does he think of his cool
        Northern rivers?

Far away, far away, to some lone lake or bay
        His lost comrades are thronging;
In fancy he follows; he hears their glad halloos
Round beautiful beaches, in bright plashy shallows:
And now his dark eye he turns up at the sky
        With wild longing.

He hears them all day, singing, winging their way,
        Over mountains and torrents,
To Canadian hills and their clear watercourses,
To the Ottawa's springs, to the Saguenay's sources;
And now they are going far down the broad-flowing
        Saint Lawrence.

Over grass-land and grove, searching inlet and cove,
        Speeds in dreams the wild gander!
He listens, he hastens, he screams on their track;
They hear him, they cheer him, they welcome him back,
They shout his proud name, and with loud clamors claim
        Their Commander!

With his consort he leads forth their young ones, and feeds
        By the pleasant morasses;
He shows them the tender young crab, and the bug,
The small tented snail, and the slow mantled slug,
And laughs as they eat the soft seeds and the sweet
        Water-grasses.

But danger is coming! Lo, strutting and drumming,
        The turkey-cock charges!
The bright fancy breaks, in the farmyard he wakes;
Nevermore he alights on the blue linkéd lakes
Of the North, or upsprings upon winnowing wings
        From their marges!

Here all the long summer abides the new-comer
        In chains ignominious,

Abandoned, companionless, far from his mate ;
But his heart is still great though dishonored his state,
And his eyes still are dreaming of glad waters gleaming
    And sinuous.

Then the rude Equinox drives before it the flocks
    Of his comrades returning ;
They sail on the gale high above the Ohio's
Broad ribbon, descending on prairies and bayous ;
And again his dark eye is turned up at the sky
    With wild yearning.

As sunward they go, far below, far below,
    Coils the pale Susquehanna !
He sees them, far off in the twilight, encamp as
A vast wingéd host upon dim, ruddy pampas ;
Or at sunrise arrayed upon green everglade
    And savanna.

So year after year, as their legions appear,
    His lost state he remembers ;
Wondering and wistful he watches their flight,
Or starts at their cries in the desolate night,
Dropped down to his hearkening ear through the darkening
    Novembers.

GREEN APPLES

PULL down the bough, Bob !   Is n't this fun ?
Now give it a shake, and — there goes one !
Now put your thumb up to the other, and see
If it is n't as mellow as mellow can be !
        I know by the stripe
        It must be ripe !
That 's one apiece for you and me.

Green, are they ?   Well, no matter for that.
Sit down on the grass, and we 'll have a chat ;
And I 'll tell you what old Parson Bute

Said last Sunday of unripe fruit.
    " Life," says he,
    " Is a bountiful tree,
Heavily laden with beautiful fruit.

" For the youth there 's love, just streaked with red,
And great joys hanging just over his head ;
Happiness, honor, and great estate,
For those who patiently work and wait ; —
    Blessings," said he,
    " Of every degree,
Ripening early, and ripening late.

" Take them in season, pluck and eat,
And the fruit is wholesome, the fruit is sweet ;
But, O my friends ! " — Here he gave a rap
On his desk, like a regular thunder-clap,
    And made such a bang,
    Old Deacon Lang
Woke up out of his Sunday nap.

Green fruit, he said, God would not bless ;
But half life's sorrow and bitterness,
Half the evil and ache and crime,
Came from tasting before their time
    The fruits Heaven sent.
    Then on he went
To his *Fourthly* and *Fifthly :* — was n't it prime ?

But, I say, Bob ! we fellows don't care
So much for a mouthful of apple or pear ;
But what we like is the fun of the thing,
When the fresh winds blow, and the hang-birds **bring**
    Home grubs, and sing
    To their young ones, a-swing
In their basket-nest, tied up by its string.

I like apples in various ways :
They 're first-rate roasted before the blaze
Of a winter fire ; and, O my eyes !

Are n't they nice, though, made into pies?
    I scarce ever saw
    One, cooked or raw,
That was n't good for a boy of my size!

But shake your fruit from the orchard tree,
And the tune of the brook, and the hum of the bee,
And the chipmonks chippering every minute,
And the clear sweet note of the gay little linnet,
    And the grass and the flowers,
    And the long summer hours,
And the flavor of sun and breeze, are in it.

But this is a hard one!　Why did n't we
Leave them another week on the tree?
Is yours as bitter?　Give us a bite!
The pulp is tough, and the seeds are white,
    And the taste of it puckers
    My mouth like a sucker's!
I vow, I believe the old parson was right!

CORN HARVEST

THE fields are filled with a smoky haze.
    The golden spears
    Of the ripening ears
Peep from the crested and pennoned maize.
All down the rustling rows are rolled
The portly pumpkins, green and gold.
    Altogether
    'T is very fine weather,
Just as the almanac foretold.

In early summer the brigand crow
    Made ruthless raids
    On the sprouting blades;
The weeds fought long with the farmer's hoe;
And the raccoons and squirrels have had their share
Of all but the good man's toil and care; —

The shy field-mouse
Has filled her house,
And the blackbirds are flocking from no one knows where.

But now his time has come : hurrah!
To the field, boys! to-day
Our work will be play.
Let the blackbirds scream, and the mad crows caw,
And the squirrels scold on the wild-cherry limb, —
We 'll take from the robbers that took from him!
Come along, one and all, boys!
Big boys and small boys,
Long-armed Amos, and Joel, and Jim!

Bring sickles to reap, or blades to strike.
Before they have lost
In sun and frost
The nourishing juices the cattle like,
Sucker and stalk must be cut from the hill;
Surround them, and bend them, then hit with a will!
Left standing too long,
They grow woody and strong;
The corn in the stook will ripen still.

Carry your stroke, lads, close to the ground.
Set the stalks upright,
And pack them tight
In pyramids shapely and stately and round.
Give the old lady's skirts a genteel spread;
Slope well the shoulders, so as to shed
The autumn rain
From the unhusked grain,
Then twist a wisp for the queer little head.

There she is, waiting to be embraced!
Reach round her who can?
'T will take a man
And a boy, at least, to clasp her waist!
Was ever a hug like that? Now draw
Tightly the girdle of good oat-straw!

With the plumpest waist
That ever was laced,
Goes the narrowest nightcap ever you saw.

We bind the corn, and leave it snug,
    Or rest in the shade
    Of the shocks we have made,
To eat our luncheon, and drink from the jug.
The children come bringing the bands, or play
Hide-and-go-seek in the corn all day,
    And now and then race
    With a chipmonk, or chase
A scared little field-mouse scampering away.

All day we cut and bind ; till at night, —
    Where a field of corn in
    The misty morning
Waved, in the level September light, —
All over the shadowy stubble-land,
The stooks, like Indian wigwams, stand.
    Compact and secure,
    There leave them to cure,
Till the merry husking-time is at hand.

Then the fodder will be to stack or to house,
    And the ears to husk.
    But now the dusk
Falls soft as the shadows of cool pine-boughs ;
Our good day's work is done ; the night
Brings wholesome fatigue and appetite ;
    Up comes the balloon
    Of the huge red moon,
And home we go, singing gay songs by its light.

THE LITTLE THEATRE

I KNOW a little theatre
    Scarce bigger than a nut.
Finer than pearl its portals are,

Quick as the twinkling of a star
   They open and they shut.

A fairy palace beams within :
   So wonderful it is,
No words can tell you of its worth, —
No architect in all the earth
   Could build a house like this.

A beautiful rose window lets
   A ray into the hall ;
To shade the scene from too much light,
A tiny curtain hangs in sight,
   Within the crystal wall.

And O the wonders there beside !
   The curious furniture,
The stage, with all its small machinery,
Pulley and cord and shifting scenery,
   In marvellous miniature !

A little, busy, moving world,
   It mimics space and time,
The marriage-feast, the funeral,
Old men and little children, all
   In perfect pantomime.

There pours the foaming cataract,
   There speeds the train of cars ;
Day comes with all its pageantry
Of cloud and mountain, sky and sea,
   The night, with all its stars.

Ships sail upon that mimic sea ;
   And smallest things that fly,
The humming-bird, the sunlit mote
Upon its golden wings afloat,
   Are mirrored in that sky.

Quick as the twinkling of the doors,
   The scenery forms or fades ;

And all the fairy folk that dwell
Within the arched and windowed shell
    Are momentary shades.

Who has this wonder holds it dear
    As his own life and limb ;
Who lacks it, not the rarest gem
That ever flashed in diadem
    Can purchase it for him.

Ah, then, dear picture-loving child,
    How doubly blessed art thou !
Since thine the happy fortune is
To have two little worlds like this
    In thy possession now, —

Each furnished with soft folding-doors,
    A curtain, and a stage !
And now a laughing sprite transfers
Into those little theatres
    The letters of this page.

THE CHARCOALMAN

THOUGH rudely blows the wintry blast,
And sifting snows fall white and fast,
Mark Haley drives along the street,
Perched high upon his wagon seat ;
His sombre face the storm defies,
And thus from morn till eve he cries,
    " Charco' ! charco' ! "
While echo faint and far replies,
    " Hark, O ! hark, O ! "
" Charco' ! " — " Hark, O ! " — Such cheery sounds
Attend him on his daily rounds.

The dust begrimes his ancient hat ;
His coat is darker far than that ;
'T is odd to see his sooty form
All speckled with the feathery storm ;

Yet in his honest bosom lies
Nor spot nor speck, though still he cries,
    "Charco'! charco'!"
While many a roguish lad replies,
    "Ark, ho! ark, ho!"
"Charco'!" — "Ark, ho!" — Such various sounds
Announce Mark Haley's morning rounds.

Thus all the cold and wintry day
He labors much for little pay;
Yet feels no less of happiness
Than many a richer man, I guess,
When through the shades of eve he spies
The light of his own home, and cries,
    "Charco'! charco'!"
And Martha from the door replies,
    "Mark, ho! Mark, ho!"
"Charco'!" — "Mark, ho!" — Such joy abounds
When he has closed his daily rounds!

The hearth is warm, the fire is bright;
And while his hand, washed clean and white,
Holds Martha's tender hand once more,
His glowing face bends fondly o'er
The crib wherein his darling lies,
And in a coaxing tone he cries,
    "Charco'! charco'!"
And baby with a laugh replies,
    "Ah, go! ah, go!"
"Charco'!" — "Ah, go!" — while at the sounds
The mother's heart with gladness bounds.

BOOK II

THE EMIGRANT'S STORY AND OTHER POEMS

Under the wintry skies,
  All pallid and still as the moon,
The cold earth slumbering lies,
  Close wound in her white cocoon.
In her shrouded and dreamless rest
  She awaits the coming of Spring:
And the soul of song in my breast
  Is dumb, — I cannot sing.

But soon at the touch, at the glance
  That thrills the bound spirit beneath,
She will wake, she will rouse from her trance,
  She will burst from her chrysalis sheath, —
All palpitating in sheen
  Of gleaming rimple and fold,
Fresh robed in sapphire and green,
  Full winged with purple and gold!

When the world, reawakened from death,
  Is wavering, throbbing in light,
And panting with perfumed breath,
  In a heaven of sound and of sight, —
O, then, with all jubilant things,
  Will my soul, that has slumbered so long,
Awake in the glory of wings,
  Arise with the rapture of song?

THE EMIGRANT'S STORY AND OTHER POEMS

THE EMIGRANT'S STORY

FRIEND, have a pipe, and a seat on the log here under the pine-tree.
Here in the cool of the day we 'll smoke, and I 'll tell you the story.

First, — do you notice the girl? the slim one helping her mother, —
Tough little tow-head, spry as a catamount, freckled as birch-bark!
Nannie her name is; — it happened the summer when she was a baby.

Times were hard in the States. We lived on the farm with the old
    folks:
There all our dear little tots had been born, and their mother before
    them.
But the old hive would n't grow with the fresh young life that was buz-
    zing
In and out of its doors; and, after much tribulation, —
Many a sleepless night I talked it over with Molly, —
We had resolved to push out, and find a new home on the prairies.

Well, it was settled at last; and, packing our pots and our kettles,
Clothing and bedding, and bags of Indian meal and potatoes,
Hen-coop, tools, — the few indispensable things to a poor man, —
Into a regular broad-beamed ark-on-wheels of a wagon,
Canvas-covered and drawn by two yoke of oxen, we started, —
Crowing cockerel, dog and cat, and chickens, and children.

Father and mother and grandmother stood and watched from the door-
    yard, —
Two generations that stayed saw two generations departing.

Molly just smothered her babies, and sobbed, and hardly looked back
    once, —

Woman all over! but I (though I broke down trying to cheer her)
Turned at the top of the hill, and gave a good stare at the old house,
Well-sweep, orchard, barn, the smoke from the chimney, and still one
Handkerchief feebly fluttering, with the great sunrise behind all.
That is the picture I saw, and see again at this minute,
Plain as if this was the hill, and down by the creek there the homestead.
Then it dropped into the past, with the life we had lived, and a new
    world
Opened before us. I tell you, 't was hard on the woman! But, stranger,
Look at her now, with her grown and half-grown daughters about her,
Smart as the best of them, setting the table and getting our supper,
Hopeful and resolute, light of heart and of hand, — and, believe me,
That 's just the way she has been ever since — after having her cry out
Over her young ones that morning — she turned a face like the sunrise
Westward; never a tear from that time nor a word of repining!

Novelty tickles the young; and the children, seeing the world move
Slowly and leisurely past, through the rolled-up sides of the canvas,
Shouted and laughed, and thought there was nothing but fun in a journey.
Tired of that, they walked, or romped with the dog by the roadside,
Racing, gathering flowers, and picking and stringing the berries;
Tired of that, sometimes they rode on the backs of the oxen;
Tired of everything else, they fell asleep in the wagon,
Spite of the jolts: — what would n't we give to sleep as a child sleeps?
Then they had something to do, when we camped at noon or at nightfall,
Gathering sticks for the fire, while I looked after the oxen.

Day after day we continued our journey, and night after night slept
Under our canvas, or lay on the ground rolled up in our blankets;
Leaving the cities behind us and pushing on into the backwoods,
Passing the scattered settlements, fording the streams: then the timber
Dwindled and disappeared; and on the great prairies the sun rose
Over the stern of our wagon and set on the horns of the oxen,
Morning and night; then forests once more; and the trail that we fol-
    lowed
Brought us into these woods. We intended to go on and settle
Over on Big Buck Branch, where one of our neighbors, John Osmond,
Going before us, had fenced his claim and rigged up a sawmill.
Here we encamped at night, and here what Molly will call God's
Hand interfered with our plans in the way I am going to tell you.

After a sultry and sweltering day in September, the night came
Breathless and close. We had halted here in the gathering twilight,
Choosing our camping-ground where fuel and water were plenty ;
Woods, great woods all about us, only on one side the creek there
Flowed through the grassy bottom much as you see it at present.
I had unyoked and watered the poor lolling cattle, and left them
Deep in the wild grass, tethered, feeding and fighting mosquitoes.
Then in the woods rang the sound of an axe, and I was the chopper,
Slashing away at the tops of a whitewood fallen in the forest,
Throwing off sticks and chips which the two boys caught up and ran with.
Molly, intent on her housekeeping, minding the baby, arranging
Everything for our comfort, was in and out of the wagon ;
Robbie already had run with a pail and brought water to cook with ;
Then in the darkening woods shot up the blaze of our camp-fire,
Home-like and cheery ; and soon the savory smell of our cooking
Made us deliciously hungry, — steaming coffee and stewing
Prairie-chickens ; I shot them that afternoon from our wagon.

After supper the little ones said their prayers to their mother,
Kneeling under the great gaunt trees, in the gleam of the firelight.
Molly then (she is one of the pious sort, did I tell you ?)
Prayed for us all, — a short prayer that we might be kept until morning.
Little the poor girl knew where the morning would find us ! It makes
    me —
Well, yes, soft is the word, when I think of that prayer and what fol-
    lowed.

Here 's the identical spot ! Here (fill your pipe again, stranger),
After preparing our bed, — that is, just spreading our blankets
On the dry ground, — we stood, the mother and I, for a long while
Hand in hand, that night, and looked at our six little shavers,
All asleep in their nests. either in or under the wagon, —
Robbie, and Johnny, and Jane, and Tommy, and Bess, and the baby, —
None of your puny sort, — cheeks brown and handsome as russets ; —
Here in the great, still woods we watched them, with curious feelings,
Asking ourselves again and again if we had done wisely
Making this journey, and was n't it all a foolhardy adventure ?
Each well enough had divined what the other was thinking : then
    Molly —
" God will take care of them and of us," says she, " if we trust him."

'T was n't for me to dispute her ; but somehow I have a notion,
Praying our best is doing our best for ourselves and each other ;
Trust in God is believing that, after we have done our part,
He will look out for the rest ; anyhow, it is useless to worry,
Whether he does or he does n't ; and so I reasoned and acted.
Though, after all has been said, there is certainly something or other,
Call it the finger of God, Fate, Providence, what you 've a mind to, —
Something that governs the cards in this game of life we are playing,
Felt oftentimes if not seen, — as it were, a Presence behind us
Planning and prompting our play, — that 's how I look at it, stranger ;
After what happened that night I 'm not the man to deny it.

I had been maybe three hours asleep, when the crow of our cooped-up
Rooster, along about midnight, awoke me ; and well I remember
What a strange night it was, — how quiet and ghostly and lonesome !
Dark as Egypt all round our little travelling household,
In the small, shadowy space half lit by our flickering night-fire.
Not a leaf rustled ; no breath, no sound, except the incessant,
Teasing noise of the vixenish katydids contradicting.
Then there was sudden commotion : the shadowy branches above us
Swayed and clashed, and the woods seemed to reel and rock for a
    moment.
Then it passed off in a roar like the sea, and again there was silence ;
Even the katydids had desisted from scolding to listen.
Nature just seemed to be holding her breath and waiting for something.

" Can't you sleep, Thomas ? " says Molly. " Are you awake, too ? " I
    said. " Yes, dear.
I have not slept for an hour, my mind is so full of forebodings.
What can it mean ? for I feel there is something dreadful impending !
Twice to-night I have dreamed that a limb from one of the trees fell
Right where we are ! Each time I awoke with a scream, — did you
    hear me ? —
Just as 't was falling on you. Sleep again I cannot and dare not,
For if I do I am sure I shall dream the same dream for a third time.
Hark ! " she exclaimed ; " what is that ? "

                                    A singular noise in the southwest ;
Not like the sound we had heard, when the wind died away in the dis-
    tance, —

Sharper and stronger than that; and, instead of dying, increasing,
Thundering onward, — a terrible rushing and howling and crashing;
Louder and louder, as if all the trees in the forest were falling;
Nearer and nearer, a deafening, deluging roar! Then I started;
"Molly!" I shrieked, "the tornado!" and made a dash at the children,
Snatching them out of their beds, all dazed and frightened and stupid,
Half in the dark, in the awfullest din and confusion.

                                            Poor Molly
Did n't know which way to turn, but flung herself on them, to shield
    them.
"Run!" I yelled; "run! — to the creek!" — In a moment the crash
    would be on us.
Catching my arms full, — one by the wrist, — the mother beside me
Bearing her part, — Heaven only knows how, we carried, we dragged
    them
Down the dark slope, in the roar of a hundred Niagaras plunging,
Blackness ahead, and the big trees screeching and breaking and clash-
    ing
Close at our heels, all about us, — the tops of one whipped us in falling!
Then the wind took us, and —

                                Well, the next minute I found myself lying
Down in the grass there, clinging, and holding on to the small fry,
In a mad storm of leaves and broken branches and hailstones, —
Howling darkness, and jaws of lightning that showed us the world all
Rushing and streaming one way. I can't say how long it lasted,
Maybe five minutes, not more; then all of a sudden the lull came.

Counting heads, I found that three of the children were with me,
Cuddled down close; but where all the while were the rest, and their
    mother?
Never a one to be seen, as I looked by the quivering flashes, —
Only the grass blown flat, ironed down, all along by the creek shore.
Soon as the tempest would let me, I rose to my feet, braced against it,
Shouted, and listened; when out of the dire confusion of noises
Came a long, dismal bellow from one of my poor frightened oxen.
Then a child cried near by. Then *her* voice: "Are you all safe there?"
"Yes. Where are you?" I cried. "Here! under the bank, by the
    water,

Tommy and Jennie — not one of us hurt — just where the wind
    dropped us.
O, what a merciful providence! Did you say — did you say *all* safe?
Baby and all?"
                "The baby!" I said.   "Have n't you got the baby?"
That brought her up from the creek with a shriek — shall I ever for-
    get it?
That, or the look she gave, as she rushed out before me? her long black
Hair flying wild in the wind, face white, in a sheet of white lightning!
"O, my baby!" she said, "you had it, — I felt its bed empty!"
"Yes, I remember — I took it, I gave it to some one — to Jennie!
Then I put both in your arms."
                 "O father!" says Jennie, "you gave me
Something wrapped up in a blanket.   I hugged it tight, but it squirmed
    so —
I was so frightened — it scratched and jumped from my arms — and,
    O father!
'T was n't the baby, I know!"   And that was the way of it: I had
Thrust my hand into the wagon, and caught up an object I found there
Under the blanket.   Consider the horrible uproar and hubbub,
Darkness and fright, and then maybe you 'll understand how a man
    can
Make such a blunder; — the baby had rolled from its place, and the
    blanket
Dropped on the cat, I suppose, when I took up the last of the children.

Well, there we were, and it 's easy to think of pleasanter places
One might prefer to be in, if he had his choice in the matter: —
Young ones shivering, crying, mother almost distracted,
None of us more than half dressed, just the clothes on which we had
    slept in;
Dark as Egypt again, not even the lightning to guide us
Into the terrible windfall in search of our camp and the baby;
Weather grown suddenly cold, and five hours yet until daylight!

All was quiet again, very much as if nothing had happened, —
Only occasional flurries of wind and spatters of cold rain;
Then I looked up, and, behold! the stars were shining; I saw them
Glance through flying clouds, and the twisted branches above me
Where I was struggling so madly to find a way back to the wagon.

I for the twentieth time had paused to hear if a child cried,
Hoping still against fate, when they shone out, O so serenely!
Over my head, those stars, looking down on my rage and impatience.
Something entered my soul with their beams, — I could never explain it;
'T was n't just what you might call a pious notion that took me, —
But from that time I was calm, under all my outward excitement;
Calm deep down in my heart, and prepared for whatever might happen.

Still it was frightful business, — tearing my way through the treetops,
Climbing about the immense crossed trunks and limbs, till a glimmer
Caught my eye through the brush, — a blinking brand of our camp-fire,
Scattered, but not quite extinguished, for all the hail and the whirlwind.
All this time I had kept up a frequent hallooing to Molly,
Brooding her half-naked young ones, just outside of the windfall,
Waiting in terror and cold to hear the worst.   Only Robbie,
Stout little fellow, was with me; wherever I clambered, he followed.
"Father!" he cried, "see the light!" and forward we scrambled to
    reach it, —
Scraped together what sticks and leaves we could feel with our fingers.
Everything, though, was so damp that, with all our puffing and blowing,
Never a blaze would start (our matches were left in the wagon), —
Till, all at once, a flash! I looked, and there was the rogue, sir,
Tearing his shirt into strips of cotton to kindle the fire with!
"Mother won't care," says he. "What's a shirt, if we only find baby?"

On went branches and bark.   There, in the still light, all around us
Lay the tremendous tangle, — timber scattered like jack-straws;
Shaggy and shadowy masses starting out of the darkness;
Upturned roots, with their cart-loads of earth, — all the work of a
    minute!
Still no sign of a wagon; no cry, in the terrible silence, —
Only the lisp of the flames, and the hiss and crackle of green stuff
Where they streamed into the hair of a giant pine-tree, and lit up
All that part of the windfall.   Near by, on a bough, a small bird sat,
Dazed: you might almost have caught it. Just then I perceived some-
    thing white gleam,
Rushed for it, tore through the brush; and there, sir, if you'll be-
    lieve me,
In a rough penfold of trees slung about in the carelessest fashion,
Safe in the midst of 'em, only the tongue smashed up and the canvas

Damaged a trifle — Excuse me, I never could get through the story,
Just along here, without being a little mite womanish! — Well, sir,
There, as I said, was the wagon, and there, as I live, was the baby,
Keeled over into a basket, and sleeping, as peaceful as could be!
That was the wonder, — to think how she had refused to be quiet
Many a night, to sleep at last through a tearing tornado!
Strange, too, — the moment I saw her she woke, and, as if she was bound to
Make up for time she had lost, set up such a musical screeching,
In the wild woods, as I guess never went to the heart of a mother
Gladder than Molly. No need for Robbie to yell, " We have found her ! "

Soon, by the help of the light, I had brought the whole tribe through the windfall.
But, after all, the thing did look mighty bad to me, stranger!
There was our poor dog killed by a tree that had crashed on our camp-fire ;
Dinner-pot smashed ; likewise the hen-coop beside it demolished ;
Wagon disabled ; and that, and all our earthly possessions,
Fast in a snarl of big logs that I never expected to cut through:
Fifteen miles to Buck Branch, and not a hand nearer to help us!

Well, I was blue! The woman of course went into hysterics,
Hugging her baby, at first ; then came to me with her comfort:
" Don't be down-hearted ! " she said. " O dear ! do look at that hen-coop!
Pull off the branches, why don't you? maybe the poor things are alive yet."
So I uncovered the rubbish ; — three pullets quite stiff ; but the rooster
Fluttered a little, got up, looked about him, and shook out his feathers,
Saw his three wives lying dead at his feet, his house all in ruins,
Hopped to a stump, where he flapped his red wings in the flush of the firelight,
Stretched up his neck and crowed! superb, courageous, defiant,
Flinging his note of cheer out into the night, till the echoes
Crowed in the distance. The frightened, huddling and shivering children
Heard it, laughed, and took heart ; and I said, " If that cockerel, after
All that has happened to him, has pluck enough left him to crow with,

What am I to despair, with my wife and children around me,
Safe, and with hands to shape our future out of this chaos ? "

Daylight came, and showed the work that was laid out before me.
There was the windfall, — a gap in the woods far off in the southwest,
Skipping the creek, then stretching as far away in the northeast, —
Just a big swath through the timber, as if a giant had mowed it !
What did I do? Went out and looked up my cattle, the first thing ;
Then set to work with my axe, getting poles and bark for a cabin ;
Drove to Buck Branch with a drag, sold one yoke of oxen, and brought
    back
Things that we needed the most ; cut grass for the cattle, come winter, —
Settled, in short, where we were, because we could n't well help it.

Watching my chance, by degrees I burned off, and logged off, the wind-
    fall,
Turning it into a wheat-lot that has n't its beat in the country.
Taken together, the woodland, and bottom, and prairie beyond there,
Make the best kind of a farm. And soon we began to have neighbors.
Table and chairs took the place of blocks and slabs in our cabin ;
Cabin itself gave way in a couple of years to a log-house ;
Log-house at last to a framed house, — this is the article, stranger ;
Not the most elegant mansion, — snug, though, and much at your ser-
    vice.
School-house and meeting-house followed. And then came the row with
    the redskins.
Terrible times ! We escaped, — and that's a strange part of my story.
Over on Big Buck Branch, where we had intended to settle,
Every man, woman, and child — except our old neighbor, John Osmond,
He was with us at the time — was murdered, or driven for refuge
Into the woods (it was winter), and all their houses and barns burnt, —
Grist-mill, saw-mill, store, there was n't a building left standing.
We on the creek took in the poor wretches, and often that winter,
Not for ourselves alone, had reason to bless the tornado, —
Or what Power soever that with the twirl of a finger,
Tied us up here in the woods, in the mighty hard knot of a windfall.

That is the story. Beg pardon ! your pipe is out. But there 's Nannie —
Baby worth saving, you think ? — just coming to call us to supper.

DOROTHY IN THE GARRET

In the low-raftered garret, stooping
    Carefully over the creaking boards,
Old Maid Dorothy goes a-groping
    Among its dusty and cobwebbed hoards ;
Seeking some bundle of patches, hid
    Far under the eaves, or bunch of sage,
Or satchel hung on its nail, amid
    The heirlooms of a bygone age.

There is the ancient family chest,
    There the ancestral cards and hatchel ;
Dorothy, sighing, sinks down to rest,
    Forgetful of patches, sage, and satchel.
Ghosts of faces peer from the gloom
    Of the chimney, where, with swifts and reel,
And the long-disused, dismantled loom,
    Stands the old-fashioned spinning-wheel.

She sees it back in the clean-swept kitchen,
    A part of her girlhood's little world :
Her mother is there by the window, stitching ;
    Spindle buzzes, and reel is whirled
With many a click : on her little stool
    She sits, a child by the open door,
Watching, and dabbling her feet in the pool
    Of sunshine warm on the gilded floor.

Her sisters are spinning all day long :
    To her wakening sense, the first sweet warning
Of daylight come, is the cheerful song
    To the hum of the wheel, in the early morning.
Benjie, the gentle, red-cheeked boy,
    On his way to school, peeps in at the gate ;
In neat, white pinafore, pleased and coy,
    She reaches a hand to her bashful mate ;

And under the elms, a prattling pair,
    Together they go, through glimmer and gloom : —

It all comes back to her, dreaming there
  In the low-raftered garret-room ;
The hum of the wheel, and the summer weather,
  The heart's first trouble, and love's beginning,
Are all in her memory linked together ;
  And now it is she herself that is spinning.

With the bloom of youth on cheek and lip,
  Turning the spokes with the flashing pin,
Twisting the thread from the spindle-tip,
  Stretching it out and winding it in,
To and fro, with a blithesome tread,
  Singing she goes, and her heart is full,
And many a long-drawn golden thread
  Of fancy is spun with the shining wool.

Her father sits in his favorite place,
  Puffing his pipe by the chimney-side ;
Through curling clouds his kindly face
  Glows upon her with love and pride.
Lulled by the wheel, in the old armchair
  Her mother is musing, cat in lap,
With beautiful drooping head, and hair
  Whitening under her snow-white cap.

One by one, to the grave, to the bridal,
  They have followed her sisters from the door ;
Now they are old, and she is their idol : —
  It all comes back on her heart once more.
In the autumn dusk the hearth gleams brightly,
  The wheel is set by the shadowy wall, —
A hand at the latch, — 't is lifted lightly,
  And in walks Benjie, manly and tall.

His chair is placed ; the old man tips
  The pitcher, and brings his choicest fruit ;
Benjie basks in the blaze, and sips,
  And tells his story, and joints his flute :
O, sweet the tunes, the talk, the laughter !
  They fill the hour with a glowing tide ;

But sweeter the still, deep moments after,
    When she is alone by Benjie's side.

But once with angry words they part:
    O, then the weary, weary days!
Ever with restless, wretched heart,
    Plying her task, she turns to gaze
Far up the road; and early and late
    She harks for a footstep at the door,
And starts at the gust that swings the gate,
    And prays for Benjie, who comes no more.

Her fault? O Benjie! and could you steel
    Your thoughts toward one who loved you so? —
Solace she seeks in the whirling wheel,
    In duty and love that lighten woe;
Striving with labor, not in vain,
    To drive away the dull day's dreariness;
Blessing the toil that blunts the pain
    Of a deeper grief in the body's weariness.

Proud, and petted, and spoiled was she:
    A word, and all her life is changed!
His wavering love too easily
    In the great, gay city grows estranged.
One year: she sits in the old church pew;
    A rustle, a murmur, — O Dorothy! hide
Your face and shut from your soul the view!
    'T is Benjie leading a white-veiled bride!

Now father and mother have long been dead,
    And the bride sleeps under a churchyard stone,
And a bent old man with grizzled head
    Walks up the long, dim aisle alone.
Years blur to a mist; and Dorothy
    Sits doubting betwixt the ghost she seems
And the phantom of youth, more real than she,
    That meets her there in that haunt of dreams.

Bright young Dorothy, idolized daughter,
    Sought by many a youthful adorer,

Life, like a new-risen dawn on the water,
  Shining, an endless vista, before her!
Old Maid Dorothy, wrinkled and gray,
  Groping under the farm-house eaves, —
And life is a brief November day
  That sets on a world of withered leaves!

FARMER JOHN

HOME from his journey Farmer John
  Arrived this morning, safe and sound.
His black coat off, and his old clothes on,
"Now I 'm myself!" says Farmer John;
    And he thinks, "I 'll look around."
Up leaps the dog: "Get down, you pup!
Are you so glad you would eat me up?"
The old cow lows at the gate, to greet him;
The horses prick up their ears, to meet him:
    "Well, well, old Bay!
    Ha, ha, old Gray!
Do you get good feed when I am away?

"You have n't a rib!" says Farmer John;
  "The cattle are looking round and sleek;
The colt is going to be a roan,
And a beauty too: how he has grown!
    We 'll wean the calf next week."
Says Farmer John, "When I 've been off,
To call you again about the trough,
And watch you, and pet you, while you drink,
Is a greater comfort than you can think!"
    And he pats old Bay,
    And he slaps old Gray; —
"Ah, this is the comfort of going away!

"For, after all," says Farmer John,
  "The best of a journey is getting home.
I 've seen great sights; but would I give
This spot, and the peaceful life I live,
    For all their Paris and Rome?

These hills for the city's stifled air,
And big hotels all bustle and glare,
Land all houses, and roads all stones,
That deafen your ears and batter your bones?
Would you, old Bay?
Would you, old Gray?
That 's what one gets by going away!

"There Money is king," says Farmer John;
"And Fashion is queen; and it 's mighty queer
To see how sometimes, while the man
Is raking and scraping all he can,
The wife spends, every year,
Enough, you would think, for a score of wives,
To keep them in luxury all their lives!
The town is a perfect Babylon
To a quiet chap," says Farmer John.
"You see, old Bay, —
You see, old Gray, —
I 'm wiser than when I went away.

"I 've found out this," says Farmer John, —
"That happiness is not bought and sold,
And clutched in a life of waste and hurry,
In nights of pleasure and days of worry;
And wealth is n't all in gold,
Mortgage and stocks and ten per cent, —
But in simple ways, and sweet content,
Few wants, pure hopes, and noble ends,
Some land to till, and a few good friends,
Like you, old Bay,
And you, old Gray!
That 's what I 've learned by going away."

And a happy man is Farmer John, —
O, a rich and happy man is he!
He sees the peas and pumpkins growing,
The corn in tassel, the buckwheat blowing,
And fruit on vine and tree;
The large, kind oxen look their thanks
As he rubs their foreheads and strokes their flanks;

The doves light round him, and strut and coo.
Says Farmer John, " I 'll take you too, —
    And you, old Bay,
    And you, old Gray,
Next time I travel so far away ! "

OLD SIMON DOLE

So, Mimy, it 's me an' you agin, is it ?
  Strange, atter so long a while, to think
I sh'd be comin' to make ye a visit,
  An' set tipped back here agin the sink,
An' tock to ye jes' 's I did, ye know, —
Wal, nigh on to forty year ago !

Le' me see ! Married in 'twenty-six ;
  'T wuz a new house then, an' ye moved right in.
Don't look quite so new to-day ! It 's slick 's
  It ever wuz, though, — neat as a pin !
I ollers telled Jerome, when he got
Our Mimy, he picked the best o' the lot.

Ye axed my advice, remember : " He ain't
  The smartis' feller in oll creation,"
Says I, " ner you wun't find him a saint ;
  Well off, though, an' that 's a consideration.
'F he gits the right kin' of a wife, he 'll let her
Manage. I guess ye can't do no better,"

Says I. An' ye found it jes' 'bout so.
  Ye begun 'ith him right, I ollers said.
'F a woman expec's to hoe her row
  With a man, — keepin' mebby a leetle ahead, —
She mus' start in season : slim chance she 'll stan',
Once give him fairly the upper han' !

Then I got married. Ah, wal, poor Mary !
  She made a good wife, though she wa'n't re'l strong.
You never looked into a han'somer dairy !
  An' she wuz as pleasant 's the day wuz long,

With jes' the pertyis' kin' of a v'ice.
I never had reason to rue my ch'ice.

I got a wife an' a farm to boot;
  Ye could n't ketch me a nappin' there!
Thinks I, " Now, s'posin' the wife don't soot?
  The farm 'll be suthin' to make that square;
No resk 'bout that! An' where 's the harm,
If the wife turns out as good as the farm? "

She 'd nat'ral larnin', — bright 's a dollar!
  It runs in the Grimeses, — she wuz clear Grimes.
I 'm 'mos' sorry I did n't foller
  Her counsels more 'n I did, sometimes.
The' wa'n't nothin' but what she understood;
An' her jedgment in matters wuz ollers good.

It might 'a' be'n well if I had, — do'no'.
  'T wa'n't never my way to be led. I hate
A woman 'at wears the breeches; an' so,
  Mebby, by tryin' to stan' too straight,
When she 'd have bent me a little, I fell
Over back now an' then, — do'no'; can't tell.

She 'd high idees! She claimed we 'd otter
  Give Simon a college edecation;
Teased me to send our secon' dotter
  (She knowed 't would cos' like all creation!)
To boardin'-school, an' have a pyaner
An' music-master for Abby an' Hanner.

I thot that notion might cool a spell.
  I never 'd sot foot inside a college,
An' I 'd rubbed through the world perty well.
  As fer the gals, a trifle o' knowledge,
Enough fer to teach, might help 'em some;
But that they could have 'thout goin' f'm hum.

" They need n't poke off to the 'cademy,
  To fin' good husban's, I 'm sure," says I.

"*You* never done that, an' you foun' *me*.
    They 'll make good wives, too, I guess, if they try,
'Thout French an' drarrin'; it don't take these
    Fer to mix a pud'n' an' set a cheese.

"I mean to bring up our Sim," says I,
    "To go to meet'n' an' Sunday-school,
An' do 's he 'd be done by, perty nigh,
    An' be a good farmer, an' nob'dy's fool,
An' give him schoolin' enough, so 's he
Can take good care of his proppity, —

"With some to take care on; then if he 's sound
    In the doctrine, and pop'lar enough fer to go
To the Gin'ral Court when the time comes round
    (Don't take much schoolin' fer that, ye know),
I sh'll consider," says I, "'t I 've done
A payrunt's hull dooty to a son.

"But drarrin' an' French an' pyaner-playin', —
    That nonsense! — I would n't give a strah
Fer gals brot up tut! An' as fer payin',"
    Says I, "bills long 's the marral lah
'T yer board'n'-schools, — when I 'm sich a dunce,
Jes' put me under guardeens to once!"

That did n't quite jibe 'ith her idee;
    An' once she could n't help flingin' out
'T the money it cost would n't come f'm me,
    Sence the farm wuz her 'n. But that wuz about
The last on 't. Tock like that! I told her
'T would make the ol' house too hot to hold her.

Singin' was well enough; an' Sim
    An' Jemimy gin'ally sot in the choir.
Then 'f they struck up a Sunday hymn,
    A settin' around a winter's fire, —
Er a good ol'-fashioned week-day song, —
Th' evenin's did n't seem quite so long.

But the sweetis' tunes wuz ollers sweeter,
  Though I do say it, if she j'ined in.
She wuz jes' the meekis', patientis' creatur'!
  I 've said it, er thot it, time an' agin.
Do'no' 's I ever spoke it out loud
To her, ' fear praisin' might make her proud.

Ye never did see sich a cute contriver
  Fer makin' things nice an' comf'table!
Work — though she wa'n't no gre't of a driver —
  Ollers, when she wuz around, went well.
Seemed 's 'ough the' wuz suthin' in her smile
'At made the wheels run as slick as ile.

Wal, bimeby Hanner she got married;
  An' Simon he begun to spark it;
An' Abby died; an' Jemimy carried
  Her wool, 's I said, to a dumb poor market;
Took up 'ith the wheelwright's son, an' went
Out West, — smart chap, but had n't a cent.

I might 'a' gi'n 'em a thousan' dollars,
  To buy 'em some land; 't would tickled mother!
They 'lotted on 't; but then she wuz ollers
  Forever a teasin' fer this un an' t' other;
I 'd got so use' ter sayin' no,
I forked out fifty, an' let 'em go.

Sim he done well, — Square Ebbitt's dotter;
  They gi'n her a han'some settin'-out!
I fixed 'em a house, an' her folks bot her
  The biggis' pyaner in town, about.
'T would do for *her*.   Sounds kin' o' nice!
She 'll play!   You 'd think her fingers wuz mice!

Childern oll married off er dead,
  It seemed some lonesome fer a spell.
We 'uz gitt'n' in years, an' wife she said
  We 'd made enough, an' I 'd otter sell, —

Give up hard work, an' settle down,
'Longside o' Simon, nigher town.

I hated, wus 'n ever a man did,
    To quit the farm; fer every year
We wuz gittin' more an' more forehanded, —
    Layin' up reg'lar suthin' clear;
An' the' 's sich a satisfaction knowin'
Yer grass an' yer bank account is growin'!

I may 'a' be'n wrong; we 're poor, frail creatur's!
    But she kep' up so 'bout her work, —
She 'd ollers jes' them delikit featur's,
    Wuz jes' so quiet, an' jes' so chirk,
(She never would fret, though she never wuz slack:
I 'd scold, but she never scolded back), —

I did n't once 'spect how low she wuz,
    Ner dream o' what wuz a-goin' to happen,
Till bimeby neighbors begun to buzz;
    An' says one to me : " Why, ye 're crazy, Cap'n!
She 'll work long 's ever she drahs breath,
An' she 's jes' workin' herself to death!"

Another said, she wuz pinin' away, —
    She did n't have s'ciety enough, —
She 'd otter go ridin' every day!
    I 'xpect I answered 'em kin o' gruff;
Though I must own I wuz gin'ally loth
To have comp'ny much, — it 's a perfick moth.

I *s'pose* I wuz wrong, — the best is li'ble
    To miss it, — an' yit I tried to do right.
I kep' the sabbath, an' read the Bible,
    An' prayed in the fam'ly marnin' an' night, —
'Thout 't wuz in hayin'-time, now an' then,
When wages wuz high, an' we 'd hired men.

We had the darktor to her; but she
    Did n't seem to have no settl' disease.

" 'T ain't 'zac'ly the lungs, Mis' Dole," says he.
" Can't be," says I, " the butter an' cheese !
An', Darktor," says I, " how *could* it come
F'm lonesomeness ?   *I* 'm ollers to hum ! "

Oll we know is, 't wuz a dispensation !
    Heavem's ways ain't our 'n — 't 's a world o' trouble !
Ye may s'arch f'm eend to eend o' the nation,
    Fer another sich evem-mated couple !
Men tock o' divorce, — that never 'd be needed,
If oll drah'd true in the yoke as she did.

It e'en a'mos' makes me shed tears, to think
    How jes' her comin' into the room —
Like a sunbeam stealin' through a chink —
    'U'd sometimes lighten up the gloom,
Though she did n't speak !   I never could git
No help that wuz savin' as she wuz yit.

So I concluded to let the place.
    'Mos' wish I 'd sold ; fer I can't go
Anigh Drake, but he sasses me to my face :
    He 's the new tenant ; he 's terrible slow !
Can't manage more 'n a fly !   I 've had
Three others, but they wuz 'bout as bad.

Men *will* ack so like the very deuse !
    Ye may plead 'ith 'em in an' out o' season,
They 're so dumb selfish 't ain't no use
    A-tryin' to make 'em hear to reason.
Evem Sim's got jes' them folts I hate !
Who he takes 'em frum, I can't consait.

I kin' o' make it my hum 'ith him,
    An' visit around among the relations ;
But the son-in-lahs is wus 'n Sim !
    Hain't none o' the dotters got the patience
The mother had.   Jemimy 's the best,
Atter all.   (They 're doin' re'l well, out West !)

You 've had your trouble as well as me ;
  We 're barn tut, ye know, as the sparks fly up'ard.
But when wus comes to wust, you 'll agree
  The' 's some comfort in a full cupboard.
Jerome he left ye perty well off, —
Though 't *wuz* a pity 'bout that cough!

Wal, here we be agin! Sich is life.
  You 've had yer Jerome, I 've had my Mary, —
He made a good husban', an' she a good wife, —
  An' now, — on'y think! — we hain't got nary!
Jes' brother an' sister once more, is it?
An' I 've come to make ye a good long visit!

AUTHOR'S NIGHT

" BRILLIANT SUCCESS ! " the play-bills said,
Flaming all over the town one day,
Blazing in characters blue and red,
  (Printed for posting, by the way,
  Before the public had seen the play!)
" Received with thunders of applause !
New Piece ! New Author ! ! Tremendous hit ! ! ! "
This was on Tuesday : still it draws,
And to-night is the Author's Benefit.

"New piece " : I 've a word to say about that.
Nine years ago, it may be more,
There came one day to the manager's door
A hopeful man, with a modest rat-tat,
Who smilingly entered, took off his hat,
And, begging the great man's pardon, slipt
Into his hand a manuscript.

In a month he came again : " The play —
Which I troubled you with — the other day " —
" The play? Oh! ah! " says the manager,
Politest of men. " Excuse me, sir ;
'T is being considered." (Safe to bet
He had n't looked at the title yet!)

"I 'll drop you a line; or you 'll confer
A favor by calling a week from now."
And he turned him out with a model bow.
Eight days later again they met, —
Modest author hopeful as ever;
But the great man finished his business thus:
"I 've read your play, sir; very clever;
But " (handing it back to him) " I regret
It is n't exactly the thing for us.
Good-morning, sir!" Politest of men!
Nine years ago, it may be ten.

Author and piece were new enough then.
But sorrow and toil and poverty
Have taken the gloss from him, you see;
And the play was afterwards knocked about
The theatres, keeping company
With dice and euchre-packs so long,
And pipes and actors' paint, it grew
To look so dingy and smell so strong,
You 'd have called it anything but new!
Till gruff and gouty old Montagu
Happened to take it up one day:
'T was after dinner; he thought, no doubt,
'T would help him to a nap. "But stay!
What in the deuce, boys! Here 's a play!"
He rubbed his glasses, forgot his gout,
And read till he started up with a shout,
" 'T is just the thing for my *protégée*,
And hang me, if I don't bring it out!"

And so it chanced, politest of men!
The play came into your hands again
Nine years later, — did I say ten?
And either age had improved its flavor,
Or you are wiser than you were then;
For now you deem it a special favor
That gouty and grouty old Montagu
Consented to bring it out with you.

"Tremendous hit!"
In the vast theatre's hollow sphere
High hangs the glittering chandelier;
     Its bright beams flash on
     Beauty and fashion;
A sea of life pours into the pit,
And cloud upon cloud piles over it,
Where Youth and Pleasure and Mirth and Passion
And Years and Folly and Wisdom and Wit
Throng to the Author's Benefit.

The orchestra leader takes his place;
Horn and serpent and oboë follow,
Violin and violoncello,
Trombone, trumpet, and double-bass.
A turning of music-leaves begins,
With a thrumming and screwing of violins;
Then the leader waves his bow, and — crash!
Kettle-drum rattles and cymbals clash,
And brass and strings and keen triangle
And high-keyed piccolo, piercing and pure,
Their many-colored chords entangle,
Weaving the wild, proud overture.

Old Montagu, with fret and frown,
All cloaked and gloved, walks up and down
Before the door of his *protégée*,
Keeping her worshippers at bay.
But he catches one who comes that way,
Gives him a gouty finger or two,
And seems quite civil: "Why did n't you
          Have a bouquet
          For my *protégée*,
In the boudoir-scene last night? 'T will do
As well to-night, though." (Straight off goes gay
Young Lothario, hunting a nosegay.)
He punches a pale reporter next
With his playful cane: "She 's terribly vext
At you, young fellow! Why did n't you get
That notice into your last Gazette?
You will in your next, eh? Don't forget!"

And gruff and snuffy old Montagu
Limps down to the curtain and peeps through :
" Boys ! what a house it is !   Thanks to me,
The fellow's fortune is made," growls he.

Then, tinkle-tinkle !   The music hushes ;
Up to the ceiling the great curtain rushes ;
            And a world of surprise
            To fresh young eyes,
A realm of enchantment, glows and flushes,
Stretching far back from the footlights' brink.
How does it look to worldly-wise
And crusty old Montagu, do you think ?

And the author, where all the while is he ?
How seems it to him ?   Were I in his place,
Turning at last my toil-worn face
From the dreary deserts of poverty,
Would n't all my heart leap high to see
The flowers of beauty and fashion and grace,
            One many-hued, gay,
            Immense bouquet,
Flaunting and fluttering here for me ?
The costumed players, even she,
            The bright young queen
            Of the radiant scene,
Speaking his speeches, living his thought ;
And all this vast, pulsating mass
Held captive by the spell he wrought, —
Held breathless, like a sea of glass
That bursts in breakers of wild applause : —
Would n't you conceive you had some cause
For an honest thrill, if you were he ?
But where, as we said, can the fellow be ?

Montagu is crabbed and old ;
And the wings are barren and gusty and cold ;
And, ah ! could the fresh young eyes behold,
            Around and under
            That vision of wonder, —

Behind the counterfeit joys and hopes,
The tinsel and paint of the players' parts, —
The barn-like vault, with its pulleys and ropes,
Shabby canvas and sheet-iron thunder,
And, O, the humanest lives and hearts!

Within the wings, just hid from view,
Snuffy and puffy old Montagu
Watches his ward, as a lynx his prey;
Wheedles her lovers, and reckons his gains;
Though naught but praise of his *protégée*,
Will he hear from another, he follows the play
With eyes that threaten and brows that rebuke her,
And lips that can chide in a fierce, sharp way,
When all is over, for all her pains.
The priest and the lover are playing euchre
In the intervals of their parts; the clown,
Dull fellow enough when the curtain is down,
                    Has had, they say,
                    Bad news to-day;
The merry ghost of the murdered man
Takes pleasant revenge on the whiskered villain
At a game of chess which they began
In the green-room, just before the killing;
The beggar is scuffling with the king;
And the lovelorn maiden is gossiping
With the misanthrope, prince of all good fellows;
And some are sad, and some are gay,
Some are in love, and some are jealous;
And there's many a play within the play!

And, O young eyes! in yonder alley,
Which the tall theatre overtops
(Its sheer crag towering above a valley
Of poor men's tenements and shops), —
Where three little cherubs, not overfed,
Are lying asleep in a trundle-bed,
While a thin, wan woman, sitting late,
Is stitching a garment beside the grate, —
You might, at this moment, see a man

Act as no paid performer can, —
In that wholly unstudied, natural way
    No one to this day
    Ever saw in a play!

Out at elbows, out at toes,
A needy, seedy, lank little man,
To and fro and about he goes,
With a vexed little bundle of infantine woes;
Sitting down, rising up, and with rocking and walking,
With hushing and tossing and singing and talking,
        Vainly trying
        To still its crying;
While a shadow behind him, huge and dim,
With a shadow-baby mimics him,
        Sketched on the wall,
        Grotesque and tall.

Anon he pauses.   Hark to the cheers!
        He laughs as he hears;
And he says, "I believe I could tell by the cheers
(If only this child would n't worry so!) —
Whether they come from above or below,
Begin in the boxes or up in the tiers, —
Which is the speech, and who is the player!"
In his keen face kindles a youthful glow, —
And lo! 't is the face of the man we know;
        'T is certainly so!
Though faded and jaded, thinner and grayer,
With a ghost of the look of long ago.
"To think," he says, "I never knew
The play was to be brought out, until
I saw it that morning on the bill!
Then did n't I hurry home to you
(I vow, this baby will never hush!
There, bite my finger, if you will!)
With the wonderful news?   And did n't I rush
Up the alley, to find old Montagu?
You would n't believe it was really true,
And you only half believe it still!"

Reason enough that she should doubt!
For has n't she witnessed, all these years,
His coming in, and his going out,
His wisdom, his weakness, his laughter and tears?
Seen him pine and seen him fret?
Eating his dinner (when dinners were had);
Serious, frivolous, hopeful, sad; —
      Why, he never could get
      A living yet,
And all that he tried has failed outright!
      Now can it be,
      Is it really he,
This poor weak man at her side, whose wit
Is making the theatre shake to-night
As if its very sides would split?

Odd, is it not? But, after all,
If you will observe, it does n't take
A man of giant mould to make
A giant shadow on the wall;
And he who in our daily sight
Seems but a figure mean and small,
Outlined in Fame's illusive light,
May stalk, a silhouette sublime,
Across the canvas of his time.

She answers with a peevish smile,
Taking stitch upon stitch the while:
" Why did n't they pay you something down
To buy you a coat and me a gown?
Then I could go to the theatre too,
And you would n't be ashamed to sit
In the private box they offered you,
Instead of sneaking in as you do.
They put you off with a benefit!
And how do I know but Montagu
Is going to cheat you out of it?"

" These women never will understand
Some things!" he cries. " How many times more

Must I explain " — A rap at the door!
A step on the creaking stairway floor!
He opens, and sees before him stand
A visitor, courteous, bland, and grand, —
His friend, the manager, true as you live!
Who puts a packet into his hand,
Very much as once we saw him give
A manuscript, with the same old bow.
(Everything seems altered now
But the model man and his model bow:
He will enter, I fancy, the other world
   In just this style, —
    With a flourish and smile,
Diamonds sparkling, and mustache curled!)

" It gives me very great pleasure: one third
Of the gross receipts " : presenting the packet.
" For a first instalment, upon my word,
Not bad, my friend! — A check, if preferred;
But I thought you might manage this," he says.
" A little seed, which I trust will grow.
The piece is certainly a success,
And, with the right management to back it,
Will run, I should say, six weeks or so.
Really, a very neat success!
We shall always be playing it more or less.
I 'm happy to say so much; although
I think I was right, nine years ago.
(Sign this little receipt, if you please?)
Times were not ripe for it then, you know;
The play would have failed, nine years ago.
Now, when can you give us another piece? "

The author, in the sudden heat
And tumult of his joy (or is it
His strange confusion at this visit?
The greatest honor of all his life!)
Partly because the said receipt
Is to be signed, and partly, maybe,
Because one arm still holds the baby,

Turns over the packet to his wife.
She tears the wrapper, and both her hands
    Amazed she raises, —
    Amazed she gazes!
The bursting treasure her broad lap fills, —
Gold and silver and good bank-bills!
Why, this at last she understands;
And now she believes in the benefit,
In the manager, and in Montagu,
In the play, and just a little bit
In her dear, old, clever husband too!

As for him, he seizes his hat, —
Wife and children must have a treat!
He follows the manager into the street,
Bent on purchasing this and that,
Something to wear and something to eat.
But the worthy man is quite too fast:
The shops are mostly closed; and at last
He comes around to the play-house door,
    Where he hears such a din
    Burst forth within,
What does he do, but just look in?

He reaches the lobby, and stands in the crowd;
By craning his neck, and tiptoeing tall,
He can see that the curtain is down, that's all.
    But still the roar
    Goes up as before,
    Shout upon shout!
Rapping and clapping and whistling and calling,
Stamping and tramping and caterwauling.
So he cries aloud to a man in the crowd,
    " *What is it about?* "
And the man in the crowd screams back as loud,
    " *Don't you know?*
    It's the end of the show!
They're trying to call the author out! "

The manager appears in his place,
Hat in hand, extremely polite,
Bowing and smiling to left and right,
(If only the author could get a sight!)
And delivers with characteristic grace
A neat little speech of about a minute,
With a plenty of pleasant nothings in it: —

" Author — unable to appear —
            Obliged — presents —
            Compliments " —
(If only the author himself could hear!
            How the people cheer!)
" Company — favorite — credit due —
My friend and the public's — Montagu —
Theatre — enterprise in securing —
Author — other plans maturing —
Public — generous appreciation —
            Gratification —
            This ovation " —

And so, with a beautiful peroration,
Just the thing for the happy occasion,
He sails away in the breeze of a grand sensation.

All is over, and out with the throng
The jostled author is borne along.
Will the fresh young eyes, I wonder, see
The crumpled man in the crowd, and note
The napless hat and the seedy coat?
Alone, unknown, he goes his way,
None so unknown and lonely as he!
While he hears at his side a sweet voice say,
" O, what would n't any one give to be
The author of that delightful play!
I know he is handsome, he must be gay,
And tall, — though of that I 'm not so certain.
Why did n't he come before the curtain?"

ONE DAY SOLITARY

I AM all right! good-by, old chap!
　Twenty-four hours, that won't be long.
Nothing to do but take a nap,
　And — say! can a fellow sing a song?
Will the light fantastic be in order, —
　A pigeon-wing on your pantry floor?
What are the rules for a regular boarder?
　Be quiet? All right! — *Cling clang* goes the door!

Clang clink, the bolts! and I am locked in.
　Some pious reflection and repentance
Come next, I suppose, for I just begin
　To perceive the sting in the tail of my sentence, —
"One day whereof shall be solitary."
　Here I am at the end of my journey,
And — well, it ain't jolly, not so very! —
　I 'd like to throttle that sharp attorney!

He took my money, the very last dollar;
　Did n't leave me so much as a dime,
Not enough to buy me a paper collar
　To wear at my trial; he knew all the time
'T was some that I got for the stolen silver!
　Why has n't he been indicted too?
If he does n't exactly rob and pilfer,
　He lives by the plunder of them that do.

Then did n't it put me into a fury,
　To see him step up, and laugh and chat
With the lying lawyers, and joke with the jury,
　When all was over, — then go for his hat, —
While Sue was sobbing to break her heart,
　And all I could do was to stand and stare!
He had pleaded my cause; he had played his part
　And got his fee; and what more did he care?

But why blame him? When I go out,
　I 'll leave plain thieving, and take to the law;

That will be safer !   These are about
  The lonesomest lodgings ever I saw !
There would n't be room for cutting a caper,
  If I was inclined ; and it 's just as well !
Wish I could ring for the morning paper !
  Can't say that I fancy this hotel.

It 's droll to think how, just out yonder,
  The world goes jogging on the same !
Old men will save and boys will squander,
  And fellows will play at the same old game
Of get-and-spend, — to-morrow, next year, —
  And drink and carouse ; and who will there be
To remember a comrade buried here ?
  I am nothing to them, they are nothing to me !

And Sue, — yes, she will forget me too !
  I know ! already her tears are drying.
I believe there is nothing that girl can do
  So easy as laughing and lying and crying.
She clung to me well while there was hope,
  Then broke her heart in that last wild sob ;
But she ain't going to sit and mope
  While I am at work on a five years' job.

They 'll set me to learning a trade, no doubt ;
  And I must forget to speak or smile.
I shall go marching in and out,
  One of a silent, tramping file
Of felons, at morning and noon and night, —
  Just down to the shops and back to the cells, —
And work with a thief at left and right,
  And feed and sleep and — nothing else ?

Was I born for this ?   Will the old folks know ?
  I can see them now on the old home-place :
His gait is feeble, his step is slow,
  There 's a settled grief in his furrowed face ;
While she goes wearily groping about
  In a sort of dream, so bent, so sad ! —

But this won't do! I must sing and shout,
    And forget myself, or else go mad.

I won't be foolish; although, for a minute,
    I was there in my little room once more.
What would n't I give just now to be in it?
    The bed is yonder, and there is the door; —
The Bible is here on the neat white stand.
    The summer-sweets are ripening now;
In the flickering light I reach my hand
    From the window, and pluck them from the bough!

When I was a child, (O, well for me
    And them if I had never been older!)
When he told me stories on his knee,
    And tossed me, and carried me on his shoulder;
When she knelt down and heard my prayer,
    And gave me in bed my good-night kiss, —
Did ever they think that all their care
    For an only son could come to this?

Foolish again! No sense in tears
    And gnashing the teeth! And yet — somehow —
I have n't thought of them so for years!
    I never knew them, I think, till now.
How fondly, how blindly, they trusted me!
    When I should have been in my bed asleep,
I slipped from the window, and down the tree,
    And sowed for the harvest that now I reap.

And Jennie, — how could I bear to leave her?
    If I had but wished — but I was a fool!
My heart was filled with a thirst and fever
    That no sweet airs of heaven could cool.
I can hear her asking, — " Have you heard? "
    But mother falters, and shakes her head:
" O Jennie! Jennie! never a word!
    What can it mean? He must be dead! "

Light-hearted, a proud, ambitious lad,
    I left my home that morning in May;

What visions, what hopes, what plans I had!
  And what have I — where are they all — to-day?
Wild fellows, and wine, and debts, and gaming,
  Disgrace, and the loss of place and friend, —
And I was an outlaw, past reclaiming :
  Arrest and sentence, and — this is the end!

Five years! Shall ever I quit this prison?
  Homeless, an outcast, where shall I go?
Return to them, like one arisen
  From the grave, who was buried long ago?
All is still; it 's the close of the week ;
  I slink through the garden, I stop by the well ;
I see him totter, I hear her shriek! —
  What sort of a tale shall I have to tell?

But here I am! What 's the use of grieving?
  Five years — will it be too late to begin?
Can sober thinking and honest living
  Still make me the man I might have been? —
I 'll sleep. O, would I could wake to-morrow
  In that old room, to find, at last,
That all my trouble and all their sorrow
  Are only a dream of the night that is past!

ONE BIRTHDAY

WHERE the willows that overhang the lane
  Make a pleasant shade in the golden weather,
Through gleams that flicker on flank and mane
  The mare and her colt come home together ;
Over them softly, one by one,
  I see the yellowing leaflets fall,
And lie like brighter spots of sun
  On the faded turf and gray stone-wall : —

Of all the scenes in my life, to-day
  That is the one that I remember ;
How sweetly on all the landscape lay
  The mellow sunlight of September !

It slept in the boughs of the hazy wood,
　　On glimmering stubble and stacks of grain:
And there at the farm-yard bars we stood
　　While the mare and her colt came up the lane.

The bright leaves fell, and over us blew
　　The fairy balloons of the air-borne thistle,
As, pricking her ears at the call she knew,
　　With whinny and prance at voice and whistle,
Coquettish and coy, she came with her foal:
　　O, well I remember, — his neck and ears
By her great gray side shone black as a coal,
　　And his legs were slender and trim as a deer's!

With hands on the bars, and curly head bare,
　　I stood, while farm boy Fred, who was taller,
Reached over and shook, at the proud, shy mare,
　　A handful of oats in my hat, to call her.
Then a form I loved came close behind,
　　A hand I loved on my shoulder lay,
And a dear voice spoke, — so gentle and kind,
　　Ah, would I could hear its tones to-day! —

"There is n't a handsomer colt in town!
　　Just look at that beautiful neck and shoulder!
His color will change to a chestnut brown,
　　To match your curls, as he grows older.
This is your birthday — let me see!"
　　The hand went higher and stroked my head:
"I 'll make you a present — what shall it be?"
　　"O father! give me the colt!" I said.

And the colt was mine — how proud was I! —
　　The doves sailed down from the sunlit gable,
The valiant cock gave a challenging cry,
　　The cockerel croaked in the open stable: —
So well I recall each sight and sound
　　That filled the heart of the happy boy,
And left one day in my memory crowned
　　Forever with color and light and joy.

THE STREAMLET

IT is only the tiniest stream,
  With nothing whatever to do,
But to creep from its mosses, and gleam
  In just a thin ribbon or two,
Where it spills from the rock, and besprinkles
  The flowers all round it with dew.

Half-way up the hillside it slips
  From darkness out into the light,
Slides over the ledges, and drips
  In a basin all bubbling and bright,
Then once more, in the long meadow-grasses,
  In silence it sinks out of sight.

So slender, so brief in its course!
  It will never be useful or grand,
Like the waterfall foaming and hoarse,
  Or the river benignant and bland,
That sweeps far away through the valley,
  And turns all the mills in the land.

Just a brooklet, so perfect, so sweet, —
  Like a child that is always a child!
A picture as fair and complete,
  And as softly and peacefully wild,
As if Nature had only just made it,
  And laid down her pencil and smiled.

The strong eagle perched on these rocks
  And dipped his proud beak, long ago;
In the gray of the morning the fox
  Came and lapped in the basin below;
By a hoof-printed trail through the thicket
  The deer used to pass to and fro.

Now the jolly haymakers in June
  Bring their luncheon, and couch on the cool

Grassy margin, and drink to the tune
  The brook makes in the pebble-lined pool, —
From grandfather down to the youngsters
  In haying-time kept out of school.

They joke and tell tales as they eat,
  While, wistful his share to receive,
The dog wags his tail at their feet ;
  Then each stout mower tucks up his sleeve,
And the farmer cries, " Come, boys ! " The squirrel
  Dines well on the crumbs which they leave.

The children all know of the place,
  And here with their basket, in search
Of wild roses, come Bertha and Grace,
  And Paul with his fish-pole and perch,
While the meadowlark sings, and above them
  The woodpecker drums on the birch.

Is the drop the bee finds in the clover
  More sweet than the liquor they quaff ?
It drips in the cup, and runs over ;
  And, sipping it, spilling it half, —
Hear their mirth ! Did Grace learn of the brooklet
  That low, lisping, crystalline laugh?

For music I 'm sure that it taught
  Its neighbor, the pied bobolink, —
Where else could the fellow have caught
  That sweet, liquid note, do you think,
Half tinkle, half gurgle ? The wren, too,
  I 'm certain has been here to drink !

O, teach me your song, happy brook !
  If I visit you yet many times,
If I put away business and book,
  And list to your fairy-bell chimes,
Will your freshness breathe into my verses,
  Your music glide into my rhymes ?

THE PHANTOM CHAPEL

I

THE night-breeze puffed our sail, as through
    The shadowy strait we steered; and soon
Along the flashing lake we flew,
    Upon the white wake of the moon.

Betwixt the islands and the shore,
    From cape to cape, we still pursued
Her sparkling keel, which sped before
    Like hopes that, laughing, still elude.

The mild night's universal smile
    Touched sheltered cove and glistening leaf;
Each shadow-girt and wooded isle
    Shook in the wind its silvered sheaf.

By day a flower, by night a bud,
    Her pure soul rocked in dreamy calms,
The lily slept upon the flood
    Her nun-like sleep with outspread palms.

From cove to cove, from cape to cape,
    We chased the hurrying moon, — when, lo!
In yonder glen, what gleaming shape
    Behind the trees uprises slow?

Between the upland and the wood,
    Half hid by elms that fringed the shore,
The semblance of a chapel stood
    Where never chapel stood before.

All still and fair, in misty air,
    The lovely miracle upsprings,
As if some great white angel there,
    Just lighted, stooped with half-shut wings.

Locked in the lonely vale, aloof
    From men, the Gothic wonder rose:

On pallid pinnacle and roof
    The quiet moonlight shed its snows.

From the dim pile, across the gray,
    Uncertain landscape, faintly came,
Through pictured panes, a stainéd ray,
    Red from some martyr's shirt of flame.

And, listening ever, we could trace
    The strains of a mysterious hymn,
Divinely cadenced, like the praise
    Of far-off quiring seraphim.

The winds were hushed : a holy calm
    Filled all the night : it seemed as if
The spirit of that solemn psalm
    Had charmed the waves that rocked our skiff.

The winds were hushed, our hearts were bowed
    In silent awe, when on the night
Rose dark and slow a wingéd cloud,
    And swept the marvel from our sight.

But, homeward voyaging, we seemed
    Like souls that leave a realm enchanted,
And all night long in memory gleamed
    That moonlit valley wonder-haunted.

II

Upon the morrow, to explore
    At dawn the mystery of the night,
We pushed once more our boat from shore,
    Through whispering flags and lilies white.

Along the widening strait we steered,
    Past windy cape and sheltered cove :
The cape we cleared, the vale we neared,
    There sloped the upland, flushed the grove ;

And, where the church had stood, behold !
The latticed wing and pointed gable
And well-sweep of a farmhouse old,
Turret and vane on barn and stable !

There at their work the housemaids sung
The songs that had entranced the night;
The farm-boy's magic-lantern hung,
A pumpkin, in the morning light !

Thereat we murmured : " Wherefore pray
For perfect knowledge ?   Better far
Than the sure insight of the day,
The moonlight's soft illusions are.

" The moon is full of fairy dreams :
She pours them from her pensile horn,
And buildeth with her silver beams
Fabrics too frail to meet the morn.

" So fade the airy hopes of youth,
And Love's young promise disappears
Before the morning gray of Truth,
The unsparing light of later years.

" So perish manhood's pillared schemes ;
And in the dawning of that day
That wakes us from this world of dreams,
Even church and faith may fade away."

But one said, " Nay, though we may miss
The cherished, changeful veil of things,
Within illusion's chrysalis
The shrouded Truth hides shining wings.

" Though we may miss the pearl and gold,
And heaven be other than we deem,
Doubt not the future will unfold
To something better than our dream.

"Last evening's bud laughs on the flood,
    A perfect flower of purest white;
And life is but a folded bud
    That still awaits the Morning Light."

Even while we spoke, a sweeter charm
    Than ever night and moonlight knew,
Breathed over all the breezy farm,
    And lurked in shade and shone in dew.

Freshness of life and pure delight
    In earth and air, in sight and sound,
Displaced the fancies of the night,
    And better than we sought we found.

The farmhouse, fairer in the glance
    Of dawn than in its moonlight vest,
Lay clasped in airs of sweet romance
    And tender human interest.

Along the dazzling waves the glory
    Of the full summer morning blazed;
From the sun-fronting promontory
    The crescent-crownéd cattle gazed.

The wild crows cawed; on great slow wings
    Up soared the heron from the brake;
The pickerel leaped in rippling rings;
    The supple swallow skimmed the lake.

O'er all, its roof the blue above,
    Its floor the common daily sod,
Walled round with light, upheld by Love,
    Arose the living Church of God.

THE CUP

THE cup I sing is a cup of gold,
Many and many a century old,
Sculptured fair, and over-filled
With wine of a generous vintage, spilled

In crystal currents and foaming tides
All round its luminous, pictured sides.

Old Time enamelled and embossed
This ancient cup at an infinite cost.
Its frame he wrought of metal run
Red from the furnace of the sun.
Ages on ages slowly rolled
Before the glowing mass was cold,
And still he toiled at the antique mould, —
Turning it fast in his fashioning hand,
Tracing circle, layer, and band,
Carving figures quaint and strange,
Pursuing, through many a wondrous change,
The symmetry of a plan divine.
At last he poured the lustrous wine,
Crowned high the radiant wave with light,
And held aloft the goblet bright,
Half in shadow, and wreathed in mist
Of purple, amber, and amethyst.

This is the goblet from whose brink
All creatures that have life must drink :
Foemen and lovers, haughty lord,
And sallow beggar with lips abhorred.
The new-born infant, ere it gain
The mother's breast, this wine must drain.
The oak with its subtile juice is fed,
The rose drinks till her cheeks are red,
And the dimpled, dainty violet sips
The limpid stream with loving lips.
It holds the blood of sun and star,
And all pure essences that are :
No fruit so high on the heavenly vine,
Whose golden hanging clusters shine
On the far-off shadowy midnight hills,
But some sweet influence it distils
That slideth down the silvery rills.
Here Wisdom drowned her dangerous thought,
The early gods their secrets brought ;

Beauty, in quivering lines of light,
Ripples before the ravished sight;
And the unseen mystic spheres combine
To charm the cup and drug the wine.

All day I drink of the wine, and deep
In its stainless waves my senses steep;
All night my peaceful soul lies drowned
In hollows of the cup profound;
Again each morn I clamber up
The emerald crater of the cup,
On massive knobs of jasper stand
And view the azure ring expand:
I watch the foam-wreaths toss and swim
In the wine that o'erruns the jewelled rim: —
Edges of chrysolite emerge,
Dawn-tinted, from the misty surge:
My thrilled, uncovered front I lave,
My eager senses kiss the wave,
And drain, with its viewless draught, the lore
That kindles the bosom's secret core,
And the fire that maddens the poet's brain
With wild sweet ardor and heavenly pain.

THE MISSING LEAF

By chance, in the dusty old library foraging,
    Seeking some food for my fancy, I drew
From its shelf a stout volume, entitled The Origin
    And End of Creation (a sort of review
Of the Works of the Lord, by a confident critic).
    "Now here should be something," I said, "that's worth saving, —
Profound, philosophical, learned, analytic," —
    Just what my insatiable soul had been craving.

I bore the rich prize to a nook by the window,
    And revelled straightway in the lore of the ages, —
Chinese, Persian, Roman, Greek, Hebrew, and Hindoo,
    With modern research to its ultimate stages:

All which, to what followed, was but the musician's
    Light touches to see if his strings were in tune, a verse
Used by the wizard to conjure his visions :
    Then opened the writer's grand scheme of the universe.

He held the round world in his hand like a watch,
    With the sun and the stars for the chain and the seal ;
Showed the cases of gold and of crystal, the notch
    Where the thing was wound up, pivot, mainspring, and wheel,
And — in short, you 'd have fancied, his knowledge was such,
    He could take it to pieces and put it together,
And set it agoing again with a touch
    Of just the right oil from his erudite feather !

I read and read on, by divine curiosity
    Fired, in pursuit of one still missing page,
One leaf, to redeem this portentous verbosity,
    Then —   Well, I just flung down the book in a rage ;
Through the window, out into the garden I sprung,
    Put screens of red roses and jasmines between us,
And cooled my hot brow and my anger among
    The dear little illiterate pinks and verbenas.

The martins that flew to their summer-house door,
    The voluble finches their little ones feeding,
The snail with his pack on his back, taught me more
    Than all the pedantic sad stuff I 'd been reading.
The river moved by without ripple or swirl,
    The world in its bosom, a wondrous illusion !
And even the slow kitchen smoke's upward curl
    Hinted beauties beyond my great author's solution.

A spider was weaving his net by the stream ;
    And in the thin gossamer's light agitation
I saw my philosopher flaunting his scheme
    Before the vast, mystical web of creation !
I watched the still swan on the water afloat,
    The sisterly birches bowed over the glass,
Their white limbs reflected, the boys in their boat,
    The colts on the bank, fetlock-deep in the grass ;

I heard, over hay-fields and clover-lots wafted,
 The lowing of kine ; and so cool was the kiss
Of the breeze on my temples, — the air, as I quaffed it,
 So sweet to my sense, — that mere breathing was bliss !
And I cried, " Who can say how this life has its being ;
 How landscape and sky with delight overfill me ;
Why sound should enchant ; how these eyes have their seeing ;
 How passion and rapture enkindle and thrill me ?

" I prize the least pebble your science can bring,
 Or whispering shell, from the shore of life's ocean ;
No word the true prophet or poet may sing,
 But deep in my heart stirs responsive emotion :
Yet who can tell aught of this afternoon glory,
 This light and this ether, this wave and this clover ?
Not a syllable lisped, of the marvellous story,
 In all your nine hundred dull pages and over !

" What moulds to my likeness these limbs and these features,
 This tangible form to the form hid within it ?
Bright robe renewed daily and nightly by Nature's
 Invisible spindles, that ceaselessly spin it,
Marble-firm fibre and milky-fine filament :
 The pulse's soft shuttle mysteriously weaving
From dust and corruption a living habiliment :
 Oldest of miracles, still past believing !

" And you — did you fancy that you could infold it,
 And label it, fast in your tissue of fallacies ?
While firm in the grasp of your reason you hold it,
 It flies, it defies your most subtile analysis !
There 's something that will not be measured and weighed,
 And brought to the test of your last sublimation ;
And this is the little mistake that you made,
 That you left it quite out of your grand calculation.

" Though other than bigots have deemed, the Creator
 Is not the blind physical force you believe him ;
Not less, O, be sure, but unspeakably greater,
 Than creeds have proclaimed, or than sages conceive him !

Of nothing comes nothing: springs rise not above
   Their source in the far-hidden heart of the mountains:
Whence then have descended the Wisdom and Love
   That in man leap to light in intelligent fountains?"

So, bathed in the sunset, I stood by the stream,
   With a heart full of joy and devout adoration,
Enwrapped in my mystery, dreaming my dream,
   Till my soul seemed dissolved in the Soul of Creation.
I looked, and saw wonder on wonder without,
   And, looking within, beheld wonder on wonder,
And trembled between, like the swan floating out,
   With one sky arched above and one sky imaged under!

THE CITY OF GOOD-WILL

As through the wood I went, by rock and spring,
   And leopard-colored banks with bright moss furred,
Careless as are the brooks, or birds that sing,
   Of any other song of brook or bird;
Heeding my own sweet thoughts, and hearkening
   To voices which no ear has ever heard;
Through moss and leaf and flickering sunbeam, seeing
A world that in my own mind had its being; —

As thus I went, the pathway ceased in light:
   Aloft upon a jutting crag I stood,
Beside a sudden torrent leaping white
   From out its lair within the darksome wood:
A sea of dazzling mist below the height
   Heaved silently; while on the solitude,
From the deep bosom of an unseen valley,
The sound of many bells broke musically.

Slowly anon, like a wind-wasted cloud,
   The veil of vapor, lifting, rolled asunder;
And through its lucent edges pierced the proud
   Spires of a vast, dim city, shining under,
Whose golden belfries, still more sweetly loud,
   Pealed forth, unmuffled, their harmonious thunder,

Beneath a full, resplendent bow, which spanned
With its swift arch all that enchanted land.

The forest path had ceased : but there, beside
    The torrent tumbling sheer athwart the brown
Crest of the crag, a stairway I descried,
    By many a vine-clad terrace winding down ;
And with the wild, white waters for my guide,
    I took that wondrous highway to the town,
Past many a cottage hanging like a nest,
Or bosomed in the mountain's verdurous vest.

So to the foot I came of that high hill ;
    And on a lofty flower-wreathed gateway saw
These sun-bright words : " THE CITY OF GOOD-WILL : "
    And through its welcoming portal went with awe.
On arch beyond high arch uprising still,
    I read, " TRUTH IS OUR TRUST," and " LOVE IS LAW."
Thus, flaming amid flowers, on every hand
Were raised the written statutes of the land.

Strange yet familiar were the streets : I seemed
    Revisiting, upon a festal day,
Some future London, or New York redeemed ;
    So sweet a peace on all that city lay !
And over all an air of gladness gleamed,
    Which never shone in Cheapside or Broadway, —
A light, methought, which came not from the sky,
But from the faces of the passers-by.

I talked with some.   They were a strong, fair race,
    Who wrought and trafficked without haste or din.
There is no prison-house in all the place ;
    For to its wise inhabitants each sin
Reveals itself so subtly in the face
    Unlighted by the heavenly beam within,
And meets such looks of searching truth and pity,
That forth it goes, self-banished, from the city.

Nor sovereignty nor servitude appears :
    Each in his place does simply what he can :

No rank, but of the soul; but all careers
    Are free to all, to woman as to man,
Of diverse gifts and attributes, yet peers
    Forever in the sacred social plan.
All in their fitting labor find enjoyment,
But deeds of love are still their best employment.

Their busy life is like a river flowing
    Between broad banks of flower-embroidered leisure;
High thoughts attend their coming and their going,
    And sweet discourse is their immortal pleasure;
A wisely serious, joyous people, knowing
    The blessedness of love, beyond all measure;
Whose proudest wishes ever at the seat
Of Justice wait, and kiss her shining feet.

No sacrifice of soul and body's health
    To Mammon or the passions' direful furies;
Nor poor, nor rich, in that pure commonwealth,
    Nor any need of wrangling courts and juries.
"Here good alone," they said, " is done by stealth,
    And only evil thoughts are held in duress.
Most blessed are they who labor most to bless,
And happiest hearts reck not of happiness."

The needful laws, which in our lower state
    Protect the many and confound the few,
The outward ties that, binding mate to mate,
    Constrain the false, and sometimes vex the true,
Have here no place; where all subordinate
    All things to charity, as angels do,
And men, through righteousness and reverence,
Dwell in an age of second innocence.

On faint winds borne, the soul of odorous balm,
    From gardens fountain-cooled, breathed everywhere;
Music, commingled with the jubilant psalm
    Of chiming golden bells, rose on the air;
And awful beauty gleamed in godlike calm,
    Where rangéd statues stood entranced and bare

Within the many-niched and pensive shades
Of pallid alabaster colonnades.

And over all, with soaring porticoes,
   And pillared dome, and glittering pinnacles, —
Of cloud, or marble pure as sculptured snows, —
   And all its tuneful towers of marvellous bells,
In frozen beauty and divine repose,
   The phantasm of a vast cathedral swells.
From far within the organ's music pours,
Deep-toned as surges upon thunderous shores.

Amidst the organ's sounding and the chime
   Of bells above, O strong, and clear, and solemn,
Ascends a thousand-voicéd chant sublime,
   By thrilling architrave and shivering column;
And silver eloquence or golden rhyme,
   From living lips or treasured script and volume,
Fills up the pauses of the chant, and stirs
With joy the souls of countless worshippers.

Their prayers, — the aspirations of the heart;
   Their worship, — good to man and thanks to Heaven;
Religion, — no sad symbol set apart,
   Or fashion to be served one day in seven,
But, lighting home and hearth and public mart,
   A constant ray for guide and solace given.
All who throng hither, ravished by its beauty,
Go forth, diffusing it in daily duty.

Whereat I cried aloud : "O life elysian!
   O mortals! love and truth alone are good!
Forsake the ways of falsehood and derision,
   And seek the holy paths of Brotherhood!"
When, lo! at sound of my own voice the vision
   Vanished, and I was walking in the wood,
Only in moss and leaf and sunbeam seeing
That brighter world which in my mind had being.

LOVE

In sad foreknowledge of man's state, that he
Might not despair, and perish utterly,
   By rude distractions hither and thither hurled,
In the beginning the dear lords above,
With infinite compassion, gave him Love;
   And Love is the sweet band that binds the world.

What holds the convex ocean in his place,
Pillars the starry vault, and guides through space
   The myriad-motioned planets swiftly whirled, —
What it may be that made and keeps them so
(If 't be not Love) I know not: yet I know
   That Love is the sweet band that binds the world.

Dreams, laughter, hope, derision, toil, and grief,
These are man's portion, and his time is brief;
   A little leaf by wild winds tossed and twirled;
In trouble and in doubt he draws his breath,
Illusion leads him, and his way is death;
   Yet Love is a sweet band that binds the world.

Strong to destroy, and very weak to save
Is man; at once a tyrant and a slave;
   And ever war's red banner is unfurled;
But, Love, since thou art left us, all is well;
If Love were banished heaven itself were hell;
   Immortal Love! sweet band that binds the world!

Bitter companions met me everywhere,
Sin-wasted Youth, and Folly with white hair,
   And keen-eyed Craft, and Scorn with sad lip curled,
Sorrows, and masks, and miseries manifold;
But, " O my heart!" I said, " be thou consoled,
   For Love is the sweet band that binds the world."

Birds build their nests: Love taught the gentle art;
The babe laughs in its mother's arms: her heart
   With Love's fresh morning thoughts is all impearled;

Chaste Comfort sits beside the household hearth;
The sun with golden girdle clasps the earth,
 And Love is the sweet band that binds the world.

COMMUNION

THERE is peace on the mountains,
  There 's joy in the glen,
For the Day, which was buried,
  Is risen again :
At the dawn, in cloud-raiment
  Too dazzling for sight,
Sits the calm, shining seraph,
  The Angel of Light.

And the air and the perfume
  Of Paradise, fanned
By invisible pinions,
  Breathe over the land :
The lost glory of Eden
  Is flooding the earth :
'T is the youth of Creation,
  The world at its birth !

Ethereal Sabbath !
  Day evermore blest !
I will walk in my garden,
  Enjoying thy rest,
While the peal from the belfry
  Is sweet on the air,
And the people are thronging
  To sermon and prayer.

The churches invite me,
  Their tables are spread
With the brightness of silver,
  The whiteness of bread;
The golden-lipped goblets
  Are dusky with wine,
And I know the Communion
  Of Christ is divine.

While to me the day's fulness
  Of glory is given,
Round, perfect, refulgent,
  Fresh coinage of heaven,
New stamped with the image
  And word of the Lord, —
Shall not I to his service
  My tribute accord?

I scorn not, I seek not,
  The wine and the bread,
Question not if the symbol
  Be living or dead:
Christ speaks from the mountain,
  Still walks on the sea;
Yonder river is Jordan,
  This lake, Galilee!

Whoso leaveth transgression
  Is cleansed by its flood;
To love, is his body,
  To serve, is his blood:
Who walk with the humble,
  The fallen lift up,
They sit at his supper,
  And drink of his cup.

I scorn not, I take not,
  The wine and the bread:
In this temple of maples
  His table is spread;
In this air, in these zephyrs,
  This world at my feet,
I have found a communion
  Most secret and sweet.

All the lightness and gladness
  That gleam in the rest
Seem but sparks of the rapture
  That burns in my breast;

I flash in the brooklet,
  I mount upon wings, —
'T is my soul in the sunbeam,
  My spirit that sings.

And I dream of a Oneness
  Pervading the Whole ;
In all nature, all nations,
  The Soul of each soul ;
One breath in all bosoms,
  A mystical chain
Whose harmony makes us
  All brothers again.

When wilt thou, dear Presence !
  Whatever thy name !
Pour out on the nations
  Thy baptism of flame
(As thou pourest this sunshine),
  And teach us to heed
The living communion
  Of truth and of deed ?

O Love ! till thou make us
  At peace with our kind,
And establish thy kingdom
  In heart and in mind ;
Till thy will in our wishes
  And actions be done ;
Man gropeth in shadow,
  And waits for the sun.

He gropeth and creepeth,
  With symbol and creed,
Till the Day of Salvation
  Be risen indeed, —
Till the strong, wingéd Seraph,
  The Angel of Light,
Roll the stone of great Darkness
  Away from the Night.

SHERIFF THORNE

Tʜᴀᴛ I should be sheriff, and keep the jail,
  And that yonder stately old fellow, you see
  Marching across the yard, should be
My prisoner, — well, 't is a curious tale,
      As you 'll agree.

For it happens, we 've been here once before
  Together, and served our time, — although
  Not just as you see us now, you know ;
When we were younger both by a score
      Of years or so.

When I was a wild colt, two thirds grown,
  Too wild for ever a curb or rein,
  Playing my tricks till — I need n't explain ; —
I got three months at breaking stone,
      With a ball and chain.

The fodder was mean, and the work was hard,
  And work and I could never agree ;
  And the discipline, — well, in short, you see,
'T was rather a roughish kind of card
      That curried me !

A stout steel bracelet about my leg,
  A cannon-shot and chain at my feet,
  I pounded the stones in the public street,
With a heart crammed full of hate as an egg
      Is full of meat.

The schoolboys jeered at my prison rig ;
  And me, if I moved, they used to call
  (For I went with a jerk, if I went at all)
A gentleman dancing the Jail-bird Jig, —
      At a public *ball*.

But once, as I sat in the usual place,
  On a heap of stones, and hammered away

At the rocks, with a heart as hard as they,
And cursed Macadam and all his race,
  There chanced that way,

Sir, the loveliest girl! I don't mean pretty;
  But there was that in her troubled eye,
  In her sweet, sad glance, as she passed me by,
That seemed like an angel's gentle pity
  For such as I.

And, sir, to my soul that pure look gave
  Such a thrill as a summer morning brings,
  With its twitter and flutter of songs and wings,
To one crouched all night long in a cave
  Of venomous things.

Down the broad green street she passed from sight;
  But all that day I was under a spell;
  And all that night — I remember well —
A pair of eyes made a kind of light
  That filled my cell.

Women can do with us what they will:
  'T was only a village girl, but she,
  With the flash of a glance, had shown to me
The wretch I was, and the self I still
  Might strive to be.

And if in my misery I began
  To feel fresh hope and courage stir, —
  To turn my back upon things that were,
And my face to the future of a man, —
  'T was all for her.

And that's *my* story.   And as for the lady?
  I saw her, — O yes, when I was free,
  And thanked her, and —   Well, just come with me;
As likely as not, when supper is ready,
  She 'll pour your tea.

She keeps my house, and I keep the jail;
  And the stately old fellow who passed just now
  And tipped me that very peculiar bow —
But that is the wonderful part of the tale,
    As you 'll allow.

For he, you must know, was sheriff then,
  And he guarded me, as I guard him;
  (The fetter I wore now fits his limb!) —
Just one of your high-flown, strait-laced men,
    Pompous and grim, —

The Great Mogul of our little town.
  But while I was struggling to redeem
  My youth, he sank in the world's esteem;
My stock went up, while his went down,
    Like the ends of a beam.

What fault?   'T was not one fault alone
  That brought him low, but a treacherous train
  Of vices, sapping the heart and brain.
Then came his turn at breaking stone,
    With a ball and chain.

It seemed, I admit, a sort of treason,
  To clip him, and give him the cap and ball,
  And that I was his keeper seemed worst of all.
And now, in a word, if you ask the reason
    Of this man's fall, —

'T was a woman again, — is my reply.
  And so I said, and I say it still,
  That women can do with us what they will:
Strong men they turn with the twirl of an eye,
    For good or ill.

AT MY ENEMY'S GATE

As I passed my enemy's gate
In the summer afternoon,

On my pathway, stealthy as Fate,
　Crept a shadow vague and chill:
The bright spirit, the rainbow grace
Of sweet, hovering Thought, gave place
To a nameless feeling of loss,
　A dark sense of something ill.

Whereupon I said, in my scorn,
" There should grow about his door
Nothing but thistle and thorn,
　Shrewd nettle, dogwood, and dock;
Or three-leaved ivy that twines
A bleak ledge with poisonous vines,
And black lichens that incrust
　The scaly crest of a rock!"

Then I looked, and there, on the ground,
Were two lovely children at play;
The door-yard turf all around
　Was bordered with pansies and pinks;
From his apple-trees showered the notes
Of a pair of ecstatic throats,
And up from the grass-lot below
　Came the gossip of bobolinks.

And, behold! like a cloud, overhead,
Flocked a multitude of white doves!
They circled round stable and shed,
　Alighting on sill and roof:
All astir in the sun, so white,
All a-murmur with love, the sight
Sent a pang to my softening heart,
　An arrow of sweet reproof.

Then I thought of our foolish strife,
And " How hateful is hate!" I said.
" Under all that we see of his life
　Is a world we never may know,
With its sorrows, and solace, and dreams;
And, even though bad as he seems,

He is what he is, for a cause,
  And Nature accepts him so.

"She gives this foeman of mine
  Of the best her bounty affords;
Sends him the rain and the shine,
  And children, whom doubtless he loves;
She fosters his horses and herds,
And surrounds him with blossoms and birds, —
  And why am I harder of heart
    To his faults than the daisies and doves?

"To me so perverse and unjust,
  He has yet in his uncouth shell
Some kernel of good, I will trust,
  Though a good I never may see.
And if, for our difference, still
He cherishes grudge and ill-will,
  The more 's the pity for him, —
    And what is his hatred to me?"

So for him began in my heart
  The doves to murmur and stir,
The pinks and pansies to start,
  And make golden afternoon.
And now, in the wintry street,
His frown, if we chance to meet,
  Brings back, with my gentler thoughts,
    The birds and blossoms of June.

RACHEL AT THE WELL

By an elm-tree half decayed,
In a skeleton of shade
  From the bird-forsaken boughs,
With the melancholy stains
Of a century of rains,
And its quaintly mended panes,
  Stands the house.

From the modern street aloof,
It uprears its olden roof
  In the sleepy summer air;
And the shadow falls across;
And the sunlight sheds a gloss
On the patches of old moss,
    Here and there.

Near the gate that guards the lane,
With its rusty hinge and chain
  Hangs, half shut, the crippled wicket.
Lilac clumps, beyond the wall,
Grow neglected, filling all
The wild door-yard with a tall
    Tangled thicket.

There 's a little path between
The encroaching ranks of green;
  Then a garden, half grown over
With striped grass and poppies red;
There the sunflower hangs her head,
And you scent somewhere a bed
    Of sweet clover.

There is fennel mixed with phlox;
And, with pinks and hollyhocks,
  Here the mistress of the place
In her lone and widowed age
Keeps her caraway and sage, —
Immemorial heritage
    Of her race.

At a pathway's end, a score
Of brief footsteps from the door,
  Is the well; and there, aslant,
Warped and cracked by sun and rain,
Stands the well-sweep in the lane,
On its one leg, like a crane
    Long and gaunt.

In her ancient bombazine,
And her hood of faded green,
  From the kitchen, on her crutch,
Comes the widow with her pail;
In the hook she hangs the bail;
And the well-sweep gives a wail
    At her touch.

With a dismal, wailing creak,
Like an almost human shriek,
  Down the slow sweep goes, and up
With the wavering pail once more;
While, in yellow pinafore,
Runs her grandchild from the door
    With a cup.

Grandchild did I say? Behold!
Like a fleece of living gold,
  Just let loose from fairy-land,
Half to perfect beauty spun,
And half flying in the sun,
Making sun and shadow one,
    See her stand!

In old Rachel can there be
Aught akin to such as she?
  Winter's snow and summer's glow!
Poor old Rachel, bent and thin, —
Withered cheeks and peakéd chin, —
Has outlived all other kin
    Long ago.

From the curb, with many a groan,
Comes the bucket to the stone;
  And her crutch is in its place;
And now, pausing at the brink,
For the elf to dip and drink,
She, poor soul, must breathe and think
    For a space.

Lo ! the cloudy years — they part
Like a morning mist : her heart
  For a moment is beguiled
With bright fancies thronging fast ;
She beholds the glowing past,
Her own girlish image, glassed
    In the child !

And will ever that sweet elf
Be a creature like herself,
  Bowed with age and grief and care ?
Can such freshness fade away
To a phantom of decay, —
Golden tresses to a gray
    Ghost of hair ?

'T was but yesterday she saw
Her own grandam go to draw
  Water, with her pail and crutch ;
And she wondered to behold
One so pitifully old ! —
Eighty years, when all is told,
    Are not much.

Like a vision of the dawn,
Youth appears, and youth is gone :
  From four summers to fourscore
Is a dream ! 'T is ever so :
Roses come and roses go,
Roses fade and roses blow
    Evermore.

Ruined petals strew the walk :
Laughing buds are on the stalk :
  Mighty Nature is consoled.
Surging life no bounds can stay :
Beauty floods the young and gay,
Life and beauty ebb away
    From the old.

We are figures on the loom:
Out of darkness, into gloom,
    We but flit across the frame;
And the gnomes that toil within
Care not for the web they spin:
Ever ending, they begin
    Still the same.

While sad Rachel dimly peers
Through the glimmering film of years,
    There the grandchild, all aglow,
Stooping, dipping, sees by chance
Her own broken countenance
In the water wave and glance
    To and fro.

Tossing arms and gleeful scream
Startle Rachel from her dream;
    And as sunshine, in dark seas,
Gilds some lone and rocky isle,
On her wrinkled face the while
Rests a heavenly light, a smile
    Of deep peace.

On her lone heart's desert place,
Golden head and gleaming grace
    Shed a radiance warm and mild.
Rachel knows not age nor care, —
Life and hope are everywhere,
As her soul goes out in prayer
    For the child.

Little fingers drop the cup
Which old Rachel must take up:
    Rachel, smiling, stoops with pain;
While away the maiden hies,
After birds and butterflies,
Clapping hands with happy cries,
    Down the lane.

TROUTING

WITH slender rod, and line, and reel,
And feather fly with sting of steel,
Whipping the brooks down sunlit glades,
Wading the streams in woodland shades,
I come to the trouter's paradise:
The flashing fins leap twice or thrice:
Then idle on this gray boulder lie
My crinkled line and colored fly,
While in the foam-flecked, glossy pool
The shy trout lurk, secure and cool.

A rock-lined, wood-embosomed nook, —
Dim cloister of the chanting brook!
A chamber within the channelled hills,
Where the cold crystal brims and spills,
By dark-browed ledges blackly flows,
Falls from the cleft like crumbling snows,
And purls and plashes, breathing round
A soft, suffusing mist of sound.

Under a narrow belt of sky
Great boulders in the torrent lie,
Huge stepping-stones where Titans cross!
Quaint broideries of vines and moss,
Of every loveliest hue and shape,
With tangle and braid and tassel drape
The beetling rocks, and veil the ledge,
And trail long fringe from the cataract's edge.
A hundred rills of nectar drip
From that Olympian beard and lip!

And see! far on, it seems as if
In every crevice along the cliff
Some wild plant grew: the eye discerns
An ivied castle: feathery ferns
Nod from the frieze and tuft the tall
Dismantled turret and ruined wall.

Strange gusts from deeper solitudes
Waft pungent odors of the woods.
The small, bee-haunted basswood-blooms
Drop in the gorge their faint perfumes.
Here all the wild-wood flowers encamp
That love the dimness and the damp.

High overhead the blue day shines;
The glad breeze swings in the singing pines.
Somewhere aloft in the boughs is heard
The fine note of some warbling bird.
In the alders dank with noonday dews
A restless catbird darts and mews.

Dear world! let summer tourists range
Your great highways in quest of change,
Go seek Niagara and the sea, —
This little nook suffices me!

So wild, so fresh, so solitary, —
I muse in its green sanctuary,
And breathe into my inmost sense
A pure, sweet, thrilling influence,
A bliss, even innocent sport would stain,
And dear old Walton's art, profane.

Here, lying beneath this leaning tree,
On the soft bank, it seems to me,
The winds that visit this lonely glen
Should soothe the souls of sorrowing men, —
The waters over these ledges curled
Might cool the heart of a fevered world!

SONG OF THE FLAIL

In the Autumn, when the hollows
  All are filled with flying leaves,
And the colonies of swallows
  Long have quit the stuccoed eaves,

And a silver mantle glistens
  Over all the misty vale,
Sits the little wife, and listens
  To the beating of the flail,
  To the pounding of the flail, —
By her cradle sits and listens
  To the flapping of the flail.

The bright summer days are over,
  And her eye no longer sees
The red bloom upon the clover,
  The deep green upon the trees ;
Hushed the songs of finch and robin,
  And the whistle of the quail,
While she hears the mellow throbbing
  Of the thunder of the flail,
  The low thunder of the flail, —
Through the amber air, the throbbing
  And reverberating flail.

In the barn the stout young thresher
  Stooping stands with rolled-up sleeves,
Beating out his golden treasure
  From the ripped and rustling sheaves : —
O, was ever knight in armor,
  Warrior all in shining mail,
Half so handsome as her farmer,
  As he plies the flying flail,
  As he wields the flashing flail ?
The bare-throated, brown young farmer,
  As he swings the sounding flail !

All the hopes that saw the sowing,
  All the sweet desire of gain,
All the joy that watched the growing
  And the yellowing of the grain,
And the love that went to woo her,
  And the faith that shall not fail,
All are speaking softly to her
  In the pulses of the flail,

Of the palpitating flail, —
Past and Future whisper to her
In the music of the flail.

In its crib the babe is sleeping,
  And the sunshine, from the door,
All the afternoon is creeping
  Slowly round upon the floor ;
And the shadows soon will darken,
  And the daylight soon must pale,
When her heart no more shall hearken
  To the tramping of the flail,
  To the dancing of the flail, —
Her fond heart no more shall hearken
  To the footfall of the flail.

And the babe shall grow and strengthen,
  Be a maiden, be a wife,
While the moving shadows lengthen
  Round the dial of their life :
Theirs the trust of friend and neighbor,
  And an age serene and hale,
When machines shall do the labor
  Of the strong arm and the flail,
  Of the stout heart and the flail, —
Great machines perform the labor
  Of the good old-fashioned flail.

But when, blesséd among women,
  And when, honored among men,
They look round them, can the brimming
  Of their utmost wishes then
Give them happiness completer ?
  Or can ease and wealth avail
To make any music sweeter
  Than the pounding of the flail ?
  O, the sounding of the flail !
Never music can be sweeter
  Than the beating of the flail !

BOOK III

———

THE BOOK OF GOLD AND OTHER POEMS

Companions of my charméd nights and days,
O songs! that on my solitary ways
Shed glimpsing glories, coy, inconstant rays;

That edged the dawns with lovelier light and dew,
Lending the heavens a yet more heavenly blue,
To life and thought a more ethereal hue,

To men a more divine humanity; —
Go forth, blithe heralds! blesséd if there be
Souls that await your solace, two or three.

THE BOOK OF GOLD AND OTHER POEMS

THE BOOK OF GOLD

A CHRISTMAS STORY

PART I

CHRISTMAS EVE

ONE snowy Christmas eve it came to pass,
As Richard Ray was turning down the gas
In the old book-shop, casting into gloom
The dusty rows on rows that lined the room,
And antique folios piled on shelf and floor,
Two strangers, meeting, halted at his door,
And entered singly.

           Short and slight the first,
In short black cloak, with ample cape reversed
Above his head to shield him from the snow —
A quaintly improvised capote ; below,
A strange bright face, large-eyed, intense, peered out :
A man of forty years or thereabout.

Lightly the snowflakes from its folds he shook,
And from his cloak produced a ponderous book.
"A fine old 'Burton'! I dare swear," said he,
"There's not another such this side the sea.
Since I am here to turn an honest penny,
I ought to laud my wares ; but what can any
Reasonably fair and candid villain say
In praise of friends he's plotting to betray ?
My rare old 'Robert Burton'! there he lies!"
Scanning the shopman with deep wondrous eyes,

Full of unspeakable great thoughts. "How much?
This leather fellow at your Midas-touch
Should turn to gold; and gold I need, Heaven knows!"

Over the counter, spectacles on nose,
Old Richard stooped: "Ah, surely; so it is!
I ought to find a purchaser for this:"
And named a price that touched the stranger's pride.

"What! sell a lifelong friend so cheap?" he cried.
"I'd sooner seek an air-hole in the ice
And drown myself!" he vowed — and took the price.
Then, with a smile so quaint it well might move
Another's tears: "Who knows but this may prove
The nucleus of a fortune? Thanks!" he said,
Flung the black cape once more above his head,
And went his way.

         In dark and silent mood,
Aside, meanwhile, the second stranger stood:
A tall fair youth, but anxious-eyed and wan;
Brows nobly arched, but all their freshness gone,
Withered and parched by fires that raged within —
The hidden fires of suffering and of sin.

Why he had entered there I scarce can tell.
He neither came to purchase nor to sell;
But, as a hunted wretch, in desperate strait,
Remorse and terror knocking at his gate,
Seeks any corner, Maurice Allanburn,
Harassed, beset, not knowing where to turn,
Had paused at Richard's door. If all were told,
Perhaps he would have clutched the old man's gold.
For Allanburn, a pious widow's son,
Affianced, loved, even to the verge had run
A secret course of ruinous excess,
Till he was ready, in his dire distress,
To fling himself on any frantic deed, —
To mount unbridled violence as a steed,
And leap the abyss, or perish utterly.

" Dishonor I will never live to see :
  When all has failed, then this ! " he said, and pressed
  A hidden vial sewed into his vest.
" The swift news of my death shall overtake
  The rumor of disgrace, and kindly break
  Their poor hearts first."

                          What hope is there?   Suspected
  Already by the house he serves, — detected,
  He fears, and tracked by spies this night, — the end
  Is menacingly nigh.   And now the friend,
  With whose forged name he has been forced to borrow
  Some thousands in his absence, comes to-morrow.
  Gold, only gold, much gold, this very night,
  Or ignominious and precipitate flight —
  Naught else can save him ; and he will not fly.
" There 's none so wretched, so ensnared, as I ! "

  So Maurice stood and watched, aloof in shade,
  The shopman and the stranger at their trade.
" What furious need of gold to such as he ? "
  He mutters.   " I could laugh at poverty,
  And welcome toil, no matter where or what,
  With but a crust by honest labor got.
  Has he staked all upon some reckless game —
  The hopes of youth, an honorable name ?
  Is life itself, and more than life, at stake —
  A mother's love, a young girl's heart to break ?
  If not, let him be happy."

                              With the air
  Of one who had a common errand there,
  Maurice drew near and cast an absent look
  Over the pages of a little book
  Which lay upon the counter, till by chance
  A single sentence riveted his glance.

  Turn back, turn back ; it is not yet too late:
  Turn back, O youth ! nor seek to expiate
  Bad deeds by worse, and save the hand from shame
  By plunging all thy soul into the flame.

He started, read again, and still again,
With a strange fascination. But just then —

" An admirable book," the old man said ;
" ' Right Thinking and Right Living : ' 't will be read,
And, I predict, be famous, centuries hence.
The author is a man of wit and sense —
Charles Masters. Out of print, I think, just now.
Only a shilling. Thank you," with a bow.
" A merry Christmas to you, and good-night ; "
And Richard Ray once more turned down the light.

And with a quick glance up and down, to learn
If he is spied and followed, Allanburn
Goes forth again into the whirling storm.

The crowd sweeps by : the shop-girl's flitting form ;
The brisk mechanic coming from his work ;
The prosperous merchant, and the honest clerk ;
The happy poor man, with his pack of toys,
The Santa Claus of his own girls and boys ;
The fatherless apprentice lad, who stops
To feast his eyes before the glittering shops —
No Christmas gifts for him, but he can fill
His dreams with presents, and be happy still ;
The sleighing parties, in their fairy shells,
The muffled drivers and the jingling bells ;
The cheery newsboy, shouting through the storm
(Blowing his finger-tips to keep them warm)
The last great forgery, the awful crime.
" Whose turn," thinks Maurice, " will it be next time ? "
And hears in fancy, " Shocking suicide ! " —
His own dread fate by all the newsboys cried.

In groups, or friendly couples, or alone,
Each with a hope and purpose of his own,
He sees them pass ; and thinks what pleasant things
The season to the humblest fireside brings,
Happy alike who give and who receive ;
And all his memories of Christmas eve —

The expectant stockings by the chimney hung ;
The sweet conspiracies of old and young ;
The Christmas tree, with its surprising fruits —
Toys, candies, picture-books, the boy's first boots ;
The days of innocence and hope and joy ;
The fond proud mother, and the proud fond boy :
And many a fault and many a broken vow
Rush over him ; and he beholds even now
In their suburban home that mother wait,
And listen for his footstep at the gate,
While with light hand some graceful task she plies,
Preparing still for him some sweet surprise.
And Maurice stifles in his throat the cry,
"There's none so wretched and so base as I."

Her image haunts him, waiting there in vain,
And conscience urges with its stinging pain ;
And Maurice, entering at a well-known door,
As on like errands, many a time before,
Snatches a pen and sets himself to write :
" Mother, do not expect me home to-night ;
Important business."

                    Flashing through the wire,
The words will find the widow by her fire ;
And she will sigh, " His work is never done.
Ah, Laura, what a husband you have won !
So faithful, so industrious, so sedate !
No wonder he is pale and worn of late,
With so much business on his hands " — the while
He hastens to a bar-room to beguile
His misery for a moment, and impart
Fresh resolution to his faltering heart.

He meets a friend ; puts on an easy air
Of gayety, and sees through his despair
A sudden gleam.   " Ah, Murdock, you're my man !
Lend me a trifle — anything you can ;
For Christmas gifts have ruined me, and I
Have still to purchase " — forging lie on lie.

The loan obtained, they chat and clink their glasses :
And Maurice notes a short slight man who passes,
Advancing to the bar with eager pace,
In short black mantle, with a strange bright face.
The wondrous eyes and the great soul within
Glow with deep fervor as he calls for gin.
He lifts with nervous hand the glass and drinks,
And pays with Richard's coin.   And Maurice thinks :
" Was this his fearful need, his mad desire,
To quench a fiery thirst with fiercer fire ?
No hope for him !   But I may yet restore
All I have perilled by one venture more."

Straight to a gaming-palace he repairs ;
Climbs with quick step the too familiar stairs ;
The hot hope mounting to his head like fumes
Of maddening wine, he walks the gilded rooms,
The scene of half his losses.   Seated there,
To Heaven, or Chance, or Fate, he breathes a prayer,
To look with favoring eyes upon his sin —
The last, he vows, if he may only win.
Not for his own, but for his mother's sake,
For Laura's, he implores ; and his last stake
On the green cloth with trembling hand lets fall,
Wins — loses — wins again — and loses all !

And all is over.   Mother's eyes no more
Shall greet him with glad welcome at the door.
No more for him the rose of love shall bloom,
And trance the senses with its charmed perfume ;
Beauty delight, or social pleasure blow
The heart's dull embers to a heavenly glow.
The world its myriad industries shall ply,
And all its vast concerns full-sailed sweep by ;
And Friendship shall endure, and Hope shall trim
Her deathless lamp, but nevermore for him.

So Allanburn upon that Christmas eve,
His ruined youth despairing to retrieve,
Locked in his melancholy lodging, sits
And meditates, or walks the room by fits,

And writes his everlasting sad farewells
To those he loves, until the Christmas bells
Peal joyously upon the stormy air —
Peal sweet and clear, and through the tumult bear
The golden tidings of the reign of Peace.
" For Love is born : let wrong and sorrow cease !
Sorrow no more ! hope evermore ! " they ring ;
" Hope evermore ! love evermore ! " they sing,
To all the world ; and all the world is blest :
To all the world but one, for whom no rest,
No respite from despair and anguish, save
A shameful death and a dishonored grave.

And after death ? He will not pause to think :
Resolved to leap, why falter on the brink ?
Folded his letters, with a strangely steady
Cold hand he seals them, and now all is ready.
He reaches for the vial at his breast,
And finds instead, forgotten in his vest,
The little book placed there some hours ago.
The leaves fall open in his hand, and, lo !
Before him, like a flaming sword that turns
All ways, once more the fiery sentence burns.

Turn back, turn back ; it is not yet too late :
Turn back, O youth ! nor seek to expiate
Bad deeds by worse, and save the hand from shame
By plunging all thy soul into the flame !

He started to his feet, dashed down the book,
And to and fro across the chamber took
Quick frenzied strides ; then hurriedly prepared
The deadly draught, and in the mirror glared
At his own spectre, ghastly pale and grim,
With glass uplifted, coldly mocking him.

" 'T is but a shadow, and what more am I ?
Come, Nothingness ! and, World and Life, good-by ! "
He raised the glass — the shadow did the same ;
He closed his eyes, and suddenly, like flame,

Leaped forth the warning to his inner sight,
In living letters read by their own light :

Turn back, turn back ; it is not yet too late.

Be it Charles Masters, Providence, or Fate,
Something has stayed his hand.   From off the floor
He takes the little book and reads once more.

When all is lost, one refuge yet remains,
One sacred solace, after all our pains :
Go lay thy head and weep thy tears, O youth !
Upon the dear maternal breast of Truth.

Still as he reads, the Christmas bells he hears,
And in their frozen sources start his tears.

Dismiss the evil counsels of Deceit,
Fling off the mask, and downward to thy feet
Let the false vesture of concealment fall,
And, owning all thy wrongs, atone for all.

At every word he feels the searching steel
That probes the quivering heart, but probes to heal.

Every false path, though fair and long it seem,
Leads to some pit ; and happy thou mayst deem
Thy wayward youth, whose lesson comes not late —
O fortunate, when most unfortunate !

So Allanburn, with soul absorbed, intent,
Reads on ; and each prophetic word seems meant
For his own heart ; such broad bright wisdom shines,
Such swift conviction lightens in the lines.
And all the while the holy bells are ringing,
The spirits of the Christmas bells are singing,
Filling the stormy world with hymns of peace.

" For love is born : let wrong and sorrow cease !
Sorrow no more ! hope evermore ! " they ring ;

"Hope evermore! love evermore!" they sing.
And all the rock of self is cleft and shaken;
And deep within, sweet blessed springs awaken
Of comfort and new courage, not to die
This coward's death, and like a traitor fly
The demons he has conjured, but to live,
Strong in the strength which only truth can give.

PART II

CHRISTMAS NIGHT

And Maurice lived.   And as a traveller — lost
By night upon some trackless prairie, crossed
By wind-driven, leaping flames, while ever nigher
Sweeps the red-maned wild hurricane of fire
With hoof of thunder and devouring breath,
And all the air is lit with lurid death —
Kindles before his feet the crisp dry grass,
And burns the path where he will safely pass;
And the flames die behind him, and the morn
Beholds him far on blackened plains forlorn:
But life is left, and hope; so Allanburn,
By frank avowal of his guilt and stern
Self-condemnation, quelled the rage of men,
Forestalled his foes, and won his friends again,
As 't were, before he lost them.

                              Desolate
And long the labor seemed, to reinstate
Fallen fortune and lost honor to restore;
But will and heart were strong, and evermore
He kept the little volume by his side —
His saviour once, and now his constant guide
And solace in the long ennobling strife,
Incarnating its wisdom in his life.

To lose with high endeavor is to win;
And they but fail who build success on sin,

Whose gilded walls of happiness shall stand
As baseless palaces on sea-washed sand.

Each day's experience taught him to construe
Its old dry truths with meanings fresh and new.

Be then thy conscience as the eternal rock,
Wave-buffeted, unmoved by every shock
Of roaring condemnation, hate, and wrong :
Set thou thereon thy pharos high and strong.

Thus as he played his arduous daily part,
He learned its lofty precepts all by heart.

Let two allied and equal laws control
Thy being — law for body and law for soul ;
As the steam-chariot, with obedient wheel,
Flies safely on its parallels of steel.

Nor prudent virtues only ; rising thence,
It taught him faith and wise beneficence.

Religion is no leaf of faded green,
Or flower of vanished fragrance, pressed between
The pages of a Bible ; but from seeds
Of love it springeth, watered by good deeds.

So passed the whirling years, some nine or ten;
And now the Christmas time brings round again
Its innocent revels, and draws near its close,
When homeward through the city Maurice goes.

Tired Nature lets her starry eyelid down,
A wintry quiet falls on all the town,
A tingling frost is in the silent air,
His own breath whitens on his beard and hair,
As Allanburn, with homeward-hasting feet,
Awakes the echoes of the icy street.

The shops, on Christmas eve ablaze with light,
Are closed and dark on this cold Christmas night.

But in the homes about him, Maurice knows
What pleasure sparkles and what comfort glows :
The dance, the song and story, told or sung ;
Smiles from the elders, laughter from the young ;
Enraptured childhood with its pictured page ;
The homely games, uniting youth and age —
Scenes which the curtained windows scarce conceal :
And all the joys which friends and kindred feel
In that glad time — with sympathizing heart,
He seems to see and hear and take a part
In all ; and now his eager fancy runs
Before to his own home and little ones.
There waits the partner of his home and life,
Their mother and (ecstatic thought !) his wife,
The ever-faithful Laura. Fondly there
His own good mother from her easy-chair
Watches the baby Maurice on the floor,
Upbuilding still, to see it fall once more,
His toppling house of blocks ; or turns to smile
On little Laura by her side the while,
Bending in the warm light her glowing head,
Hushing her doll and putting it to bed.

The last house falls in ruins ; in the box
Are packed at last the bright new Christmas blocks ;
The doll's asleep, the cradle put away ;
And so the happy children end their play.
And in imagination now he sees
Two cherubs in white nightgowns on their knees,
Mingling their curls before the mother's chair,
Lisping with dewy lips their evening prayer.
How sweet the picture ! Suddenly the past
Rises to dash it ; and he starts aghast,
Seeing his own pale spectral image stand
Within a mocking mirror, glass in hand.

While thus amid his blessings he must think
Of perils passed, and shudder at the brink
Of one black gulf, the dark remembrance makes
What is seem brighter ; as he sometimes wakes

At midnight from the hideous dream, to press
More closely his dear present happiness.

He hurries on with eased and thankful heart;
And of a sudden sees before him start
From a by-street the figure of a child,
A wretched girl in rags, who puts up wild
Entreating hands, and cries out piteously,
" Oh, sir! who is there — who will come and see
My father? He is very sick! I fear " —
" My child, I will go with you. Is it near? "
And, comprehending what she scarce can say,
He follows where she quickly leads the way.
Down the by-street where red-eyed rum-shops glare,
And with hot breath defile the evening air,
Where pines pale Poverty, while Vice and Crime
With lurid orgies vex the hallowed time;
Across a court and upward through the gloom
Of creaking stairs, she leads to a cold room,
Ill-odored with foul drugs and misery,
Where from his couch a man starts up to see
A stranger come.

" Art thou the Christ? " he cries;
And in the wan white face and wondrous eyes,
Where now the awful fires of fever burn,
Is something which recalls to Allanburn
Old Richard's book-shop and one long-ago
White Christmas eve. " Art thou the Christ or no? "

" Not I," said Maurice, as amazed he stood,
" But in His name I come to do you good."

" Idle your labor, if you be not He.
No Christ at second-hand will do for me.
For know you who I am? — Sir, a lost soul!
Hear overhead Jehovah's thunder roll!
It mutters — do you mark it? — ' Woe! woe! woe!'"

Maurice replied: " I do not hear it so.
It says you shall be saved. For Christ is here:

In me He comes to bring you help and cheer,
For you and for your child."

                              " For her indeed !
And, sir, I thank you ; she has woful need.
But I am driven about the desert world
By my own burning ; hither and thither whirled
Forever, a wailing, wandering ghost of sin,
Through regions where Lord Christ has never been.
And yet I was a master once, and taught
Divine Philosophy ; preached, wrote, and brought
Refreshment to some hearts, I verily think.
Now I am perishing for a little drink ;
And if you bear a charitable mind,
As I must deem — for in your face I find
A certain eloquence — give me some gin.
You 'll tell me that has been my special sin :
Not so : it was the world-consuming thirst
For fresher power and larger life which first
Fevered my soul ; then, in the sacred name
Of inspiration, sovereign Opium came.
In gorgeous dreams he stalks, the Lord of Pain :
Gin is a little page that bears his train.
In pomp before us to the feast he goes,
But ever, at the pageant's sorrowful close,
Puts off his robes of fantasy and dream,
And in his naked death's-head grins supreme.

" You 're right : that little hunchback last held rum ;
That other bottle smells of laudanum.
To purchase that my little girl was sent
Starved through the street, and our last coin was spent.
Now curse me for a fool, and go your way ;
But in your censure don't forget to say,
'HE WAS THE BOUND THRALL OF LORD OPIUM.' "

"Unhappy man ! think you that I have come
With judgment to condemn you ?   What am I ? "
Says Maurice, as he puts the bottles by,
And takes the sick man's hot dry hand in his.
" A fellow-man, to whom all miseries

Through his own sin and suffering are made known;
Who censures no man's folly but his own."

" And have you kissed Temptation ? in the cup
Of madness drunk all hope and manhood up ?
I am more guilty; yet I am the same
Who once, and with some reason, bore the name
Of Genius ; for my spirit, in my youth,
Explored all knowledge and conceived all truth.
And — let me whisper it — I had a wife,
Won from a pleasant home and gentle life :
A violet just opened in the air
Of the sweet May is not so sweet and fair.
And we were happy, and I loved her well ;
And hers was greater love ; and when I fell,
She strove with me, strove for me, and forgave me,
And would have saved, if mighty love could save me,
Pleading with Heaven and men and me my cause.
But all my resolutions were as straws
That bind a sleeping lion when he wakes.
Why, sir, for her and our dear children's sakes
To prudence I a thousand times was pledged ;
And with that venom-thought the tooth is edged
That gnaws me here.   But now her sleep is sound,
Under the buttercups, in the cool ground,
While I am burning.   Where are you, my girl ?
Fidelia ! child ! my brain is all awhirl.
I cannot see you well."

                              She nestles near :
" Oh, father ! don't you know me ?   I am here."

With feeble hand he takes her thin wan shoulder,
And for an eager moment seems to hold her
In his soul's steadfast gaze : he sees the sad
And patient little face that never had
Its share of smiles ; small features, which should be
All freshness, pinched with early penury.
And eyes — still like her mother's, tender blue,
Through every trial heavenly deep and true

In their affection — at this moment dim
With piteous tears, not for herself, but him.

He held her there, and fondly gazed, and smiled
With mournful pathos : " My poor orphan child !
You 've had no parent since your mother died."

" Oh, father ! I have you." But he replied,
" Your own good father died some years ago.
I *was* that father ; but this man of woe,
Who chides, neglects you, makes your dear heart bleed,
I pray you think it is not I indeed.
A father should have cherished this frail flower,
And nourished it in gentle sun and shower,
And kept it, with a father's manifold
Fond troubles, from rude winds and wintry cold.

" I dreamed just now that it was Christmas day ;
And I saw troops of children at their play,
And you among them, and your little brother —
He had not died of hunger. And your mother,
All hope and happy smiles, was at my side.
And with unutterable love and pride
We watched and kept you ever in our sight,
And all was happiness and warmth and light.
You were not cold or hungry any more ;
You were like other children. Then the roar
Of laughing fiends awoke me, and I saw
My darling shivering on her bed of straw.
But do not mind. When I am gone, for you,
My poor Fidele, the vision may come true.
Then you 'll forgive your father. Do not weep.
I am too weak and ill. Now let me sleep."

So saying, he sunk back upon his bed.

And Maurice drew the child aside, and said,
" Have you no friends, no kindred, who should know ?
Nor other home to which you two can go ? "

"My mother's friends; but they are far away.
They would have had me go to them and stay —
Forsake my father!" weeping, she replied.
"But mother left him to me when she died.
'Be good to him; be always good and true,'
That was her charge, and so what could I do?
They call him wicked. Oh, it is not so!
But, good or wicked, this is all I know:
He is my father, and has need of me."

"And you do well," cries Maurice, cheerily.
"Your little heart is very brave and strong.
Now watch till I return; 't will not be long."

Five minutes takes him to a coach; ten more,
And he alights in haste at his own door.
There busy hands in ample baskets pack
Fuel and food, and he is whirling back;
Finds a physician by the way; and, lo!
Into that dismal chamber steals a glow
Of comfort. Kindlings crackle in the grate;
The table beams with bounty, where of late
Only the rank-breathed empty bottles stood;
While in the child the sense of gratitude
For gifts that seem by Heavenly Mercy sent
Is lost in wonder and bewilderment.

"Eat, child!" But now beside the patient's bed
The doctor sits; and ere she touches bread,
Though from long fasting weak in every limb,
She trembling waits for words of hope from him.

As when an infant gone astray has climbed
Some dizzy height, and any act ill-timed
Of rescuing friends may cause its hold to miss,
And dash it down the dreadful precipice,
But slowly, step by step, with toil and pain,
The way it climbed must it descend again:
So this strayed soul has groped along the ledge
Of life-o'er-death, till at the very edge

He swoons, suspended in the giddy air ;
And only tender love and utmost care
And all the skill which ever science gave
Can save him, if indeed even such can save.

The wise physician, seated at his task —
His kindly features moulded to a mask
Of calm grave thought, through which no faintest ray
To kindle expectation finds its way —
Counts pulse, and ponders symptoms, and prepares
The patient's powders, while the patient glares
Delirious ; then takes leave ; but at the door,
Seeing the child's eyes question and implore,
Puts off the doctor and resumes the man,
And speaks what comfortable words he can.

And now Fidele is pacified and fed.
She sleeps, and Maurice watches in her stead
Through weary hours ; till, just as morning breaks,
The patient from a fitful slumber wakes,
But cannot move for utter weariness.
" Fidele ! " he whines, in querulous distress ;
Sees the strange watcher there, and at the sight
Gropes feebly in his memories of the night
To find again the half-remembered face.

" Let the child rest ; command me in her place,"
Says Maurice, pillowing the patient's head.

" Something I do recall," the sick man said.
" But solve me now the riddle if you can :
You are, I deem, a prosperous gentleman ;
I, the forlorn self-ruined wretch you see,
Not worth your thought ; and yet you waste on me
Your time and thought.   We 've met, I think, before ?
Nay, speak, or I shall only talk the more."

" You are a man — enough for me to know
I can relieve a fellow-mortal's woe.

But you are more to me than common men.
Once, twice, indeed, we 've met; " and how and when
(To soothe his patient) Allanburn relates.
" That night the subtle circles of our fates
Appeared to touch ; so that in memory
I 've seen you still, and wondered what might be
Your fortunes since.   Dark as they were that night,
My own were in a far more evil plight.
And I was saved — almost by chance it seemed —
So mere a chance that often I have dreamed
It was your path of life, not mine, it crossed,
And you were saved instead, and I was lost."

The other sighed, " No chance !   Our destiny,
With its heaven-reaching branches, is a tree
Which grows from little seeds in our own hearts ;
The elements strengthen, bend, or rend the parts,
As they are sound or flawed.   My will was weak,
The very pith and root of all.   But speak ! "

" What was my chance or providence ?   A book,
Which from the counter carelessly I took —
A little faded volume, thumbed and old,
But to my life and need a BOOK OF GOLD."

The sick man groaned.   " Talk not of books to me !
If they could save, be sure I should not be
This burnt-out wick ; but a lamp glorified,
Set in the windows of the Lord, to guide
Benighted souls, to cheer the tempest-tossed,
And show the Way of Life, which I have lost."

Quoth Allanburn : " All that you say, and more,
My author in his book has said before.

" *Good books are pearl and gold ; yet not of them*
Is builded bright the New Jerusalem :
Hear thou thyself the Voice the prophets heard,
And shape in thine own life the shining Word.

" But now, we talk too much, and you must rest."

In the pale face a vivid gleam expressed
Surprise, hope, doubt. " I had wellnigh forgot
That such a book was written. Is it not
' Right Thinking and Right Living ' ? "

        Maurice cried,
" You know it ! " And a look almost of pride
And joy into the strange bright visage stole.

" Thank Heaven, if it has helped a single soul !
Enough, O friend ! But you are here to gain
A deeper lesson than its leaves contain ;
Since he whose words can save, himself may be
Among the lost."

    " Charles Masters ! "

        " I am he :
Be not too much amazed and grieved ; for I
Am happy, and contented now to die."

" Dear soul ! and have I sought you far and near,"
Cries Allanburn, " at last to find you here ?
My benefactor ! *'T is not yet too late !*
All that I have, life, happiness, estate,
I owe to you ; and, help me, Heaven ! I yet
Will pay some portion of the precious debt
In love and service to your child and you."

" I am repaid," Charles Masters said, and drew
A long deep sigh of peace. " You bring me rest,
And almost make me feel that I am blessed.
Cherish my child — she has a heart of gold.
But all your prayers and patience cannot hold
This bruised reed up, and make it grow again.
Seek not to keep my memory among men,
But set these warning words above my grave :
' OTHERS HE SAVED, HIMSELF HE COULD NOT SAVE.' "

THE WRECK OF THE FISHING-BOAT

PART I

CAPE PORPOISE is a little fishing town :
  Where the tide billow, which the Atlantic rolls
Foaming on reef and beach, glides rippling down
  Through sinuous creeks and over shining shoals,
Floating a few light craft, upon the brown
    Impassive ooze careened with slanting poles,
Or, refluent, leaves all slack and bare again, —
It nestles in the rocky coast of Maine.

In their unchanging, ancient village hived —
  Few drones in that compact community —
The hardy fisher-folk have wived and thrived,
  Drawing a scant subsistence from the sea,
Through many generations ; and survived
    Tempest and wreck, and dire calamity
Of war — French, English, Indian — and embargo,
And British cruisers catching crew and cargo.

Few drones, I said : there will be, now and then,
  Some good-for-nothing idlers found amid
The best communities of bees and men ;
  Nor could Cape Porpoise ever quite get rid
Of such unthrifty fellows as Wild Ben —
    A youth of shining talents, which he hid
In Scriptural earth of self-indulgent sloth —
Under a punch-bowl or a tavern cloth.

A natural boatman — nimble with the sail,
  The oar, the seine ; no lad more skilled than he
To calk a leak, splice rope, or brave the gale :
  A very imp he seemed of the wild sea.
Handy to help, yet never within hail
    When needed most ; but he was sure to be
Off with his cronies somewhere, getting drunk
Over in Biddeford or Kennebunk.

Ben's father was a fisherman — Job Nelson.
  He set the scapegrace to repair, one day,
The foremast step — or socket on the kelson —
  Of their small craft, the *Lark*, moored in the bay.
" Do it right now," he said, " and do it well, son,
  Or the next blow will bear it quite away.
'T is wrenched and parted; and I 'm in no hurry
To risk dismasting in another flurry.

" I 'll put that catch of codfish on the flakes;
    Then you must help me underrun the trawl."
Ben from the shelf the saw and hatchet takes,
    When round the cove he hears a comrade call;
To go with whom his task he soon forsakes,
    Careless who mends the boat or helps to haul
The lines that night.   Hatchet and saw are left
Upon the shore, hid in a rocky cleft.

The fish were put upon the flakes to dry;
    Then Job, all ready for the voyage, looked round,
And searched the little seaport low and high,
    And called; but Ben was nowhere to be found.
'T was only the wild loon that laughed reply,
    Over by Redin's Island — dreary sound!
That far, half-human call which sometimes mocks
The seeker for some lost one mid the rocks.

Ben's father stormed, and gave him up at last,
    But would not leave the trawl another day.
The afternoon and tide were going fast;
    The *Lark* would soon be stranded where she lay.
" I wonder did the rogue secure the mast?
    Whether he did or not, I cannot stay;
I 'll take the tools and mend the step myself,
If need be."   But the tools had left the shelf.

Job Nelson raved, and on the absent one
    Volleys of violent invective poured.
But goodwife Jane, who loved her wayward son,
    Stood pale and quiet while her husband roared;

Then mildly said, " I 'm sure he must have done
  The task you bid, and left the tools aboard.
So say no more.   I always like to go
And help you with the trawl, and that you know."

The young ones were just coming in from school —
  A girl of six, two boys of eight and ten ;
A babe there was beside — as seemed the rule
  In every house — of that sweet season when
Babes first begin to push a chair or stool:
  A little brood much younger than Wild Ben.
(Three others in the rocky hills were laid,
Where you would think a grave could scarce be made.)

The mother soon their simple supper spread,
  And nursed her babe, and hastened to prepare
For sea, with more of pleasure than of dread,
  And gave the infant to the others' care,
And left them with their bowls of milk and bread,
  And started ; but went back and kissed them where,
Grouped in the open cottage door, they stood
To see her off, and charged them to be good, —

Again, and still again — she knew not why ;
  But as she quickly turned to go, there gushed
A sudden tender torrent to her eye ;
  And over her a fearful feeling rushed,
As if some great calamity were nigh,
  And that dear babe might nevermore be hushed
And comforted on her warm breast at night ;
But soon she laughed such fancies out of sight.

" You 'll see us coming with the tide at dark,"
  She promised them, and hurried to the pier,
Where Job already had his little bark ;
  And down the steep wharf-ladder to the sheer
Groped with slow feet, and stepped aboard the *Lark ;*
  Then listened, as they pushed away, to hear
The happy children shouting from the door,
And watched, until her home was seen no more.

The breeze was fair, the passage smooth and swift;
    And, huddled in the doorway, side by side,
The children saw the little vessel drift
    Among the islands scattered far and wide,
Where broke the sea through many a foaming rift —
    A feather wafted by the wind and tide
Away, away, to veer at last from sight
Round Folly Island, by Goat Island Light.

The children ate their meal of milk and bread,
    And played at wreck and raft with bowl and spoon;
And Job, the oldest, put the babe to bed;
    Then, as the slow, full-freighted afternoon
Went down the west with wake all fiery red,
    And over isle and inlet sailed the moon,
They waited for their parents, anxious-eyed,
To see them coming with the coming tide.

Pulse of the world! hoarse sea with heaving breath,
    Swaying some grief's great burden to and fro!
Fierce heart that neither hears nor answereth,
    Sounding its own eternal wail of woe!
Punctual as day, unheeding life or death,
    Wasting the ribs of earth with ceaseless throe;
Remorseless, strong, resistless, resting never,
The tides come in, the tides come in forever!

The tide came in, and flooded creek and cove,
    And spread on marsh and meadow far away
Under the moon; and many a dim sail hove
    Softly in sight, and gleamed along the bay,
And folded its pale wing, no more to rove;
    And hearths were bright, and, blithe from breeze and spray
And chasing breakers, fathers, sons, and brothers
Went home to happy children, wives, and mothers.

The tide came in, and shoulder-deep the pier
    Wallowed in waves that lapped and leaped and glistened;
And still, to see one longed-for sail appear,
    The lonesome little watchers gazed and listened

Until their fluttering hearts were filled with fear,
  And beat against the bars like birds imprisoned.
Their parents came not with the coming tide;
And now the hungry babe awoke and cried.

The others cried for sympathy or fright,
  Till little Job assumed a manly air,
And brushed his tears, and said, " The moon is bright;
  We 'll hurry to the wharf to meet them there;
I 'm sure by that time they will be in sight.
  I 'll carry Baby; Willie, you 'll take care
That Sissy does n't fall. Of course, you know,
It 's the big catch of fish that keeps them so."

He soothed the babe, and tied his sister's hood,
  And led them forth with childish words of cheer:
" Don't cry! you know she told us to be good!"
  Then to the wharf, shuddering with cold and fear.
The tide was in; the steep wharf-ladder stood
  Plunged in the deep wide flood, which lashed the pier,
And brimmed the bay, and gleamed among the isles,
And silvered shores and shoals for glittering miles.

But over all that bright expanse no sail.
  The wind had freshened, and was blowing strong;
And well those little ones might quake and quail,
  Harking to catch their father's cheery song,
To hear the waves instead, and rising gale:
  No sound beside, but evermore the long
Roll of the thundering breakers far away.
The night was chill: it was the month of May.

They find a skiff careened upon the pier,
  And into this the trembling wretches creep,
And cuddle close, eager for warmth and cheer,
  And still their long and lonesome vigil keep,
Scanning the troubled waters far and near,
  Till all but Job have cried themselves to sleep.
He wraps his shivering sister in his coat,
Then falls asleep himself, there in the boat.

PART II

And now, half sobered from his late carouse,
  Wild Ben went slowly sauntering up the street.
Thinking of home and wrath with sullen brows,
  He sidled to the door with stealthy feet,
But stared amazed to find an empty house —
  A lamp still burning in the window-seat,
Which Job had set, upon the seaward side,
To cheer his parents coming with the tide.

Ben glowered and growled, and searched both house and shed,
  Then stood and studied, in a sort of maze,
The vacant cradle and each empty bed.
  The lamp flame, flickering to a dying blaze,
Leaped, quivered, vanished, and the moon instead
  Poured through the quiet panes its haunting rays,
While in his flesh and stirring hair the youth
Felt a cold, curdling horror of the truth.

He from the cupboard brought a loaf and bowl,
  And tried to eat; and cursed and swore a little,
To still the rising terrors of his soul;
  But strove in vain to solve the fearful riddle.
Then like some conscious murderer, he stole
  From the deserted house. It was the middle
Of the dread night: the village slept; afar
The savage ocean roared on reef and bar.

The smacks, sails furled, and headed all one way,
  Veered on the tide in the strong wind which drove
Now tempest-like athwart the little bay :
  Only the *Lark* was absent from the cove,
And, tethered to the buoy where late she lay,
  The dory reared and champed, as if it strove,
Frighted, to fly.   Ben seemed to see and hear
In every object sight or sound of fear.

Then all his faults, the counsels he had spurned,
  Thronged on his heart, like fiends, to chide and mock.

The one bright eye of the lone light-house burned
  Far off. What does it see on wave or rock,
Or in the burying surf ? The tide has turned ;
  White in the moon, the wild, fleet waters flock,
From shoals and creeks, back to their deep sea caves —
Realm of strewn wrecks and cold, uncovered graves.

In his strange horror and bewildering fear
  He seeks the landing, and discovers there,
In the old boat abandoned on the pier,
  A living heap — Job's face, with tangled hair,
And in the moonlight on that face a tear ;
  He notes, beside, Job's little arms, half bare,
And, closely nestled, covered by his coat,
The others, all asleep there in the boat.

He saw the small breasts heave ; he felt them breathe :
  A shadow in the moonlight, dark and dumb,
He watched them for a moment from beneath
  Remorseful brows, while every sense seemed numb
With inward agony ; then gnashed his teeth.
  Job staggered up — " Oh, father, have you come ? "
But no kind father's eyes looked down on him ;
Only his brother stood there, pale and grim.

" What are you doing here so late at night ?
  Where 's mother ? "   " Why, she went instead of you.
Oh, Ben, I hope you did the mending right !
  The tools were gone, and what could father do ? "
Ben gave a groan ; recoiling with affright,
  The little boatman wakes his little crew ;
And Ben, arousing from his stupor, tries
To quiet them with well-intended lies.

He launched a skiff, and, cursing smack and trawl,
  Leaped in, and sent the trembling wretches home,
And rowed till on the outmost island wall
  He saw the gathering surges burst and comb,
Loud-booming, and the angered sea was all
  One awful waste of tumbling waves and foam :

No sail, nor any lonesome thing afloat,
Save him, in his own tide-borne, tossing boat.

Stoutly he pulled, and strained his eyes across
    The running surf and restless rolling sea,
By Vaughan's low isle and lonely Albatross;
    But only rock and ocean can he see.
Tumultuously the hoary waters toss
    Their mighty plumes, careering endlessly;
And the beaked breakers with loud rustling wings
Flap on the reef like wild, infuriate things.

Ah many a time as to a mad carouse
    Had he rowed forth, to feel the rush, the thrill,
The towering surge come tumbling on his bows;
    The boat, held firm by its bold rider's will —
The mind's electric presence, which endows
    Even wood with life and senseless things with skill —
Rising triumphant, flinging off the wave;
Man the sole master, even the sea his slave!

But now there is a fury in his brain:
    The frolic purpose and the joy are gone,
And but the practised power and will remain.
    Brows drenched with spray and sweat, wild-eyed and wan,
He mounts the surges, resolute to gain
    The open sea, and to the trawl pulls on;
Finds the long line of tossing floats still there,
But living object never anywhere.

But what is this the slow great seas uplift,
    Weltering, low-sunken, glimmering in the dim
Sad rays of the drooping moon?   A wreck adrift,
    With heaving, wave-washed side turned up at him,
And through the gaping ribs a ghastly rift:
    Some foundered boat capsized.   His senses swim;
Madly he gazes round; on every side
Rolls billowy desolation wild and wide.

PART III

'T was now some hours since Job his lines had hauled,
    Secured the captured fish, and dropped once more
His freshly baited hooks ; while Jane, installed
    As mate to her brave captain, prompt with oar,
Boat-hook, or bait to help him, scarce recalled
    The doubts that shook her at the cottage door.
The tiller grasped, the wind abeam, the sails
Fill, strain, swell proudly, and the rushing rails

Sweep through the water, bowing to the bubbles,
    Upon the cheery homeward track at last.
The lucky fisherman forgets his troubles,
    And hopefully he eyes the swaying mast
And sunlit canvas, as the *Lark* redoubles
    Her wingéd speed in the increasing blast ;
And the glad mother turns across the foam
Her yearning gaze with tender thoughts of home.

Then, in the midst of pleasant talk, they feel
    A sudden shock, a lurch, and hear a crash.
The staggering foremast, parted from the keel,
    Drops slantwise down, and tears a hideous gash
In the *Lark's* side, through which the waters steal,
    Rising about their feet with ominous splash,
As pitching heavily she lies, brought to,
And sinking, spite of all that Job can do.

And so the worst — far worse than aught he feared —
    Had come to pass.   Too terrified to speak,
Jane bailed the gushing water, while he cleared
    The wreck, and strove to stanch the dreadful leak.
Still, as the cruel ice-cold waters neared
    Her knees, her waist, she did not start nor shriek,
But bailed amidst the fish that swam about,
Till a great wave washed in, and they swam out.

She saw the escaping fish as in a dream,
    And frantically still the bucket plied.

But now the vessel, settling on her beam,
   Turned to the sky her glistening, splintered side:
This too she noticed ; and in that supreme
   Dread moment thought of many things beside —
Her home, her babes, three little hill-side graves,
And her and Job there struggling in the waves.

Fast to the wreck they cling; but every sea
   Deluges them with waters deadly cold.
They sink, they rise, they gaze despairingly
   Round the wide waste of waters to behold
Some sail; but only far-off sails they see,
   Faintly suffused with pale ethereal gold.
Across the fluctuating gilded swells,
The sun is setting over York and Wells.

"Job, are we lost?" said Jane. "Cling for your life!"
   He cried. "I'll save you." Round the sunken deck
He swam, and cut the halyards with his knife,
   And, working in the water to his neck,
Lashed spar to spar ; then caught his sinking wife
   Just as a great wave swept her from the wreck,
And drew her forth, half drowned, with streaming hair,
Upon his little raft, and bound her there —

On the drenched canvas stretched, a dripping heap.
   And still the sails descried were few and far.
And so the day went down upon the deep,
   And the moon shimmered, and the light-house star
Pencilled its ruddy beam across the sweep
   Of wandering waters ; while, with breast to spar,
Shaping his course to reach the nearest shore,
Job swam, and pushed his laden raft before.

"Oh, Job," said Jane, "I am so cold! I ache
   In every bone. Dear Job, if I should die,
Be gentle with the children for my sake.
   Oh, now I think, I wish to live, that I
May do my duty better. If you take
   Another wife, I hope that she will try

To love our dear ones, and be kind to you.
Forgive poor Ben for what he failed to do."

" Don't talk of dying and of other wives
    Quite yet," cries Job; " I 'll get you safe to land."
But, terribly and strongly as he strives,
    Not all the might of manhood can withstand
The wrenching seas and sharp cross-wind that drives
    The raft away towards some more distant strand.
Still, for a while he bravely struggles, loath
To quit the raft, which will not bear them both.

Off the dim cape of moonlit Arundel [1]
    Slowly they drift, scarce fifty rods away,
Soon to be swept by wind and drenching swell
    Helplessly on, across an open bay,
As Job, in fierce despair, foresees too well.
    " Oh, Jane," he says, " there is no other way,
But I must leave you. I will swim ashore
For help — God help us! " He could say no more.

" I thought of that. If you are sure to reach
    The rock and save yourself, I pray you, go.
But, oh," she said, " for *their* sake, I beseech,
    Take care. The sea is terrible, you know,
On those sharp ledges."   " There 's a pebbly beach
    Close in the point. I 'll rest a minute. Oh,
Now must I leave you? "   " Touch me first," said Jane,
" Dear Job, for we may never meet again."

[1] *Arundel* is the name under which the township of Kennebunkport (in York County, Maine) was incorporated in 1717, and by which it was known for over a hundred years; when it was discarded, and for fifty years more disappeared from the vocabulary of the coast. It has recently been restored, however, to the broad, green, wood-crested promontory — now a favorite summer resort — lying immediately east of the mouth of the Kennebunk River, and called *Cape Arundel* when it is not called *Ocean Bluff*. The " open bay " alluded to in this stanza is Wells Bay. The " long dark river pier," mentioned farther on, is the immense granite breakwater at the mouth of the Kennebunk. " Old Fort Beach " is on Cape Arundel, not far from the " Spouting Rock: " it is a natural sea-wall of pebbles and smooth stones, from which many a ship has been ballasted. The village of Cape Porpoise is near the other — that is to say, the eastern — extremity of the township of Kennebunkport, and is one of the oldest settlements on the coast.

So they touched hands upon the cold wet mast
   With quick, convulsive pressure, and with wan,
Strange faces in the moonlight looked their last,
   And said their last farewells — and Job was gone:
Forth from her side a slow dark object passed,
   Tossed by the sweeping waves; and, drifting on,
She watched him from her raft, and held her breath,
And prayed, " Oh, save him, save him, Lord, from death ! "

She watched him sink, and mount, and disappear ;
   Then strained each aching sense to see him gain
The gray grim shore, his signal shout to hear,
   Forgetting her own peril and sharp pain ;
Broke from her bonds, half rising from her bier,
   And gazed and shrieked and wrung her hands in vain,
In unimaginable wild distress —
Alone in the vast ocean's loneliness.

No answering shout, no dim emerging shape —
   Or they are lost in the perpetual roar
Of waters and the formless glooms that drape
   The solitary coast.   And evermore
The raft is slowly drifting from the cape ;
   And still no dory from the inner shore
And long dark river pier, nor boatman's cry,
Brings hope that *he* is safe and help is nigh.

Dying she seems ; and, like one dying, sums
   Her good and evil days in manifold
Visions of home and love ; till life becomes
   A dream of misery and mortal cold,
And mercifully pain itself benumbs
   The sense of pain.   And so the night grows old ;
And, like a shuttle of the wind, which shifts
Sharply about, back towards the cape she drifts.

PART IV

The night grows old, the moon is low, the stars
  Drowse in the liquid depths of heaven. And now,
With hope rewakened by the missing spars,
  Ben searches sea and shore, and drives his bow
Amidst the breakers of the rocks and bars;
  Darting with desperate speed his daring prow
At any shape or shadow, which may be
Shadow or shape he longs, yet dreads, to see.

He rounds the cape, from cove to cove he rows,
  And, as the moon is setting, comes at last
To Old Fort Beach, which, half in shadow, shows
  A long low shape upon the shingle cast.
Through tumbling kelp, rolled in the undertow's
  Enormous foaming jaws that hold it fast,
He shoots his skiff ashore, and stoops beside
That long low shape left stranded by the tide:

A mass of spars and twisted ropes, still wet
  From the receding wave, with flecks of spume on
The dark, drenched sail, and something darker yet —
  A shadow in the shadow, ghastly, human,
Stretched on the raft. Mother and son have met.
  Cold to the touch, appalling, droops the woman.
He lifts her from the raft, and, kneeling there,
Bends over her in terror and despair.

"Mother! — O God! you are not dead!" He takes
  A rum-flask from his coat in furious haste,
And for the first time in his wild youth makes
  Wise use of its bad contents. At the taste
She gives a little moan of pain, and wakes
  Slowly to consciousness of strong arms placed
Around her, and a shadowy visage bowed
Above her in a sort of dreamy cloud.

And, for the first time in his life, he prays —
  To Heaven, to her, with mingled oaths, as if

Profanity and prayer were kin. He lays
  Full half his garments on her in the skiff,
And pushes off in the moon's faint last rays;
  And rows away by sombre cove and cliff,
And on through flashing surge and shadowy air,
Under the light-house lantern's streaming glare.

Meanwhile the little ones lie sunk in deep
  And restful slumber, till, with direful din,
Which fills the house and wakes them from their sleep,
  A sudden headlong force comes bursting in.
Staring with fear, upright the youngsters leap,
  And see what seems their brother Benjamin
Bearing a great black burden on his arm
In the gray dawn, and shouting loud alarm.

" Quick! for the doctor, for the neighbors, run!
  Mother is drowned! " Half naked, from the shed,
With sobs of terror, speeds the oldest one.
  The others, wondering, whispering, " Is she dead? "
Clasp their small hands, while the remorseful son
  Is getting her into their soft warm bed.
Too weak for words, she gives a pitying sigh
And faint sweet smile, to hear her baby cry.

She had not thought that ever she should hear
  That cry again. And now she seems half blessed:
Ben is so good, her little home so dear!
  Now, if she dies, she feels that this is best —
To fold her palms with friends and kindred near,
  In her dear home, and then be laid to rest
By gentle hands beside those little graves,
And not to perish in the cold dark waves.

If only Job were safe! That thought again,
  With throbbing life's return, distracts her mind.
The neighbors now come hurrying, earnest men
  And white-faced, eager women, all so kind.
Some stay to serve the sick, and some, with Ben,
  Put forth in boats and scour the coast to find

The missing man ; while springs triumphantly
The glorious sun from out the glorious sea.

Its far-off flag of smoke a steamship trails
    Across the fiery orb ; and here and there,
On the blue dome of ocean, tacking sails
    Darken and brighten in the purple air.
Forgetting death and wreck and ruthless gales,
    The broad bright sea is marvellously fair !
With quivering scales and panting side, lies curled
The azure dragon round about the world.

Such beauty seems a mockery of their quest.
    The frolic waters well their secret keep,
And hide grim death beneath a lovely breast.
    Down in the green recesses of the deep,
Where, to and fro, in noiseless dark unrest,
    The slow mysterious plumes of sea-weed sweep,
With upturned face and sightless, staring eyes,
Beckoning with spectral hand, the dead man lies.

Five days they search in vain ; upon the last,
    A farmer gathering sea-weed hears a yelp
Of terror from his cur, and starts aghast
    At something hideous tangled in the kelp.
Ox-goad and fork down on the beach are cast ;
    And from the nearest farm runs ready help.
'T is done : the slow, unwieldy oxen start,
With a dread burden oozing in the cart.

Beside the little graves is shaped another ;
    Then the sad burial.   Her own life scarce won
From death, at home still lay the weak, wan mother ;
    But with the children walked the oldest son,
His hat plucked fiercely on his brow — their brother
    From that time forth, and father, both in one —
Rage in his heart, and on his bowed soul set
The thorny crown of sorrow, vain regret.

AUNT HANNAH

She is known to all the town, in her quaintly fashioned gown,
  And wide bonnet — you would guess it at the distance of a mile ;
With her little sprigs of smilax, and her lavender and lilacs,
  Snowy napkins and big basket, and serenely simple smile.

She is just a little queer ; and few gentlefolk, I fear,
  In their drawing-rooms would welcome that benignant, beaming face ;
And the truth is, old Aunt Hannah's rather antiquated manners
  In some fashionable circles would seem sadly out of place.

Yet there's something quite refined in her manners and her mind,
  As you presently discover ; and 't is well enough to know,
Everything that now so odd is in the bonnet and the bodice
  Was the very height of fashion five-and-forty years ago.

She was then a reigning belle ; and I 've heard old ladies tell
  How at all the balls and parties Hannah Amsden took the lead :
Perfect bloom and maiden sweetness, lily grace of rare completeness,
  Though the stalk stands rather stiffly now the flower has gone to seed.

She had all that love could give, all that makes it sweet to live —
  Fond caresses, jewels, dresses ; and with eloquent appeal
Many a proud and rich adorer knelt — in metaphor — before her :
  Metaphorically only does your modern lover kneel.

If she heeded, 't was because, in their worship, their applause,
  Her perfection was reflected, and a pleasing music heard ;
But she suffered them no nearer than her goldfinch or her mirror,
  And she hardly held them dearer than her pier-glass or her bird.

But at last there came a day when she gave her heart away —
  If that rightly be called giving which is neither choice nor will,
But a charm, a fascination, and a wild sweet exultation —
  All the fresh young life outgoing in a strange ecstatic thrill.

At a city ball, by chance, she first met his ardent glance.
  He was neither young nor handsome, but a man of subtle parts,
With an eye of such expression as your lover by profession
  Finds an excellent possession when he goes a-hunting hearts.

It could trouble, it could burn; and when first he chanced to turn
  That fine glance on Hannah Amsden, it lit up with swift desire,
With a sudden dilatation, and a radiant admiration,
  And shot down her soul's deep heaven like a meteor trailing fire.

How was any one to know that those eyes had looked just so
  On a hundred other women, with a gaze as bright and strange?
There are men who change their passions even oftener than their fash-
    ions,
  And the best of loving always, to their mind, is still to change.

Nay, it was not base deceit: his own conquest seemed complete.
  They were soon affianced lovers; and her opening life was filled
With the flush of flame-lit fancies, morning's rosy-hued romances,
  All the dews of hope and rapture love's delicious dawn distilled.

Home the country maiden went; and a busy summer spent
  All in bridal preparations, blissful troubles, happy woes;
Fitting dresses, filling presses, little crosses and distresses —
  Those preliminary prickles to the hymeneal rose.

Never, since the world began, course of true love smoother ran;
  Not an eddy of dissension, nor the ripple of a doubt.
All the neighbors and relations came with kind congratulations,
  And a hundred invitations to the wedding-feast went out.

All the preparations thrived, and the wedding-day arrived:
  Pleased but pensive moved the mother; and the father, with a smile
Broad and genial as the summer, gave a welcome to each comer:
  All things turned on golden hinges, all went merry, for a while.

And the lovely bride, arrayed all in laces and brocade,
  Orange blossoms in her tresses (strange as now the story seems),
Quite enchanting and enchanted, in her chamber blushed and panted,
  And but one thing now was wanted to fulfil her darling dreams.

For the clergyman was there, to unite the happy pair,
  And the guests were all assembled, and the company sat dumb;
And the banquet was belated, and the maid was still unmated,
  And the wedding waited, waited, for a coach that did not come.

Then a few began to sneer, and a horror and a fear
  Fell on friends and anxious parents ; and the bride with cheek aflame,
All too rudely disenchanted, in her chamber paced and panted ;
  And the one thing still was wanted ; and the one thing never came.

Glassy smiles and feeble chat — then the parson took his hat,
  And the wedding guests departed, glad to breathe the outer air ;
Till the last farewell was taken, kind word offered, kind hand shaken ;
  And the great house stood forsaken in its shame and its despair.

With a firmness justified less by hope, perhaps, than pride,
  All her misery, all their pity, Hannah bore without complaint ;
Till her hasting mother met her, pale and breathless, with a letter,
  And she saw the superscription, and shrieked " Frederick ! " and grew
    faint.

With quick hand the seal she broke, and she neither breathed nor spoke,
  But a sudden ashy paleness all her fair face overspread ;
And a terror seemed to hold her, and her cheek grew cold and colder,
  And her icy fingers rattled in the paper as she read.

In her chamber once alone, on the floor she lay like stone,
  With her bridal gear about her — all that idle, fine array ;
And the white moon, white and holy, to her chamber bar climbed slowly,
  And looked in upon the lowly, wretched lady where she lay.

Why the letter was delayed, what the poor excuse he made,
  Mattered little there to Hannah lying on the moonlit floor.
'T was his heart that had miscarried ; for some new toy he had tarried :
  In a fortnight he was married, and she never saw him more.

Came the glorious autumn days — golden hills, cerulean haze —
  And still Hannah kept her chamber with her shame and her despair ;
All the neighbors and relations came and offered consolations,
  And the preacher preached up patience, and remembered her in prayer.

Spite of all that they could say, Hannah Amsden pined away.
  Came the dull days of November, came the winter, wild and white :
Lonely, listless, hours together she would sit and watch the weather,
  Or the cold bright constellations pulsing in the pallid night.

For a twelvemonth and a day so poor Hannah pined away.
Came once more the fatal morning, came the dread hours that had
    been :
All the anguish she lived over, waiting, wailing for her lover.
Then the new dawn shone about her, and a sweeter dawn within.

All her soul bleached white and pure, taught by suffering to endure,
    Taught by sorrow to know sorrow, and to bind the bleeding heart,
Now a pale and placid sister in the world that lately missed her —
    Sweetly pale where Peace had kissed her — patient Hannah chose her
    part.

To do good was her delight, all her study day and night;
    And around her, like a fragrance in the halo round a saint,
Breathed the holy exhalation of her life and occupation.
    But the rising generation soon began to call her quaint.

For her self-forgetfulness even extended to her dress ;
    Milliner and mantua-maker never crossed her threshold more ;
But the bodice, and the bonnet with the wondrous bow upon it,
    Kept their never-changing fashion of the faded years before.

So she still goes up and down on her errands through the town ;
    And sometimes a school-girl titters, or an urchin stops to grin,
Or a village cur barks at her ; but to her 't is little matter —
    You may fleer or you may flatter — such deep peace her soul is in.

Among all the sick and poor there is nobody so sure
    Of a welcome and a blessing ; and who sees her once appear,
Coming round some poor man's trellis with her dainty pots of jellies,
    Or big basket brimmed with bounty, soon forgets that she is queer.

For her pleasant words, addressed to the needy and distressed,
    Are so touching and so tender, full of sympathy and cheer,
By the time your smile is ready for the simple, dear old lady,
    It is pretty sure to tremble in the balance with a tear.

TOM'S COME HOME

WITH its heavily rocking and swinging load,
The stage-coach rolls up the mountain road.
The mowers lean on their scythes and say,
"Hullo! what brings Big George this way?"
The children climb the slats and wait
To see him drive past the door-yard gate;
When, four in hand, sedate and grand,
He brings the old craft like a ship to land.
At the window, mild grandmotherly eyes
Beam from their glasses with quaint surprise,
Grow wide with wonder, and guess, and doubt;
Then a quick, half-stifled voice shrieks out,
       "Tom! Tom's come home!"

The face at the casement disappears,
To shine at the door, all joy and tears,
As a traveller, dusty and bearded and brown,
Over the wheel steps lightly down.
"Well, mother!" "My son!" And to his breast
A forward-tottering form is pressed.
She lies there, and cries there; now at arm's-length
Admires his manly size and strength
(While he winks hard one misty eye);
Then calls to the youngsters staring nigh —
"Quick! go for your gran'ther! run, boys, run!
Tell him your uncle — tell him his son —
       Our Tom's come home!"

The stage-coach waits; but little cares she
What faces pleasantly smile to see
Her jostled glasses and tumbled cap.
Big George's hands the trunk unstrap
And bear it in; while two light-heeled
Young Mercuries fly to the mowing field,
And shriek and beckon, and meet half-way
The old gran'ther, lame, and gaunt, and gray,
Coat on arm, half in alarm,
Striding over the stony farm.

The good news clears his cloudy face,
And he cries, as he quickens his anxious pace,
      "Tom?   Tom come home?"

With twitching cheek and quivering lid
(A soft heart under the hard lines hid),
And "Tom, how d'e do?" in a husky voice,
He grasps with rough, strong hand the boy's —
A boy's no more!   "I should n't have known
That beard."   While Tom's fine barytone
Rolls out from his deep chest cheerily,
"You 're hale as ever, I 'm glad to see."
In the low back porch the mother stands,
And rubs her glasses with trembling hands,
And, smiling with eyes that blear and blink,
Chimes in, "I never!" and "Only think!
      Our Tom 's come home!"

With question and joke and anecdote,
He brushes his hat, they dust his coat,
While all the household gathers near —
Tanned urchins, eager to see and hear,
And large-eyed, dark-eyed, shy young mother, —
Widow of Tom's unlucky brother,
Who turned out ill, and was drowned at the mill:
The stricken old people mourn him still,
And the hope of their lives in him undone;
But grief for the dissolute, ruined son —
Their best-beloved and oldest boy —
Is all forgotten, or turned to joy,
      Now Tom 's come home.

Yet Tom was never the favored child,
Though Tom was steady, and Will was wild;
But often his own and his brother's share
Of blows or blame he was forced to bear;
Till at last he said, "Here is no room
For both — I go!"   Now he to whom
Scant grace was shown has proved the one
Large-hearted, upright, trusty son;

And well may the old folks joy to find
His brow so frank and his eye so kind,
No shadow of all the past allowed
To trouble the present hour, or cloud
      His welcome home.

His trunk unlocked, the lid he lifts,
And lays out curious, costly gifts;
For Tom has prospered since he went
Into his long self-banishment.
Each youngster's glee, as he hugs his share,
The widow's surprise, and the old folks' air
Of affectionate pride in a son so good,
Thrill him with generous gratitude.
And he thinks, " Am I that lonely lad
Who went off friendless, poor, and sad,
That dismal day from my father's door?"
And can it be true he is here once more
      In his childhood's home?

'T is hard to think of his brother dead,
And a widow and orphans here in his stead —
So little seems changed since they were young!
The row of pegs where the hats were hung;
The checkered chimney and hearth of bricks;
The sober old clock with its lonesome ticks
And shrill, loud chime for the flying time;
The stairs the bare feet used to climb,
Tom chasing his wild bedfellow Will;
And there is the small low bedroom still,
And the table he had when a little lad:
Ah, Tom, does it make you sad or glad,
      This coming home?

Tom's heart is moved. " Now don't mind me!
I am no stranger guest," cries he.
" And, father, I say!" — with the old-time laugh —
" Don't kill for me any fatted calf!
But go now and show me the sheep and swine,
And the cattle — where is that colt of mine? —

And the farm and crops — is harvest over ?
I 'd like a chance at the oats and clover !
I can mow, you 'll find, and cradle and bind,
Load hay, stow away, pitch, rake behind ;
For I know a scythe from a well-sweep yet.
In an hour I 'll make you quite forget
        That I 've been from home."

He plucks from its peg an old farm hat,
And with cordial chat upon this and that,
Tom walks with his father about the place.
There 's a pensive grace in his fine young face
As they loiter under the orchard trees,
As he breathes once more the mountain breeze,
And looks from the hill-side far away,
Over pasture and fallow and field of hay,
To the hazy peaks of the azure range,
Which change forever, yet never change.
The wild sweet winds his welcome blow :
Even old Monadnock seems to know
        That Tom 's come home.

The old man stammers and speaks at last :
" You notice your mother is failing fast,
Though she can't see it.   Poor Will's disgrace
And debts, and the mortgage on the place ;
His sudden death — 't was a dreadful blow ;
She could n't bear up like a man, you know.
She 's talked of you since the trouble came :
Some things in the past she seems to blame
Herself for ; what, it is hard to tell.
I marvel how she keeps round so well,
For often all night she lies awake.
I 'm thankful, if only for her sake,
        That you 've come home."

They visit the field ; Tom mows with the men ;
And now they come round to the porch again.
The mother draws Tom aside, lets sink
Her voice to a whisper, and — " What do you think ?

You see," she says, " he is broken quite.
Sometimes he tosses and groans all night ;
And, Tom, it is hard, it is hard indeed !
The mortgage, and so many mouths to feed !
But tell him he must not worry so,
And work so hard, for he don't know
That he has n't the strength of a younger man.
Counsel him, comfort him, all you can,
   While you 're at home."

Tom's heart is full ; he moves away,
And ponders what he will do and say.
And now at evening all are met,
The tea is drawn, the table set ;
But when the old man, with bended head,
In reverent, fervent tones has said
The opening phrase of his simple grace,
He falters, the tears course down his face ;
For the words seem cold, and the sense of the old
Set form is too weak his joy to hold ;
And broken accents best express
The upheaved heart's deep thankfulness,
   Now Tom 's come home.

The supper done, Tom has his say :
" I heard of some matters first to-day ;
And I call it a shame — you 're both to blame —
That a son, who has only to sign his name,
To lift the mortgage and clear the score,
Should never have had that chance before.
From this time forth you are free from care !
Your troubles I share ; your burdens I bear.
So promise to quit hard work, and say
That you 'll give yourselves a holiday.
Now, father ! now, mother ! you can't refuse ;
For what 's a son for, and what 's the use
   Of his coming home ? "

And so there is cheer in the house to-night.
It can hardly hold so much delight.

Tom wanders forth across the lot,
And, under the stars — though Tom is not
So pious as boys sometimes have been —
Thanks Heaven, that turned his thoughts from sin,
And blessed him, and brought him home once more.
And now he knocks at a cottage door,
For one who has waited many a year
In hope that thrilling sound to hear ;
Who, happy as other hearts may be,
Knows well there is none so glad as she
　　　That Tom 's come home.

THE BALLAD OF ARABELLA

'T WAS the good fast yacht, The Mermaid, that went sailing down the
　　　bay,
With a party predetermined to be jolly, one would say,
By the demijohns and boxes, by the lemons and the beer,
And the ice, that went aboard her just before she left the pier.

With the wind upon her quarter, how she courtesies and careens
To the nodding, laughing billows ! how her tower of canvas leans !
Past the headland, by the islands, with the flying gulls she flew,
And her long wake lay behind her like a stripe across the blue.

And I guess that all were happy on her deck, except, perhaps,
Mr. Brown — one of your poetizing, sentimental chaps :
In the midst of joy and juleps he sits spiritless and pale,
With his chin upon his knuckles and his elbow on the rail —

Quite Byronic, I assure you — and his mournful gaze intent
On the fascinating features of Miss Arabella Bent.
That is she beside the mast there, with the tumbler and the straw :
Such a laugh you hear but seldom, and such teeth you never saw.

Teeth so fine you might suspect them, but that curious eyes behold
" In their Milky Way of whiteness just one little star of gold " —
That is what our poet called it in a sonnet that he wrote,
Which 't is much to be regretted that we have n't room to quote.

She has had a hundred lovers, and she held them cheap as dirt —
For I grieve to say she's been a most unconscionable flirt.
But they fell away to sixty, and they dwindled down to six,
And now, having passed the forest, she must make a choice of sticks.

Only two at last are left her — Colonel Birch and Mr. Brown.
It was long a question which should be the envy of the town.
For a while it seemed the poet; now it certainly is Birch,
And at ten o'clock next Tuesday she will marry him in church.

There he is — and not by any means a crooked stick is he:
It is wonderful how very straight an old Bent beau can be!
He has fought his country's battles — in a commissary's tent;
And he still is young and handsome — in the eyes of Bella Bent.

Well might her perfidious conduct drive a poet-lover mad!
After all his sighs and sonnets, it was really too bad.
Although poor, and six-and-thirty, and his last book has n't sold,
'T was her teeth that took his fancy, and he cares not for her gold.

Calmly sipping, sits the Colonel; and he keeps his eye the while
On his heiress; and you read it in his half-developed smile,
Cold and quiet as his sabre's edge just started from its sheath —
'T was her gold that fired his fancy, and he cares not for her teeth.

So the yacht sailed down the harbor to a favorite fishing-ground,
Where the skipper dropped an anchor; for the gentlemen were bound
Just to try their hands at cod, and have a chowder.   There she lay
Rocking on the ocean billows that came rolling up the bay;

And the hooks went down with clam bait, and — in short, the luck was
      fine;
Even Brown grew interested in an unpoetic line;
And he smiled; but Arabella grew as suddenly quite pale,
Leaned her cheek upon her hand, and laid her arm upon the rail.

Like the lady in the ballad, she grew sick as he grew well;
With the heaving of the billows her fair bosom heaved and fell:
He is actually jolly, when, at every sudden lurch,
Dizzy, dreadful, dying qualms oppress the future Mrs. Birch.

She is bending by the gunwale — all at once you hear a scream :
From her lips, in anguish parted, with a glitter and a gleam,
Something darts into the flashing wave, and disappears beneath,
While in strangely altered accents, " Oh, my teeth ! " says she, " my
    teeth ! "

Then as she is wildly leaning, gazing downward in despair,
One mad breeze has snatched her bonnet, and another has her hair.
It all happened in a moment : in the ocean sink the pearls,
And far off upon the water float the bonnet and the curls.

And could that be Arabella, the pale ghost that shrieking fled ? —
All below, a lovely woman, but above, a spectral head !
Something sadder than sea-sickness now disturbed the maiden's breast,
And it was n't her lost tresses that had left her so distressed.

Brown was busy with his fishing, and just then he had a bite ;
The sharp line it cut his fingers, but he pulled with all his might.
" Help ! " he shouted.   'T was a monster, but at last it flopping lay
In the yacht, just at the moment they were getting under way.

" Now what 's up ? " says Brown.   " The anchor — and a big fish on
    your line !
Don't you know ?   Why, Arabella gave her salt tears to the brine,
And her hairpins to the sculpins, and, the oddest thing of all,
What should fall into the water but her thundering waterfall ! "

Much amazed was Brown to hear it (though the worst had not been said),
When up spoke the jovial skipper, " Now let 's put for Porpoise Head ;
There we 'll land and have our chowder ; we have fish enough," says he.
" First the locks are to be rescued ; we will run then for the quay.

" Steer for yonder bobbing buoy ! "   It was the chignon that he meant.
Soon the yacht was laid alongside ; out from her a paddle went.
Vastly pleased were all to see it, and indeed they had been dull
Not to smile at woman's tresses dripping from The Mermaid's scull.

Then they made for Porpoise Landing.   In the cabin, Birch the while
Pleaded fondly with his lady : " Dearest, let me see you smile !
Here 's your beautiful new bonnet, and your very wavy hair."
But she said, " Oh, what 's a bonnet ? and oh, Colonel ! what is hair ? "

From her interesting features then her handkerchief she took,
Opened wide those lovely lips of hers, and hoarsely whispered, "Look!"
All that dazzling row had vanished! Birch's blood within him froze;
But he quickly said, "I love you — love you still, in spite of those!"

"But you do not, oh! you do not, see the point, dear Colonel, yet:
Full five weeks it took my dentist to get up that splendid set;
And, alas! I 've been and lost 'em where you can't go down and search,
And how *can* a woman give her hand — without her teeth — in church?

"All the world expects the wedding, and next Tuesday is the day;
I was going to look so stunning, and — oh! what will people say?
Then there 's Brown — think what a triumph it will surely be to him!"
"I must say it is a fix!" replies the Colonel, looking grim.

Then the ladies crowded round her: "We are coming to the pier!
Are you better? Bite this cracker; it will do you good, my dear.
Pretty soon we 'll have our chowder — you are fond of that, you know."
But the maid behind her muffler only moaned and murmured, "No!

"Leave me here!" And so they left her, with the Colonel by her side:
Never sat so glum a bridegroom by so dismal-faced a bride.
All the rest went, laughing, romping, on the shore, just out of reach
Of the breakers that came dashing their white foreheads on the beach.

All but Brown: up to the cottage through the glaring sand he trod,
Proudly following the varlet who bore off the monster cod.
"For," says he, "I hooked the fellow, and I 'm bound to see him
        weighed."
That is done, and still he lingers, "just to see a chowder made."

Through the fellow's long white waistcoat slides the steward's polished
        knife;
Stops at something: "Here 's a — Bless me! what in time? Upon
        my life!"
Now I know you won't believe me; but there, grinning from within,
Through a very broad incision, with a cool, sarcastic grin,

Stowed away with stolen clam bait, crab and shrimp and octopod,
In the belly of that careless, undiscriminating cod,

Was the strangest, oddest, queerest, most amazing prize, which he
For some shining bait had swallowed as it wriggled through the sea.

" Arabella's teeth, by Heaven ! " — Brown has seized them, and, behold !
In their " Milky Way of whiteness " there 's his little " star of gold,"
Where the dentist, more completely to disguise the vulgar truth,
By a masterly device had plugged an artificial tooth !

Out rushed Brown — with tragic gestures he ran down upon the shore,
His fine eyes in frenzy rolling as they never rolled before ;
In his hand he grasped the treasure. " Oh, I see it all ! " says he ;
" Without these she can't be married, and she 'll maybe yet have me."

Then up went his hand to hurl them, but as quickly it came down :
After all, there was a streak of magnanimity in Brown.
" Oh, deceitful Arabella ! falsest of all womankind !
I was going to fling 'em farther, but I guess I 'll change my mind.

" Though she 's treated me so meanly, and I know she loves me not,
I won't be too hard upon her " — and he started for the yacht.
" Cruel, cruel Arabella ! now your fate is in my hand ! "
And he thrust it in his pocket as he strode along the strand.

In the gloomy little cabin the unhappy couple sat :
Arabella, lightly shrieking, dropped her chignon and her hat,
Upon which she had been making indispensable repairs,
As with sudden clank and clatter Brown came stumbling down the
　　stairs.

Then upleaped her faithful Colonel, in no amicable mood ;
Face to face, with lowering foreheads, the two rivals, stooping, stood,
For they both were rather tallish, and the cabin roof was low.
" Sir," says Brown, "you do not know me, or you would n't meet
　　me so.

" I have come to do a service to that lady weeping there ;
For, Miss Bent, I know your secret, and I beg you won't despair.
You shall go to church on Tuesday ; you shall wear your bridal wreath ! "
And from out his trousers pocket he produced the missing teeth.

"Mine!" (upspringing, Arabella gave her head a fearful thump).
"Brown! oh, Brown! where did you get them? I declare, you are a
    trump!
I had lost them in the ocean!" "And I found them on the shore!"
For he did n't deem it kindness at the time to tell her more.

"Why, what *did* you think?" "At first," said he, "I thought it was a
    spoon."
She replied, "Who would have thought that they could wash ashore so
    soon!"
And she dipped them in a tumbler, turned her back upon the two —
(While Brown whispered to the Colonel: "H—m!" "You don't
    say!" "Yes, I do!")

For a moment; then she turned again, and, to be brief, she had
No more cause to use a muffler, nor occasion to be sad.
Then the Colonel spoke: "Excuse me, Brown; I did n't understand;
You 're an honorable fellow, and I offer you my hand."

With a smile the other took it, while the grateful lady said,
As before The Mermaid's mirror she arrayed her graceful head,
"Brown, I wish I could reward you, but I cannot marry two;
But some other time I trust that I may do as much for you."

"Do not think of it, I beg you. Though it 's been a bitter cup,
I 've been cured of some illusions, and I freely give you up.
I shall change my occupation, and do better now, I hope:
I am going out of poetry, and going into soap."

"And you 'll be our friend?" says Bella. "So we 've settled this
    affair!
Now let 's go and have some chowder, for I 'm hungry as a bear."
And she joined the merry party, and she shook her dewy curls,
And the lightning of her laughter was a dazzling flash of pearls.

And at ten A. M. on Tuesday she and Colonel Birch were wed:
'T was a cheerful, glad occasion — for his creditors — 't is said.
All admired his manly bearing, so serenely calm was he,
And collected — as 't was hoped that now those little bills might be.

She was just one cloud of loveliness, from bridal wreath and veil
To the vast voluminous flounces, and the drifted, snowy trail.
Brown was present, and he could n't for his life repress a smile,
As he saw the white teeth glitter halfway down the shady aisle.

And he whispered to the lady who sat blushing by his side
('T was the old soap-maker's daughter, who was soon to be his bride)
That there could have been no wedding — though the fact seemed very
    odd —
If it had n't been for him and that accommodating cod.

BOOK IV

A HOME IDYL AND OTHER POEMS

Above the roofs of the lowly let Poesy hover and glance,
And set by the humblest highway the finger-post of Romance;
Strong in the wisdom that counsels and glad with the faith that con-
   soles,
To guide men ever upward to higher and nobler goals,
To cheer with chants of the morning, or soothe with songs of the night, —
So live, a beguiler of sorrows and minister of delight.

A HOME IDYL AND OTHER POEMS

A HOME IDYL

I

OVER the valley the storm-clouds blow,
Dark and low ;
The wild air whitens with flying snow.

Through the timber two lovers ride,
Side by side,
Wrapped in a shaggy buffalo-hide.

The winter has paved for their sleigh a track
Over the back
Of the river rolling deep and black.

Encircled by trees which the axe has spared,
In a bared
White space by the bank is their home prepared.

There Love in the wilderness far aloof
Wove the roof :
Boughs and bark are the warp and woof.

A small rude hut amid stumps and knolls, —
Cabin of poles,
With sticks and clay for the chinks and holes.

To that lonely door his bride he brings :
Back it swings :
The fire is kindled, the kettle sings.

Though wooden platter and pewter plate
Indicate
Lowly station and small estate ;

And happy they if their little hoard
Will afford
Daily bread for that rough-hewn board ;

Though the snow, whirled round their cabin, sifts
Through the rifts,
And up to the window climb the drifts,

Let the forest roar and the tempest blow !
Drive the snow !
In the heart of the hut is a heavenly glow.

Love that is mighty and Hope that is great,
Consecrate
Wooden platter and pewter plate.

Not to mansions where abide
Wealth and pride,
Comes ever a happier Christmas-tide.

In the privacy of their safe retreat
It is sweet
To hear the rush of the whirlwind's feet;

To hear the tempest's whistling lash
Smite the sash,
And the mighty hemlocks howl and clash.

II

Far from the city, its life and din,
Friends and kin,
Is the fresh new world which they begin.

In and about with busy feet,
Light and fleet,
She keeps his cabin cozy and neat.

With shouldered axe I see him go
                    Through the snow,
To clear the land for harrow and hoe.

Over his roof-tree curls the smoke,
                    While the stroke
Of his axe resounds on ash and oak.

From the log at his feet, to left and right,
                    Fly the bright
Splintered chips in the wintry light.

When the warm days come in early spring,
                    She will bring
Her work to the woods and sew and sing.

'T is pleasant to feel her watching near,
                    Joy to hear
Her voice in the woodland, high and clear!

Together they talk in the new-fallen tree,
                    And foresee
The work of their hands in the days to be.

Where the beech comes crashing down, and the lithe
                    Branches writhe,
He will turn the furrow and swing the scythe.

A rose by the doorway she will set,
                    Nor forget
Pansies and pinks and mignonette.

He will burn the clearing and plant the corn;
                    She will adorn
Their house for him and their babe unborn.

III

Swiftly ever, without a sound,
                    Earth goes round,
Air and ocean and solid ground.

Swiftly for them as for you and me,
Till they see
What they foresaw in the fallen tree.

Before their door in the summer morn,
Waves the corn.
'T is Christmas again, and a babe is born.

Not for the glories of wealth and art,
Would they part
With that small treasure of home and heart.

Dear Heaven! what springs of bliss are stirred,
When is heard
Its laugh or its first low lisping word!

A flower let fall by the Infinite
Love has lit
In their path, and brought God's peace with it.

IV

The world goes round, and year by year
Still appear
Children that add to the household cheer.

Now a daughter and now a son,
One by one
They are cradled, they creep, they walk, they run.

Sons and daughters, until behold!
Young and old,
A Jacob's-ladder with steps of gold!

A ladder of little heads! each fair
Head a stair
For the angels that visit the parent pair.

V

Blesséd be childhood! Even its chains
Are our gains!
Welcome and blesséd, with all the pains,

Losses, and upward vanishings
                    Of light wings, —
With all the sorrow and toil it brings,

All burdens that ever those small feet bore
                    To our door, —
Blesséd and welcome for evermore!

VI

What new delight, when over their toys
                    Girls and boys
In the Christmas dawn make a joyous noise!

Floor-boards clatter and roof-boards ring,
                    When they spring
To the chimney-nook where the stockings swing.

What glee, whenever with wild applause
                    One withdraws
Some wonderful gift of Santa Claus!

Let the happy little ones shout and play
                    All the day!
But the hearts of the parents, where are they?

No new-made home in the woods, but, lo!
                    Swift or slow,
The same griefs follow, the same weeds grow.

To the virgin wilderness, toward the far
                    Evening star,
Though we flee, there the wind-blown evils are.

The lovers had dreamed of a home without
                    Pain and doubt;
But Sorrow and Death have found them out.

The loveliest child of their love is laid
                    In the shade
Of the lonely pines, more lonely made

By the little grave where the vague winds blow,
  And the snow
Curves mockingly over the mound below.

Let the children all the Christmas Day
  Shout and play !
But the hearts of the parents turn away,

By tenderly mournful thoughts subdued,
  To the rude,
Low grave in the vast gray solitude.

VII

The world goes round with its sorrow and sin :
  Now begin
The boys to plough and the girls to spin.

Gone long ago the hut of poles,
  Stumps and knolls :
A frame-house now is the shelter of souls.

By the river are farms all up and down,
  And the crown
Of its steeples shows the neighboring town.

There, market and mill for the farmer's crops,
  Schools and shops,
And white spires over the orchard-tops.

No more, to the terror of flocks and fowls,
  Hoot the owls
In the woods near by, nor the gaunt wolf howls.

Where the antlered buck on the tender boughs
  Used to browse,
Sheep come to shed and the cattle house.

Where the panther pounced on the passing fawn,
  Lies the lawn
With its untracked dew in the chill gray dawn.

Highways are braided and swamps reclaimed ;
Towns are named ;
Life is softened, manners are tamed.

For youthful culture and social grace
Soon replace
The first rude life of a pioneer race ;

And men are polished, through act and speech,
Each by each,
As pebbles are smoothed on the rolling beach.

VIII

The farmer has hands both strong and skilled,
Fair fields tilled,
A house well kept and big barns filled.

In the porch at sunrise he will stand,
Flushed and tanned,
And view well pleased his prosperous land.

Crib and stable and pear-shaped stacks,
Stalls and racks,
Have come in the track of the fire and axe.

Cider in cask and fruit in bin
Are laid in
For the gloomy months that will soon begin.

Sons and daughters, a gathering throng,
Fair and strong,
Fill the old house with life and song.

With threshing and spinning, wheat and wool,
House and school,
Heads are busy and hands are full.

Then spelling-matches and evening calls,
Country balls,
And sleighing-parties when the snow falls.

IX

Footprints of some shy lover show,
   Where they go
From village to farm, in the morning snow.

The farmer, florid and well-to-do,
   Blusters, " Who
Is that bashful boy comes here to woo ? "

With burning blushes and down-dropt eyes,
   Nellie tries
To tell her trouble, but only cries.

The simple secret which poor Nell
   Cannot tell,
The anxious mother interprets well ;

And out of a wise and tender heart
   Takes the part
Of her child with gentle, persuasive art.

" Somebody once came wooing me,
   Shy as he !
They may be poor, but so were we.

" ' No matter for wealth and grand display,'
   You would say :
' We can be happy ! '   Then why can't they ?

" We are proud, who were humble then ; but, oh !
   High or low,
Happier days we shall never know ! "

" Pooh, pooh ! well, well ! "   He yields assent,
   But must vent
His grudging fatherly discontent,

That she, their child, so jealously reared,
   So endeared
By all they have borne for her, hoped and feared,

From them and their love should turn away,
To obey
The same old law, in the same old way,

And, placing her hand in the hand of a man,
Work and plan,
Beginning the world as they began.

X

He yields assent : the bright heaven clears
As she hears ;
The red dawn breaks through her doubts and fears.

The days bring signs of a coming change :
What is the strange
New raiment the busy hands arrange ?

The patterns they shape and the seams they sew ?
In the glow
Of the clear dusk, over the rosy snow,

The lover comes to the farmer's door ;
Shy no more,
Shy and abashed, as heretofore,

But manly of mien and open-browed,
Happy and proud
That his love is approved and his suit allowed.

For the father, who frowned, at last has smiled,
Reconciled,
On the modest youth who has won his child.

"Right sort of chap ; I like his way !
What d' ye say ?
We 'll have him at dinner Christmas Day."

XI

A wild white world lies all around,
Winter-bound ;
River and roof and tree and ground.

And the windows are all, at Christmas-time,
Thick with rime.
But the poultry is fat and the cider prime.

The thankful mother brings forth her best
For their guest;
And the farmer is merry with tale and jest.

Ruby jellies in autumn stored
Crown the board;
The goose is carved and the cider poured.

The house shows never in all the year
Better cheer,
For guest more honored or friend more dear.

Here the doctor has sat, and as he quaffed,
Praised the draught;
At those old stories the parson has laughed.

And there with his host by the fire, the great
Magistrate
Has puffed, in familiar tête-à-tête.

The daughter listens, and glad is she,
Glad to see
Father and lover so well agree.

She listens and watches with joy and pride,
When beside
The glorious chimney, glowing wide,

They bask in the blaze of the bounteous oak,
Bask and smoke,
And the young man laughs at the elder's joke.

Lover's laughter that will not fail,
Though the tale
Be sometimes dull, or the joke be stale.

He will laugh and jest, or in graver mood
          Hearken to good
Sagacious counsel, as young men should.

He reasons well; and his wit is found
          Sweet and sound;
He can pass opinion and stand his ground.

Feats of strength and of foolery, too,
          He can do,
When he joins in the games of the younger crew.

He opens his watch for the boys to see,
          On his knee;
And sings them a merry song, may be.

She shares his triumph, and thrilled to tears
          Overhears
Words meant for only the mother's ears.

" Well, yes," says the farmer, all aglow,
          Speaking low;
" As likely a fellow as any I know!"

To her pleased fancy the sweetest word
          Ever heard —
His praise of the man her love preferred!

And well may parent and child rejoice,
          When the voice
Of prudence approves the young heart's choice!

XII

In spring the lovers pass elate
          Through the gate
With golden hinges and bolts of fate.

The gate swings open; the gate is passed;
          And at last,
For evil or good, the bolts are fast.

She may bid farewell, or linger still;
And at will
Her feet may often recross the sill,

And tread again the familiar floor ;
Yet a door
Has closed behind her for evermore.

XIII

'T is the exodus of youth begun ;
One by one,
Now a daughter and now a son,

They are wooed, they woo, they pass elate
Through the gate
With golden hinges and bolts of fate.

Some fall by the way : alas, for those
Shall unclose
The door of the Darkness no man knows !

Two ways forever the house of breath
Openeth,
The way of life and the way of death.

Once, may be twice, a maid shall ride,
Now a bride,
Now in a pale robe by no man's side.

Two phantoms, traced upon every wall,
Wait for all,
A shining bridal, a low black pall.

Though blessed the dwellers and charmed the spot,
Palace or cot,
No home is exempt from the common lot.

XIV

Laurels in life's first summer glow
Rarely grow ;
But honors thicken on heads of snow.

There is a lustre of swords and shields,
Well-fought fields;
The power the statesman or patriot wields;

The glory that gleams from righted wrongs,
Or belongs
To the prophet's words or the poet's songs, —

High thoughts that shine like the Pleiades
Over seas!
But worthy of worship, even with these,

Is the fame of an honest citizen,
Now and then;
The good opinion of plain good men.

The farmer, solid and dignified,
Through the wide,
Fair valley on many affairs shall ride:

Through highway and by-way, country and town,
Up and down,
He shall ride in the light of his own renown.

In the halls of state, with outstretched hand,
He shall stand,
And counsel the Solons of the land.

Neighbors, wearying of the law's
Quirks and flaws,
To his good sense submit their cause.

Their cause with wary, impartial eye
He will try,
And many a snarl of the law untie.

If simple and upright men there be,
Such is he:
A life like a broad, green, sheltering tree,

For shade in the wayside heat and dust :
　　　All men trust
His virtue, and know his judgments just.

　　　　　XV

Not all the honors that come with age
　　　　　Can assuage
The pains of its long late pilgrimage.

The world's fair offerings, great and small,
　　　　　What are they all,
When the heart has losses and griefs befall ?

One by one to the parents came
　　　　　Babes to name :
One by one they have passed the same.

Hither and thither, each to his own,
　　　　　All have flown,
Like birds from the nest when their wings have grown.

Beginning again the same old strife ;
　　　　　Husband and wife
Twisting the strands of the cord of life ;

Weaving ever the endless chain,
　　　　　Pleasure and pain,
The gladness of action, the joy of gain.

Hither and thither, over the zone,
　　　　　All have flown,
Like thistledown by the four winds blown.

One has power, and one has wealth
　　　　　Got by stealth :
Happiest they who have hope and health.

Into the farther and wilder West
　　　　　Some have pressed ;
Some are weary, and some are at rest.

Hither and thither, like seed that is sown,
Each to his own!
What pangs of parting these doors have known!

The tears of the young who go their way,
Last a day ;
But the grief is long of the old who stay

Within these gates, where they have been left,
Long bereft,
With fond ties broken and old hearts cleft,

They have stood, and gazing across the snow,
Felt the woe
Of seeing the last of their children go.

Now all are scattered, like leaves that are strewn :
Through the lone,
Forsaken boughs let the wild winds moan!

XVI

But new life comes as the old life goes,
Life yet glows!
In children's children the fresh tide flows.

The heart of the homestead warms to the core,
When once more
Little feet patter on path and floor.

In the best-wrought life there is still a reft,
Something left
Forever unfinished, a broken weft.

But merciful Nature makes amends,
When she sends
Youth, that takes up our raveled ends,

Our hopes, our loves, that they be not quite
Lost to sight,
But leave behind us a fringe of light.

XVII

Age is a garden of faded flowers,
                    Ruined bowers,
Peopled by cares and failing powers;

Where Pain with his crutch and lonely Grief
                    Grope with brief,
Slow steps over withered stalk and leaf.

But the love of children is like some rare
                    Heavenly air,
That makes long Indian summer there;

A youth in age, when the skies yet glow,
                    Soft winds blow,
And hearts keep glad under locks of snow.

XVIII

So the old couple long abide
                    In the wide
Old-fashioned house by the river side.

Is life but a pool of trouble and sin?
                    Theirs has been
As a cup to pour Heaven's mercies in!

Happy are they who, calm and chaste,
                    Freely taste
Each day's brimmed measure, nor haste nor waste;

Who love not the world too well, nor hate;
                    But await
With faith the coming of unknown fate;

Pleased amid simple sights and sounds,
                    In these bounds
Of a life which Infinite Life surrounds!

With doubt and bitterness and ennui,
Life can be
But an ashy fruit by the heart's Dead Sea.

To cheerful endeavor and sacrifice
It shall rise
Each day forever a new surprise.

XIX

Now daughters and sons, from far and near,
Reappear,
And the day of all golden days is here.

Experienced matrons, world-wise men
Come again:
They are seven to-day who once were ten.

Are these the children who left your door?
Look once more!
O mother! are these the babes you bore?

Where's she, who was once so fresh and fair?
Nell is there,
A grandmother now with silvered hair!

And is this the lover who came to woo?
Now he too
Is solid and florid and well-to-do.

One has acres and railroad shares,
But no heirs;
One, a house full of children and poor man's cares.

But all distinction in life to-day
Falls away,
Like costume dropped with the parts they play.

Here all, whatever success they claim,
Rank the same;
And the half-forgotten household name,

As in old days, rings out again :
          Now as then
It is *Tom* and *Nellie* and *Sallie* and *Ben.*

All smiles, all tears, through a shining haze,
          In a maze
Of wonder and joy, the old folks gaze.

Three generations around them stand,
          Hand in hand,
As the petals of some vast flower expand.

Sons, daughters, husbands and wives inclose
          Younger rows,
Children's children, and children of those :

Whose children may yet with a living girth
          Circle earth :
Oh, infinite marvel of life and birth !

This is the crowning hour that cheers
          Failing years,
This is the solace of many tears.

Past sorrows, viewed from that sunset height
          Fade from sight,
Or glimmer far off in softened light.

Remembered mercies and joys increase,
          Trials cease,
And all is blessedness, all is peace.

XX

The world goes round with its hopes and fears,
          Joys and tears :
'T is Christmas again, in the latter years.

To the white graveyard, through the snow,
          Dark and slow,
I see a solemn procession go.

Where first he hollowed the mould and piled,
In the wild
Great woods, the mound of his little child, —

Softly muffled to sight and tread,
Lies outspread
The field of the unremembering dead.

Neighbor with neighbor sleeps below,
Foe with foe,
Their quarrels forgotten long ago.

Once more, with its burden that goes not back,
Moves the black
Far-followed hearse, on its frequent track,

To the voiceless bourne of all the vast
Peopled past:
Thither, from all life's ways at last,

From all its raptures and all its woes,
Thither goes
The old patriarch to his long repose.

Close by where children and wife are laid,
Leans a spade
By the dark heaped earth of a grave just made.

The heavily laden firs, snow-crowned,
Droop around,
With tent-like branches that sweep the ground.

The slow procession makes halt amid
Slabs half-hid,
Snow-mantled tablet and pyramid;

Whose fairest marble looks poor and pale
By the frail
And careless sculpture of snow and gale.

The trestles are set, the bier they place
In mid-space,
And lift the lid from the upturned face, —

Still smiling, as when the soul took flight
In a bright
Last vision of sudden angelic light.

Where, scheming world, are your triumphs now?
All things bow
Before Death's pallid and awful brow.

Hearts are humbled and heads are bare,
While the prayer
Is wafted far on the wintry air.

Friends gather and pass, and tears are shed
Over the dead:
They gather and pass with reverent tread.

They have looked their last and turned away;
From the day
Veil forever the face of clay!

The glory that gilds this wondrous ball,
Lighting all,
No more forever on him shall fall.

The throng moves outward; clangs the great
Iron gate:
All's ended: lonely and desolate

Appears, in the white and silent ground,
One dark mound;
And the world goes round, the world goes round.

OLD ROBIN

SELL old Robin, do you say? Well, I reckon not to-day!
I have let you have your way with the land,
With the meadows and the fallows, draining swamps and filling hollows,
And you 're mighty deep, Dan Alvord! but the sea itself has shallows,
And there *are* things that you *don't* understand.

You are not so green, of course, as to feed a worn-out horse,
Out of pity or remorse, very long!
But as sure as I am master of a shed and bit of pasture,
Not for all the wealth, I warn you, of a Vanderbilt or Astor,
Will I do old Robin there such a wrong.

He *is* old and lame, alas! Don't disturb him as you pass!
Let him lie there on the grass, while he may,
And enjoy the summer weather, free forever from his tether.
Sober veteran as you see him, we were young and gay together:
It was I who rode him first — ah, the day!

I was just a little chap, in first pantaloons and cap,
And I left my mother's lap, at the door;
And the reins hung loose and idle, as we let him prance and sidle,—
For my father walked beside me with his hand upon the bridle:
Yearling colt and boy of five, hardly more.

See him start and prick his ears! see how knowingly he leers!
I believe he overhears every word,
And once more, it may be, fancies that he carries me and prances,
While my mother from the doorway follows us with happy glances.
You may laugh, but — well, of course, it 's absurd!

Poor old Robin! does he know how I used to cling and crow,
As I rode him to and fro and around?
Every day as we grew older, he grew gentler, I grew bolder,
Till, a hand upon the bridle and a touch upon his shoulder,
I could vault into my seat at a bound.

Ah, the nag you so disdain, with his scanty tail and mane,
And that ridge-pole to shed rain, called a back,

Then was taper-limbed and glossy, — so superb a creature was he!
And he arched his neck, so graceful, and he tossed his tail, so saucy,
Like a proudly waving plume long and black!

He was light of hoof and fleet, I was supple, firm in seat,
And no sort of thing with feet, anywhere
In the country, could come nigh us; scarce the swallows could outfly us;
But the planet spun beneath us, and the sky went whizzing by us,
In the hurricane we made of the air.

Then I rode away to school in the mornings fresh and cool;
Till one day, beside the pool where he drank,
Leaning on my handsome trotter, glancing up across the water
To the judge's terraced orchard, there I saw the judge's daughter,
In a frame of sunny boughs on the bank.

Looking down on horse and boy, smiling down, so sweet and coy,
That I thrilled with bashful joy, when she said, —
Voice as sweet as a canary's, — " Would you like to get some cherries?
You are welcome as the birds are; there are nice ones on this terrace;
These are white-hearts in the tree overhead."

Was it Robin more than I, that had pleased her girlish eye
As she saw us prancing by? half I fear!
Off she ran, but not a great way: white-hearts, black-hearts, sweethearts
        straightway!
Boy and horse were soon familiar with the hospitable gateway,
And a happy fool was I — for a year.

Lord forgive an only child! All the blessings on me piled
Had but helped to make me wild and perverse.
What is there in honest horses that should lead to vicious courses?
Racing, betting, idling, tippling, wasted soon my best resources:
Small beginnings led to more — and to worse.

Father? happy in his grave! Praying mothers cannot save; —
Mine? a flatterer and a slave to her son!
Often Mary urged and pleaded, and the good judge interceded,
Counseled, blamed, insisted, threatened: tears and threats were all un-
        heeded,
And I answered him in wrath: it was done!

Vainly Mary sobbed and clung; in a fury out I flung,
To old Robin's back I sprung, and away!
No repentance, no compassion; on I plunged in headlong fashion,
In a night of rain and tempest, with a fierce, despairing passion, —
Through the blind and raving gusts, mad as they.

Bad to worse was now my game : my poor mother, still the same,
Tried to shield me, to reclaim — did her best.
Creditors began to clamor ; I could only lie and stammer ;
All we had was pledged for payment, all was sold beneath the hammer —
My old Robin there, along with the rest.

Laughing, jeering, I stood by, with a devil in my eye,
Watching those who came to buy : what was done
I had then no power to alter ; I looked on and would not falter,
Till the last man had departed, leading Robin by the halter ;
Then I flew into the loft for my gun.

I would shoot him! no, I said, I would kill myself instead!
To a lonely wood I fled, on a hill.
Hating Heaven and all its mercies for my follies and reverses,
There I plunged in self-abasement, there I burrowed in self-curses ;
But the dying I put off — as men will.

As I wandered back at night, something, far off, caught my sight,
Dark against the western light, in the lane ;
Coming to the bars to meet me — some illusion sent to cheat me!
No, 't was Robin, my own Robin, dancing, whinnying to greet me!
With a small white billet sewed to his mane.

The small missive I unstrung — on old Robin's neck I hung,
There I cried and there I clung! while I read,
In a hand I knew was Mary's — " One whose kindness never varies
Sends this gift : " no name was written, but a painted bunch of cherries
On the dainty little note smiled instead.

There he lies now! lank and lame, stiff of limb and gaunt of frame,
But to her and me the same dear old boy!
Never steed, I think, was fairer!   Still I see him the proud bearer
Of my pardon and salvation ; and he yet shall be a sharer —
As a poor dumb beast may share — in my joy.

It is strange that by the time I, a man, am in my prime,
He is guilty of the crime of old age !
But no sort of circumvention can deprive him of his pension :
He shall have his rack and pasture, with a little kind attention,
And some years of comfort yet, I 'll engage.

By long service and good-will he has earned them, and he still
Has a humble place to fill, as you know.
Now my little shavers ride him, sometimes two or three astride him ;
Mary watches from the doorway while I lead or walk beside him ; —
But his dancing all was done long ago.

See that merry, toddling lass tripping to and fro, to pass
Little handfuls of green grass, which he chews,
And the two small urchins trying to climb up and ride him lying ;
And, hard-hearted as you are, Dan, — eh ? you don't say ! you are crying ?
Well, an old horse, after all, has his use !

PLEASANT STREET

'T is Pleasant, indeed,
As the letters read
On the guideboard at the crossing.
Over the street
The branches meet,
Gently swaying and tossing.

Through its leafy crown
The sun strikes down
In wavering flakes and flashes,
As winding it goes
Betwixt tall rows
Of maples and elms and ashes.

There, high aloof
In the gilded roof,
Are the pewee and vireo winging
Their fitful flight
In the flickering light ;
The hangbird's basket swinging.

By many a great
And small estate,
And orchard cool and pleasant,
And croquet-ground,
The way sweeps round,
In many a curve and crescent.

In crescents and curves
It sways and swerves,
Like the flow of a stately river.
On carriage and span,
On maiden and man,
The dappling sunbeams quiver.

It winds between
Broad slopes of the green
Wood-mantled and shaggy highland,
And shores that rise
From the lake, which lies
Below, with its one fair island.

The long days dawn
Over lake and lawn,
And set on the hills ; and at even
Above it beam
All the lights that gleam
In the starry streets of heaven.

But not for these,
Lake, lawns and trees,
And gardens gay in their season, —
Its praise I sing
For a sweeter thing,
And a far more human reason.

Children I meet
In house and street,
Pretty maids and happy mothers,
All fair to see ;
But one to me
More beautiful than all others !

One whose pure face,
With its glancing grace,
Makes every one her lover ;
Charming the sight
With a sweeter light
Than falls from the boughs above her.

Though on each side
Are the homes of pride,
And of beauty, — here and there one, —
The dearest of all,
Though simple and small,
Is the dwelling of my fair one.

You will marvel that such
A gay sprite so much
Of a grave man's life engages,
And smile when I
Confess with a sigh
The differences in our ages.

Must love depart
With our youth, and the heart,
As we grow in years, become colder ?
My love is but four,
While I am twoscore,
And may be a trifle older.

With her smile and her glance,
And her curls that dance,
No one could ever resist her.
If anywhere
There 's another so fair,
Why, that must be her sister.

With screams of glee
At the sight of me,
Together forth they sally
From under the boughs
That screen the house
That stands beside the valley.

It is scenes like these,
  As they clasp my knees
And clamor for kiss and present,
  That still must make
  Our street by the lake
More pleasant — oh, most pleasant!

  Ride merrily past,
  Glide smoothly and fast,
O throngs of wealth and of pleasure!
  While sober and slow
  On foot I go,
Enjoying my humble leisure.

  O world, before
  My lowly door
Daily coming and going;
  O tide of life,
  O stream of strife,
Forever ebbing and flowing!

  By the show and the shine
  No eye can divine
If you be fair or hateful;
  I only know,
  As you come and go,
That I am glad and grateful.

  So here, well back
  From the shaded track,
By the curve of its greenest crescent,
  To-day I swing
  In my hammock, and sing
The praise of the street named *Pleasant*.

MENOTOMY LAKE [1]

THERE 's nothing so sweet as a morning in May,
  And what is so fair as the gleam of glad water?
Spring leaps from the brow of old Winter to-day,
  Full-formed, like the fabled Olympian's daughter.

A breath out of heaven came down in the night,
  Dispelling the gloom of the sullen northeasters ;
The air is all balm, and the lake is as bright
  As some bird in brave plumage that ripples and glisters.

The enchantment is broken which bound her so long,
  And Beauty, that slumbered, awakes and remembers ;
Love bursts into being, joy breaks into song,
  In a glory of blossoms life flames from its embers.

I row by steep woodlands, I rest on my oars
  Under banks deep-embroidered with grass and young clover ;
Far round, in and out, wind the beautiful shores —
  The lake in the midst, with the blue heavens over.

The world in its mirror hangs dreamily bright ;
  The patriarch clouds in curled raiment, that lazily
Lift their bare foreheads in dazzling white light,
  In that deep under-sky glimmer softly and hazily.

Far over the trees, or in glimpses between,
  Peer the steeples and half-hidden roofs of the village.
Here lie the broad slopes in their loveliest green ;
  There, crested with orchards, or checkered with tillage.

There the pines, tall and black, in the blue morning air ;
  The warehouse of ice, a vast windowless castle ;
The ash and the sycamore, shadeless and bare ;
  The elm-boughs in blossom, the willows in tassel.

In golden effulgence of leafage and blooms,
  Far along, overleaning, the sunshiny willows

[1] The Indian name for Arlington Lake, or Spy Pond.

Advance like a surge from the grove's deeper glooms, —
The first breaking swell of the summer's green billows.

Scarce a tint upon hornbeam or sumach appears,
The arrowhead tarries, the lily still lingers;
But the flag-leaves are piercing the wave with their spears,
And the fern is unfolding its infantile fingers.

Down through the dark evergreens slants the mild light:
I know every cove, every moist indentation,
Where mosses and violets ever invite
To some still unexperienced, fresh exploration.

The mud-turtle, sunning his shield on a log,
Slides off with a splash as my paddle approaches;
Beside the green island I silence the frog,
In warm, sunny shallows I startle the roaches.

I glide under branches where rank above rank
From the lake grow the trees, bending over its bosom;
Or lie in my boat on some flower-starred bank,
And drink in delight from each bird-song and blossom.

Above me the robins are building their nest;
The finches are here, — singing throats by the dozen;
The catbird, complaining, or mocking the rest;
The wing-spotted blackbird, sweet bobolink's cousin.

With rapture I watch, as I loiter beneath,
The small silken tufts on the boughs of the beeches
Each leaf-cluster parting its delicate sheath,
As it gropingly, yearningly opens and reaches,

Like soft-wingèd things coming forth from their shrouds.
The bees have forsaken the maples' red flowers
And gone to the willows, whose luminous clouds
Drop incense and gold in impalpable showers.

The bee-peopled odorous boughs overhead,
With fragrance and murmur the senses delighting;

The lake-side, gold-laced with the pollen they shed
  At the touch of a breeze or a small bird alighting ;

The myriad tremulous pendants that stream
  From the hair of the birches, — O group of slim graces,
That see in the water your silver limbs gleam,
  And lean undismayed over infinite spaces ! —

The bold dandelions embossing the grass ;
  On upland and terrace the fruit-gardens blooming ;
The wavering, winged, happy creatures that pass, —
  Pale butterflies flitting, and bumble-bees booming ;

The crowing of cocks and the bellow of kine ;
  Light, color, and all the delirious lyrical
Bursts of bird-voices ; life filled with new wine, —
  Every motion and change in this beautiful miracle,

Springtime and Maytime, — revive in my heart
  All the springs of my youth, with their sweetness and splendor :
O years that so softly take wing and depart !
  O perfume ! O memories pensive and tender !

As lightly I glide between island and shore,
  I seem like an exile, a wandering spirit,
Returned to the land where 't is May evermore,
  A moment revisiting, hovering near it.

Stray scents from afar, breathing faintly around,
  Are something I 've known in another existence ;
As I pause, as I listen, each image, each sound,
  Is softened by glamour, or mellowed by distance.

From the hill-side, no longer discordant or harsh,
  Comes the cry of the peacock, the jubilant cackle ;
And sweetly, how sweetly, by meadow and marsh,
  Sounds the musical jargon of blue jay and grackle !

O Earth ! till I find more of heaven than this,
  I will cling to your bosom with perfect contentment.

O water ! O light ! sky-enfolding abyss !
  I yield to the spell of your wondrous enchantment.

I drift on the dream of a lake in my boat ;
  With my oar-beat two pinion-like shadows keep measure ;
I poise and gaze down through the depths as I float,
  Seraphic, sustained between azure and azure.

I pause in a rift, by the edge of the world,
  That divides the blue gulfs of a double creation ;
Till, lo, the illusion is shattered and whirled
  In a thousand bright rings by my skiff's oscillation !

THE INDIAN CAMP

OUT from the Northern forest, dim and vast ;
        Out from the mystery
Of yet more shadowy times, a pathless past,
        Untracked by History ;

Strangely he comes into our commonplace,
        Prosaic present ;
And, like a faded star beside the bay's
        Silvery crescent,

Upon the curved shore of the shining lake
        His tent he pitches —
A modern chief, in white man's wide-awake
        And Christian breeches.

Reckless of title-deeds and forms of law,
        He freely chooses
Whatever slope or wood-side suits his squaw
        And lithe papooses.

Why not ?   The owners of the land were red,
        Holding dominion
Wherever ranged the foot of beast or spread
        The eagle's pinion ;

And privileged, until they welcomed here
  Their fair-faced brother,
To hunt at will, sometimes the bear and deer,
  Sometimes each other.

How often to this lake, down yonder dark
  And sinuous river,
The painted warriors sailed, in fleets of bark,
  With bow and quiver!

This lank-haired chieftain is their child, and heir
  To a great nation,
And well might fix, you fancy, anywhere
  His habitation.

Has he too come to hunt the bear and deer,
  To trap the otter?
Alas! there's no such creature stirring here,
  On land or water.

To have a little traffic with the town,
  Once more he chooses
The ancient camping-place, and brings his brown
  Squaw and papooses.

No tent was here in yester-evening's hush;
  But the day, dawning,
Transfigures with a faint, a roseate flush,
  His dingy awning.

The camp-smoke curling in the misty light,
  And canvas slanting
To the green earth, all this is something quite
  Fresh and enchanting;

Viewed not too closely, lest the glancing wings,
  The iridescent
Soft colors of romance, give place to things
  Not quite so pleasant.

The gossamers glistening on the dewy turf;
  The lisp and tinkle

Of flashing foam-bells, where the placid surf
    Breaks on the shingle;

The shimmering birches by the rippling cove;
    A fresh breeze bringing
The fragrance of the pines, and in the grove
    The thrushes singing,

Make the day sweet. But other sight and sound
    And odor fill it,
You find, as you approach their camping-ground
    And reeking skillet.

The ill-fed curs rush out with wolfish bark;
    And, staring at you,
A slim young girl leaps up, smooth-limbed and dark
    As a bronze statue.

A bare papoose about the camp-fire poles
    Toddles at random;
And on the ground there, by the blazing coals,
    Sits the old grandam.

Wrinkled and lean, her skirt a matted rag,
    In plaited collar
Of beads and hedgehog quills, the smoke-dried hag
    Squats in her squalor,

Dressing a marmot which the boys have shot;
    Which done, she seizes
With tawny claws, and drops into the pot,
    The raw, red pieces.

The chief meanwhile has in some mischief found
    A howling urchin,
Who knows too well, alas! that he is bound
    To have a birching.

The stoic of the woods, stern and unmoved,
    Lays the light lash on,
Tickling the lively ankles in approved
    Fatherly fashion.

The boy slinks off, a wiser boy, indeed —
    Wiser and sorrier.
And is this he, the chief of whom we read,
    The Indian warrior?

Where hangs his tomahawk? the scalps of tall
    Braves struck in battle?
Why, bless you, sir, his band is not at all
    That kind of cattle!

In ceasing to be savages, they chose
    To put away things
That suit the savage : even those hickory bows
    Are merely playthings.

For common use he rather likes, I think,
    The white man's rifle,
Hatchet, and blanket; and of white man's drink,
    I fear, a trifle.

With neighbors' scalp-locks, and such bagatelles,
    He never meddles.
Bows, baskets, and I hardly know what else,
    He makes and peddles.

Quite civilized, you see.   Is he aware
    Of his beatitude?
Does he, for all the white man's love and care,
    Feel proper gratitude?

Feathers and war-paint he no more enjoys;
    But he is prouder
Of long-tailed coat, and boots, and corduroys,
    And white man's powder.

And he can trade his mink and musquash skins,
    Baskets of wicker,
For white man's trinkets; bows and moccasins
    For white man's liquor.

His Manitou is passing, with each strange,
    Wild superstition:
He has the Indian agent for a change,
    And Indian mission.

He owns his cabin and potato patch,
    And farms a little.
Industrious? Quite, when there are fish to catch,
    Or shafts to whittle.

Though all about him, like a rising deep,
    Flows the white nation,
He has — and while it pleases us may keep —
    His Reservation.

Placed with his tribe in such a paradise,
    'T is past believing
That they should still be given to petty vice,
    Treachery, and thieving.

Incentives to renounce their Indian tricks
    Are surely ample,
With white man's piety and politics
    For their example.

But are they happier now than when, some night,
    The chosen quotas
Of tufted warriors sallied forth to fight
    The fierce Dakotas?

Still under that sedate, impassive port,
    That dull demeanor,
A spirit waits, a demon sleeps — in short,
    The same red sinner!

Within those inky pools, his eyes, I see
    Revenge and pillage,
The midnight massacre that yet may be,
    The blazing village.

When will he mend his wicked ways, indeed,
    Kill more humanely —
Depart, and leave to us the lands we need?
    To put it plainly.

Yet in our dealings with his race, in crimes
    Of war and ravage,
Who is the Christian, one might ask sometimes,
    And who the savage?

His traits are ours, seen in a dusky glass,
    And but remind us
Of heathenism we hardly yet, alas!
    Have left behind us.

Is right for white race wrong for black and red?
    A man or woman,
What hue soever, after all that's said,
    Is simply human.

Viewed from the smoke and misery of his dim
    Civilization,
How seems, I'd like to ask — how seems to him
    The proud Caucasian?

I shape the question as he saunters nigh,
    But shame to ask it.
We turn to price his wares instead, and buy,
    Perhaps, a basket.

But this is strange!   A man without pretense
    Of wit or reading,
Where did he get that calm intelligence,
    That plain good-breeding?

With him long patience, fortitude unspent,
    Untaught sagacity :
Culture with us, the curse of discontent,
    Pride, and rapacity.

Something we gain of him and bear away
    Beside our purchase.
We look awhile upon the quivering bay
    And shimmering birches —

The young squaw bearing up from the canoes
    Some heavy lading;
Along the beach a picturesque papoose
    Splashing and wading;

The withered crone, the camp-smoke's slow ascent,
    The puffs that blind her;
The girl, her silhouette on the sunlit tent
    Shadowed behind her;

The stalwart brave, watching his burdened wife,
    Erect and stolid:
We look, and think with pity of a life
    So poor and squalid!

Then at the cheering signal of a bell
    We slowly wander
Back to the world, back to the great hotel
    Looming up yonder.

AN IDYL OF HARVEST TIME

SWIFT cloud, swift light, now dark, now bright, across the landscape
    played;
And, spotted as a leopard's side in chasing sun and shade,
To far dim heights and purple vales the upland rolled away,
Where the soft, warm haze of summer days on all the distance lay.

From shorn and hoary harvest-fields to barn and bristling stack,
The wagon bore its beetling loads, or clattered empty back;
The leaning oxen clashed their horns and swayed along the road,
And the old house-dog lolled beside, in the shadow of the load.

The children played among the sheaves, the hawk went sailing over,
The yellow-bird was on the bough, the bee was on the clover,

While at my easel by the oak I sketched, and sketched in vain : —
Could I but group those harvesters, paint sunshine on the grain !

While everywhere, in the golden air, the soul of beauty swims,
It will not guide my feeble touch, nor light the hand that limns.
(The load moves on — that cloud is gone ! I must keep down the glare
Of sunshine on my stubble-land. Those boys are my despair !)

My fancies flit away at last, and wander like the gleams
Of shifting light along the hills, and drift away in dreams ;
Till, coming round the farm-house porch and down the shady lane,
A form is seen, half hid, between the stooks of shaggy grain.

Beside my easel, at the oak, I wait to see her pass.
'T is luncheon-time : the harvesters are resting on the grass.
I watch her coming to the gap, and envy Master Ben
Who meets her there, and helps to bear her basket to the men.

In the flushed farmer's welcoming smile, there beams a father's pride.
More quiet grows, more redly glows, the shy youth by his side :
In the soft passion of his look, and in her kind, bright glance,
I learn a little mystery, I read a sweet romance.

With pewter mug, and old brown jug, she laughing kneels : I hear
The liquid ripple of her lisp, with the gurgle of the beer.
That native grace, that charming face, those glances coy and sweet,
Ben, with the basket, grinning near — my grouping is complete !

The picture grows, the landscape flows, and heart and fancy burn, —
The figures start beneath my brush ! (So you the rule may learn :
Let thought be thrilled with sympathy, right touch and tone to give,
And mix your colors with heart's blood, to make the canvas live.)

All this was half a year ago : I find the sketch to-day, —
Faulty and crude enough, no doubt, but it wafts my soul away !
I tack it to the wall, and lo ! despite the winter's gloom,
It makes a little spot of sun and summer in my room.

Again the swift cloud-shadow sweeps across the stooks of rye ;
The cricket trills, the locust shrills, the hawk goes sailing by ;

The yellow-bird is on the bough, the bee is on the thistle,
The quail is near — "Ha hoyt!" — I hear his almost human whistle!

THE OLD BURYING-GROUND

PLUMED ranks of tall wild-cherry
     And birch surround
The half-hid, solitary
     Old burying-ground.

All the low wall is crumbled
     And overgrown,
And in the turf lies tumbled,
     Stone upon stone.

Only the school-boy, scrambling
     After his arrow
Or lost ball, — searching, trampling
     The tufts of yarrow,

Of milkweed and slim mullein, —
     The place disturbs;
Or bowed wise-woman, culling
     Her magic herbs.

No more the melancholy
     Dark trains draw near;
The dead possess it wholly
     This many a year.

The headstones lean, winds whistle,
     The long grass waves,
Rank grow the dock and thistle
     Over the graves;

And all is waste, deserted,
     And drear, as though
Even the ghosts departed
     Long years ago!

The squirrels start forth and chatter
    To see me pass ;
Grasshoppers leap and patter
    In the dry grass.

I hear the drowsy drumming
    Of woodpeckers,
And suddenly at my coming
    The quick grouse whirs.

Untouched through all mutation
    Of times and skies,
A by-gone generation
    Around me lies :

Of high and low condition,
    Just and unjust,
The patient and physician,
    All turned to dust.

Suns, snows, drought, cold, birds, blossoms,
    Visit the spot ;
Rains drench the quiet bosoms,
    Which heed them not.

Under an aged willow,
    The earth my bed,
A mossy mound my pillow,
    I lean my head.

Babe of this mother, dying
    A fresh young bride,
That old, old man is lying
    Here by her side !

I muse : above me hovers
    A haze of dreams :
Bright maids and laughing lovers,
    Life's morning gleams ;

The past with all its passions,
　　Its toils and wiles,
Its ancient follies, fashions,
　　And tears and smiles;

With thirsts and fever-rages,
　　And ceaseless pains,
Hoarding as for the ages
　　Its little gains!

Fair lives that bloom and wither,
　　Their summer done;
Loved forms with heart-break hither
　　Borne one by one.

Wife, husband, child and mother,
　　Now reck no more
Which mourned on earth the other,
　　Or went before.

The soul, risen from its embers,
　　In its blest state
Perchance not even remembers
　　Its earthly fate;

Nor heeds, in the duration
　　Of spheres sublime,
This pebble of creation,
　　This wave of time.

For a swift moment only
　　Such dreams arise;
Then, turning from this lonely,
　　Tossed field, my eyes

Through clumps of whortleberry
　　And brier look down
Toward yonder cemetery,
　　And modern town,

Where still men build, and marry,
    And strive, and mourn,
And now the dark pall carry,
    And now are borne.

A STORY OF THE "BAREFOOT BOY"

WRITTEN FOR J. G. WHITTIER'S SEVENTIETH BIRTHDAY

"I was once a barefoot boy." — J. G. WHITTIER

ON Haverhill's pleasant hills there played,
    Some sixty years ago,
In turned-up trousers, tattered hat,
Patches and freckles, and all that,
    The Barefoot Boy we know.

He roamed his berry-fields content;
    But while, from bush and brier
The nimble feet got many a scratch,
His wit, beneath its homely thatch,
    Aspired to something higher.

Over his dog-eared spelling-book,
    Or school-boy composition,
Puzzling his head with some hard sum,
Going for nuts, or gathering gum,
    He cherished his ambition.

He found the turtles' eggs, and watched
    To see the warm sun hatch 'em;
Hunted, with sling, or bow and arrow,
Or salt, to trap the unwary sparrow;
    Caught fish, or tried to catch 'em.

But more and more, to rise, to soar —
    This hope his bosom fired.
He shot his shaft, he sailed his kite,
Let out the string and watched its flight,
    And smiled, while he aspired.

"Now I 've a plan — I know we can ! "
　　He said to Mat — another
　Small shaver of the barefoot sort :
　His name was Matthew ; Mat, for short ;
　　Our barefoot's younger brother.

"What ! fly ? " says Mat.　"Well, not just that."
　　John thought : " No, we can't fly ;
　But we can go right up," says he,
" Oh, higher than the highest tree !
　　Away up in the sky ! "

" Oh, do ! " says Mat ; " I 'll hold thy hat,
　　And watch while thee is gone."
　For these were Quaker lads, and each
　Lisped in his pretty Quaker speech.
　　"No, *that* won't do," says John.

" For thee must help ; then we can float,
　　As light as any feather.
　We both can lift ; now don't thee see ?
　If thee 'll lift me while I lift thee,
　　We shall go up together ! "

An autumn evening ; early dusk ;
　　A few stars faintly twinkled ;
　The crickets chirped ; the chores were done ;
　'T was just the time to have some fun,
　　Before the tea-bell tinkled.

They spat upon their hands, and clinched,
　　Firm under-hold and upper.
" Don't lift too hard, or lift too far,"
　Says Mat, " or we may hit a star,
　　And not get back to supper ! "

" Oh, no ! " says John ; " we 'll only lift
　　A few rods up, that 's all,
　To see the river and the town.
　Now don't let go till we come down,
　　Or we shall catch a fall !

" Hold fast to me ! now ; one, two, three !
  And up we go ! " They jerk,
They pull and strain, but all in vain !
A bright idea, and yet, 't was plain,
  It somehow would n't work.

John gave it up ; ah, many a John
  Has tried and failed, as he did !
'T was a shrewd notion, none the less,
And still, in spite of ill success,
  It somehow has succeeded.

Kind nature smiled on that wise child,
  Nor could her love deny him
The large fulfillment of his plan ;
Since he who lifts his brother man
  In turn is lifted by him.

He reached the starry heights of peace
  Before his head was hoary ;
And now, at threescore years and ten,
The blessings of his fellow-men
  Waft him a crown of glory.

RECOLLECTIONS OF " LALLA ROOKH "

READ AT THE MOORE BANQUET IN BOSTON, MAY 27, 1879

WHEN we were farm-boys, years ago,
  I dare not tell how many,
When, strange to say, the fairest day
  Was often dark and rainy ;

No work, no school, no weeds to pull,
  No picking up potatoes,
No copy-page to fill with blots,
  With little o's or great O's ;

But jokes and stories in the barn
  Made quiet fun and frolic ;

Draughts, fox-and-geese, and games like these,
    Quite simple and bucolic ;

Naught else to do, but just to braid
    A lash, or sing and whittle,
Or go, perhaps, and set our traps,
    If it "held up" a little ;

On one of those fine days, for which
    We boys were always wishing,
Too wet to sow, or plant, or hoe,
    Just right to go a-fishing, —

I found, not what I went to seek,
    In the old farm-house gable, —
Nor line, nor hook, but just a book
    That lay there on the table,

Beside my sister's candlestick
    (The wick burned to the socket) ;
A handy book to take to bed,
    Or carry in one's pocket.

I tipped the dainty cover back,
    With little thought of finding
Anything half so bright within
    The red morocco binding ;

And let by chance my careless glance
    Range over song and story ;
When from between the magic leaves
    There streamed a sudden glory —

As from a store of sunlit gems,
    Pellucid and prismatic —
That edged with gleams the rough old beams,
    And filled the raftered attic.

I stopped to read ; I took no heed
    Of time or place, or whether

The window-pane was streaked with rain,
  Or bright with clearing weather.

Of chore-time or of supper-time
  I had no thought or feeling;
If calves were bleating to be fed,
  Or hungry pigs were squealing.

The tangled web of tale and rhyme,
  Enraptured, I unraveled;
By caravan, through Hindostan,
  Toward gay Cashmere, I traveled.

Before the gate of Paradise
  I pleaded with the Peri;
And even of queer old Fadladeen
  I somehow did not weary;

Until a voice called out below:
  "Come, boys! the rain is over!
It's time to bring the cattle home!
  The lambs are in the clover!"

My dream took flight; but day or night,
  It came again, and lingered.
I kept the treasure in my coat,
  And many a time I fingered

Its golden leaves among the sheaves
  In the long harvest nooning;
Or in my room, till fell the gloom,
  And low boughs let the moon in.

About me beamed another world,
  Refulgent, oriental;
Life all aglow with poetry,
  Or sweetly sentimental.

My hands were filled with common tasks,
  My head with rare romances;
My old straw hat was bursting out
  With light locks and bright fancies.

In field or wood, my thoughts threw off
  The old prosaic trammels ;
The sheep were grazing antelopes,
  The cows, a train of camels.

Under the shady apple-boughs,
  The book was my companion ;
And while I read, the orchard spread
  One mighty branching banyan.

To mango-trees or almond-groves
  Were changed the plums and quinces.
I was the poet, Feramorz,
  And had, of course, my Princess.

The well-curb was her canopied,
  Rich palanquin ; at twilight,
'T was her pavilion overhead,
  And not my garret skylight.

Ah, Lalla Rookh! O charmèd book!
  First love, in manhood slighted !
To-day we rarely turn the page
  In which our youth delighted.

Moore stands upon our shelves to-day,
  I fear a trifle dusty ;
With Scott, beneath a cobweb wreath,
  And Byron, somewhat musty.

But though his orient cloth-of-gold
  Is hardly now the fashion,
His tender melodies will live
  While human hearts have passion.

The centuries roll ; but he has left,
  Beside the ceaseless river,
Some flowers of rhyme untouched by Time,
  And songs that sing forever.

FILLING AN ORDER

READ AT THE HOLMES BREAKFAST, BOSTON, DECEMBER 3, 1879

To Nature, in her shop one day, at work compounding simples,
Studying fresh tints for Beauty's cheeks, or new effects in dimples,
An order came : she wiped in haste her fingers and unfolded
The scribbled scrap, put on her specs, and read it, while she scolded.

" From Miss Columbia ! I declare ! of all the upstart misses !
What will the jade be asking next ?   Now what an order this is !
Where 's Boston ?   Oh, that one-horse town out there beside the ocean !
She wants — of course, she always wants — another little notion !

" This time, three geniuses, A 1, to grace her favorite city :
The first a bard ; the second wise ; the third supremely witty ;
None of the staid and hackneyed sort, but some peculiar flavor,
Something unique and fresh for each, will be esteemed a favor !
Modest demands ! as if my hands had but to turn and toss over
A Poet veined with dew and fire, a Wit, and a Philosopher !

" But now let 's see ! "   She put aside her old, outworn expedients,
And in a quite unusual way began to mix ingredients, —
Some in the fierce retort distilled, some pounded by the pestle, —
And set the simmering souls to steep, each in its glowing vessel.
In each, by turns, she poured, she stirred, she skimmed the shining
        liquor,
Threw laughter in, to make it thin, or thought, to make it thicker.
But when she came to choose the clay, she found, to her vexation,
That, with a stock on hand to fill an order for a nation,
Of that more finely tempered stuff, electric and ethereal,
Of which a genius must be formed, she had but scant material —
For three ?   For one !   What should be done ?   A bright idea struck
        her ;
Her old witch-eyes began to shine, her mouth began to pucker.

Says she, " The fault, I 'm well aware, with genius is the presence
Of altogether too much clay, with quite too little essence,
And sluggish atoms that obstruct the spiritual solution ;
So now, instead of spoiling these by over-much dilution,

With their fine elements I 'll make a single, rare phenomenon,
And of three common geniuses concoct a most uncommon one,
So that the world shall smile to see a soul so universal,
Such poesy and pleasantry, packed in so small a parcel."

So said, so done ; the three in one she wrapped, and stuck the label :
Poet, Professor, Autocrat of Wit's own Breakfast-Table.

THE OLD MAN OF THE MOUNTAIN [1]

ALL round the lake the wet woods shake
   From drooping boughs their showers of pearl ;
From floating skiff to towering cliff
   The rising vapors part and curl.
The west wind stirs among the firs
   High up the mountain side emerging ;
The light illumes a thousand plumes
   Through billowy banners round them surging.

A glory smites the craggy heights ;
   And in a halo of the haze,
Flushed with faint gold, far up, behold
   That mighty face, that stony gaze !
In the wild sky upborne so high
   Above us perishable creatures,
Confronting Time with those sublime,
   Impassive, adamantine features.

Thou beaked and bald high front, miscalled
   The profile of a human face !
No kin art thou, O Titan brow,
   To puny man's ephemeral race.
The groaning earth to thee gave birth,
   Throes and convulsions of the planet ;
Lonely uprose, in grand repose,
   Those eighty feet of facial granite.

[1] Profile Notch, Franconia, N. H. The "Profile" is formed by separate projections of the cliff, which, viewed from a particular point, assume the marvellous appearance of a colossal human face.

Here long, while vast, slow ages passed,
Thine eyes (if eyes be thine) beheld
But solitudes of crags and woods,
Where eagles screamed and panthers yelled.
Before the fires of our pale sires
In the first log-built cabin twinkled,
Or red men came for fish and game,
That scalp was scarred, that face was wrinkled.

We may not know how long ago
That ancient countenance was young;
Thy sovereign brow was seamed as now
When Moses wrote and Homer sung.
Empires and states it antedates,
And wars, and arts, and crime, and glory;
In that dim morn when Christ was born
Thy head with centuries was hoary.

Thou lonely one! nor frost, nor sun,
Nor tempest leaves on thee its trace;
The stormy years are but as tears
That pass from thy unchanging face.
With unconcern as grand and stern,
Those features viewed, which now survey us,
A green world rise from seas of ice,
And order come from mud and chaos.

Canst thou not tell what then befell?
What forces moved, or fast or slow;
How grew the hills; what heats, what chills,
What strange, dim life, so long ago?
High-visaged peak, wilt thou not speak?
One word, for all our learnèd wrangle!
What earthquakes shaped, what glaciers scraped,
That nose, and gave the chin its angle?

Our pygmy thought to thee is naught,
Our petty questionings are vain;
In its great trance thy countenance
Knows not compassion nor disdain.

With far-off hum we go and come,
  The gay, the grave, the busy-idle;
And all things done to thee are one,
  Alike the burial and the bridal.

Thy permanence, long ages hence,
  Will mock the pride of mortals still.
Returning springs, with songs and wings
  And fragrance, shall these valleys fill;
The free winds blow, fall rain or snow,
  The mountains brim their crystal beakers;
Still come and go, still ebb and flow,
  The summer tides of pleasure-seekers:

The dawns shall gild the peaks where build
  The eagles, many a future pair;
The gray scud lag on wood and crag,
  Dissolving in the purple air;
The sunlight gleam on lake and stream,
  Boughs wave, storms break, and still at even
All glorious hues the world suffuse,
  Heaven mantle earth, earth melt in heaven!

Nations shall pass like summer's grass,
  And times unborn grow old and change;
New governments and great events
  Shall rise, and science new and strange;
Yet will thy gaze confront the days
  With its eternal calm and patience,
The evening red still light thy head,
  Above thee burn the constellations.

O silent speech, that well can teach
  The little worth of words or fame!
I go my way, but thou wilt stay
  While future millions pass the same:
But what is this I seem to miss?
  Those features fall into confusion!
A further pace — where was that face?
  The veriest fugitive illusion!

Gray eidolon! so quickly gone
   When eyes, that make thee, onward move;
Whose vast pretence of permanence
   A little progress can disprove!
Like some huge wraith of human faith
   That to the mind takes form and measure;
Grim monolith of creed or myth,
   Outlined against the eternal azure!

O Titan, how dislimned art thou!
   A withered cliff is all we see;
That giant nose, that grand repose,
   Have in a moment ceased to be;
Or still depend on lines that blend,
   On merging shapes, and sight, and distance,
And in the mind alone can find
   Imaginary brief existence!

UNDER MOON AND STARS

From the house of desolation,
From the doors of lamentation,
I went forth into the midnight and the vistas of the moon;
   Where through aisles high-arched and shady
   Paced the pale and spectral lady,
And with shining footprints silvered the deep velvet turf of June.

In the liquid hush and coolness
Of the slumbering earth, the fulness
Of my aching soul was solaced; till my senses, grown intense,
   Caught the evanescent twinkle,
   Caught the fairy-footed tinkle,
Of the dew-fall raining softly on the leafage cool and dense.

The sad cries, the unavailing
Orphans' tears and woman's wailing,
In the shuttered house were buried, and the pale face of the dead;
   From the chambers closed and gloomy
   Neither sight nor sound came to me,
But great silence was about me, and the great sky overhead.

As a mighty angel leaneth
His calm visage from the zenith,
Gazed the moon: my thoughts flew upward, through the pallid atmosphere,
To the planets in their places,
To the infinite starry spaces,
Till despair and death grew distant, and eternal Peace drew near.

Then the faith that oft had failed me,
And the mad doubts that assailed me,
Like two armies that had struggled for some fortress long and well,
Both as by a breath were banished;
Friend and foe together vanished,
And my soul sat high and lonely in her solemn citadel.

Peace! and from her starry station
Came white-pinioned Contemplation,
White and mystical and silent as the moonlight's sheeted wraith;
Through my utter melancholy
Stole a rapture still and holy,
Something deeper than all doubting, something greater than all faith.

And I pondered: "Change is written
Over all the blue, star-litten
Universe; the moon on high there, once a palpitating sphere,
Now is seamed with ghastly scissures,
Chilled and shrunken, cloven with fissures,
Sepulchres of frozen oceans and a perished atmosphere.

"Doubtless mid yon burning clusters
Ancient suns have paled their lustres,
Worlds are lost with all their wonders, glorious forms of life and thought,
Arts and altars, lore of sages,
Monuments of mighty ages,
All that joyous nature lavished, all that toil and genius wrought.

"So this dear, warm earth, and yonder
Sister worlds that with her wander
Round the parent light, shall perish; on through darkening cycles run,

Whirling through their vast ellipses
Evermore in cold eclipses,
Orphaned planets roaming blindly round a cold and darkened sun !

"This bright haze and exhalation,
Starry cloud we call creation,
Glittering mist of orbs and systems, shall like mist dissolve and fall, —
Seek the sea whence all ascendeth,
Meet the ocean where all endeth :
Thou alone art everlasting, O thou inmost Soul of all !

"Through all height, all depth, all distance,
All duration, all existence,
Moves one universal nature, flows one vast Intelligence,
Out of chaos and gray ruin
Still the shining heavens renewing,
Flashing into light and beauty, flowering into form and sense.

"Veiled in manifold illusion,
Seeming discord and confusion,
Life's harmonious scheme is builded : earth is but the outer stair,
Is but scaffold-beam and stanchion
In the rearing of the mansion.
Dust enfolds a finer substance, and the air, diviner air.

"All about the world and near it
Lies the luminous realm of spirit,
Sometimes touching upturned foreheads with a strange, unearthly
sheen ;
Through the deep ethereal regions
Throng invisible bright legions,
And unspeakable great glory flows around our lives unseen ;

"Round our ignorance and anguish,
Round the darkness where we languish,
As the sunlight round the dim earth's midnight tower of shadow
pours,
Streaming past the dim, wide portals,
Viewless to the eyes of mortals
Till it flood the moon's pale islet or the morning's golden shores.

" Round the world of sense forever
　　Rolls the bright, celestial river :
Of its presence, of its passing, streaks of faint prophetic light
　　Give the mind mysterious warning,
　　Gild its clouds with gleams of morning,
Or some shining soul reflects it to our feeble inner sight."

　　So by sheen and shade I wandered ;
　　And the mighty theme I pondered
(Vague and boundless as the midnight wrapping world and life and man)
　　Stooped with dewy whispers to me,
　　Breathed unuttered meanings through me,
Of man's petty pains and passions, of the grandeur of God's plan !

　　And I said, " Thou one all-seeing,
　　Perfect, omnipresent Being,
Sparkling in the nearest dewdrop, throbbing in the farthest star ;
　　By the pulsing of whose power
　　Suns are sown and systems flower ;
Who hast called my soul from chaos and my faltering feet thus far !

　　" What am I to make suggestion ?
　　What is man to doubt and question
Ways too wondrous for his searching, which no science can reveal ?
　　Perfect and secure my trust is
　　In thy mercy and thy justice,
Though I perish as an insect by thine awful chariot-wheel !

　　" Lo ! the shapes of ill and error,
　　Lo ! the forms of death and terror,
Are but light-obstructing phantoms, which shall vanish late or soon,
　　Like this sudden, vast, appalling
　　Gloom on field and woodland falling
From the wingèd, black cloud-dragon that is flying by the moon ! "

　　Downward wheeled the dragon, driven
　　Like a falling fiend from heaven ;
And the silhouettes of the lindens, on the peaceful esplanade,
　　Lay once more like quiet islands
　　In the moonlight and the silence ;
And by softly silvered alleys, leafy mazes, still I strayed,

Till, through boughs of sombre maples,
With the pale gleam on its gables,
Lo! the house of desolation, like a ghost amid the gloom!
Then the thought of present sorrow,
Of the palled, funereal morrow,
Filled anew my heart with anguish and the horror of the tomb.

And I cried, " Is God above us?
Are there Powers that guard and love us,
Pilots to the blissful havens?   Do they hear the tones of woe,
Death and pain and separation,
Wailing through the wide creation?
Will the high heavens heed or help us; do they, can they feel and
know?"

Ah! the heart is very human;
Still the world of man and woman,
Love and loss, throbs in and through us!   For the radiant hour is rare,
When the soul from heights of vision
Views the shining plains Elysian,
And in after-times of trouble we forget what peace is there.

SONNETS

I

NATIVITY

Thistle and serpent we exterminate,
    Yet blame them not; and righteously abhor
    The crimes of men with all their kind at war,
Whom we may stay or slay, but not in hate.
By blood and brain we are predestinate
    Each to his course; and unawares therefor
    The heart's blind wish and inmost counselor
Makes times and tides; for man is his own fate.
Nativity is horoscope and star!
    One innocent egg incloses song and wings;
    One, deadly fangs and rattles set to warn.

Our days, our deeds, all we achieve or are,
  Lay folded in our infancy; the things
  Of good or ill we choose while yet unborn.

II

CIRCUMSTANCE

STALKING before the lords of life, one came,
  A Titan shape! But often he will crawl,
  Their most subservient, helpful, humble thrall;
Swift as the light, or sluggish, laggard, lame;
Stony-eyed archer, launching without aim
  Arrows and lightnings, heedless how they fall, —
  Blind Circumstance, that makes or baffles all,
Happiness, length of days, power, riches, fame.
Could we but take each wingèd chance aright!
  A timely word let fall, a wind-blown germ,
    May crown our glebe with many a golden sheaf;
A thought may touch and edge our life with light,
  Fill all its sphere, as yonder crescent worm
    Brightens upon the old moon's dusky leaf.

III

PROVIDENCE

WEARY with pondering many a weighty theme,
  I slept; and in the realm of vision saw
  A mighty Angel reverently updraw
The cords of earth, all woven of gloom and gleam,
Wiles, woes, and many a silver-threaded stream
  Of sighs and prayers, and golden bands of law,
  And ties of faith and love, with many a flaw
Riven, but reunited in my dream.
These the great Angel, gathering, lifted high,
  Like mingled lines of rain and radiance, all
    In one bright, awful braid divinely blended,
That reached the beams of heaven, — a chain whereby
  This dimly glorious, shadow-brooding ball
    And home of man hung wondrously suspended.

THE TRAGEDY QUEEN

HER triumphs are over, the crown
　　Has passed from her brow ;
And she smiles, " To whom now does the town
　　My poor laurels allow ? "
It has wept for her, dying, a hundred times,
With mimic passion, in mimic crimes :
Who cares for her lying discrowned and dying
　　In earnest now ?

Only those who have known her strange story,
　　And watched her through all,
So serene in the day of her glory,
　　So grand in her fall, —
In the sphere beyond all tragic art
Playing her own deep woman's part, —
A few faithful, befriend her, still cherish, attend her,
　　And come at her call.

And so, when to-night the old fire
　　Flamed up in her eye,
And she said, " 'T is a childish desire,
　　I cannot deny,
To see the old boards and the footlights again,
To feel the wild storm of the plaudits of men !
But grant me this pastime, you know 't is the last time,"
　　What could we reply ?

Her form to the carriage we bore
　　In dark mantle and veil ;
On my arm, at the gloomy side-door,
　　She hung, lily-like, frail ;
But, treading the old, familiar scene,
She moved majestic, she walked a queen —
The rouged ballet-girls staring to see her high bearing,
　　So proud and so pale !

At the wing, her swift glance as we waited
　　Swept royally round :

I could feel how she thrilled and dilated,
      And how at the sound,
The brief commotion that intervenes
In the busy moment of shifting scenes,
The creaking of pulleys, the shrill shrieking *coulisse*,
      Her heart gave a bound.

      The manager hastes and unlocks
         The small door from the wing;
      To the deep-curtained, crimson-lined box
         Our dear lady we bring.
All a-flutter with life, all a-glitter with light,
The vast half-circle burst on the sight;
The fairy stage showing amidst, like a glowing
      Great gem in its ring.

      The strong soul in the weak woman's face
         Flashes forth to behold
      The gay world that assembled to grace
         Her own triumphs of old.
The vision brings back her bright young days —
For her the loud tumult, the showered bouquets;
And her fancy is ravished with joy amid lavished
      Glory and gold.

      In that moment of dream disappear
         Sorrow, sickness, and pain:
      Airy hopes, a romantic career,
         Beam and beckon again.
Alas! but the life itself could last
No more than the dream: and the dream is past —
'T is gone with the quickness of breath, while the sickness
      And sorrow remain.

      We saw her, pain-stricken and white,
         Sink back in her place:
      Could a pang of sharp envy so smite
         The brief joy from her face?
Lo, the queen of the ballet! she wavers and glides;
Upon floods of strong music triumphant she rides,

And laughingly pillows each movement on billows
Of beauty and grace.

And there, in his orchestra stall,
The stage-vampire is seen,
Foremost once, most devoted of all,
In the train of our queen.
Still seeking a fresh young heart to devour,
Still following ever the queen of the hour,
Enrapt by so rare a sight, sits the gray parasite,
Ogling the scene.

Not envy — her heart is too great.
But for her, for all these,
Whose fortunes, like flatterers, wait
On their power to please,
Whose unsubstantial happiness draws
Its air-plant life from the breath of applause,
The powers soon jaded, the flowers all faded
And withered she sees;

The unworthy contentions, the strife;
Feet lured from the goals,
Hands stayed in the contest of life,
By the hour that cajoles
With its wayside-scattered apples of joy;
The sunshine that pampers, the storms that destroy,
And all the besetting temptations benetting
These butterfly souls.

And naught, as we know, can assuage
Her keen anguish of heart,
Seeing thus from her dearly loved stage
The true grandeur depart.
Now the people prefer these wonder-shows,
Scant costume, antics, and flushed tableaux;
For tinsel and magic, forgetting her tragic
Magnificent art.

" Let us go ! " she entreats ; " I am ill ! "
    And unnoticed withdraws
    From the theatre, thundering still
      With the surge of applause.
As slowly she turns behind the scene
For a parting glance, comes the gay new queen,
By fairies attended, all glowing and splendid
      In spangles and gauze.

    From the footlights, arms filled with bouquets,
      One is hurrying back ;
    One gazes with cold marble face
      From the veil's tragic black :
And there at the manager's beck they meet ;
The new queen stoops at the old queen's feet,
With all her soft graces, and sweet commonplaces
      Of greeting no lack.

    Before her the great lady stood,
      So gracious, so grand !
    " You are lovely — I think you are good :
      O child, understand !
Be prudent, yet generous ; false to none ;
Keep the pearl of the heart ; be true to one ;
Be wise, oh, be gentle ! " and from the dark mantle
      She reached forth her hand.

    And they parted. All freshness and fire,
      One passed in her bloom,
    Feet swift with delight and desire,
      Arms shedding perfume !
From the cold dim coach one looks her last
At the theatre lights and the joyous past,
As away in the lurid wet night we are hurried,
      Through rain-gust and gloom.

THE OLD LOBSTERMAN

CAPE ARUNDEL, KENNEBUNKPORT, MAINE

JUST back from a beach of sand and shells,
    And shingle the tides leave oozy and dank,
Summer and winter the old man dwells
    In his low brown house on the river bank.
Tempest and sea-fog sweep the hoar
And wrinkled sand-drifts round his door,
Where often I see him sit, as gray
And weather-beaten and lonely as they.

Coarse grasses wave on the arid swells
    In the wind ; and two bright poplar-trees
Seem hung all over with silver bells
    That tinkle and twinkle in sun and breeze.
All else is desolate sand and stone :
And here the old lobsterman lives alone :
Nor other companionship has he
But to sit in his house and gaze at the sea.

A furlong or more away to the south,
    On the bar beyond the huge sea-walls
That keep the channel and guard its mouth,
    The high, curved billow whitens and falls ;
And the racing tides through the granite gate,
On their wild errands that will not wait,
Forever, unresting, to and fro,
Course with impetuous ebb and flow.

They bury the barnacled ledge, and make
    Into every inlet and crooked creek,
And flood the flats with a shining lake,
    Which the proud ship ploughs with foam at her beak :
The ships go up to yonder town,
Or over the sea their hulls sink down,
And many a pleasure pinnace rides
On the restless backs of the rushing tides.

I try to fathom the gazer's dreams,
  But little I gain from his gruff replies;
Far off, far off the spirit seems,
  As he looks at me with those strange gray eyes;
Never a hail from the shipwrecked heart!
Mysterious oceans seem to part
The desolate man from all his kind —
The Selkirk of his lonely mind.

He has growls for me when I bring him back
  My unused bait — his way to thank;
And a good shrill curse for the fishing-smack
  That jams his dory against the bank;
But never a word of love to give
For love, — ah! how can he bear to live?
I marvel, and make my own heart ache
With thinking how his must sometimes break.

Solace he finds in the sea, no doubt.
  To catch the ebb he is up and away.
I see him silently pushing out
  On the broad bright gleam at break of day;
And watch his lessening dory toss
On the purple crests as he pulls across,
Round reefs where silvery surges leap,
And meets the dawn on the rosy deep.

His soul, is it open to sea and sky?
  His spirit, alive to sound and sight?
What wondrous tints on the water lie —
  Wild, wavering, liquid realm of light!
Between two glories looms the shape
Of the wood-crested, cool green cape,
Sloping all round to foam-laced ledge,
And cavern and cove, at the bright sea's edge.

He makes for the floats that mark the spots,
  And rises and falls on the sweeping swells,
Ships oars, and pulls his lobster-pots,
  And tumbles the tangled claws and shells

In the leaky bottom; and bails his skiff;
While the slow waves thunder along the cliff,
And foam far away where sun and mist
Edge all the region with amethyst.

I watch him, and fancy how, a boy,
    Round these same reefs, in the rising sun,
He rowed and rocked, and shouted for joy,
    As over the boat-side one by one
He lifted and launched his lobster-traps,
And reckoned his gains, and dreamed, perhaps,
Of a future as glorious, vast, and bright
As the ocean, unrolled in the morning light.

He quitted his skiff for a merchant ship;
    Was sailor-boy, mate, — gained skill and command;
And brought home once from a fortunate trip
    A wife he had found in a foreign land:
So the story is told: then settled down
With the nabobs of his native town, —
Jolly old skippers, bluff and hale,
Who owned the bottoms they used to sail.

Does he sometimes now, in his loneliness,
    Live over again that happy time,
Beguile his poverty and distress
    With pictures of his prosperous prime?
Does ever, at dusk, a fond young bride
Start forth and sit by the old man's side;
Children frolic, and friends look in;
With all the blessings that might have been?

Yet might not be! The same sad day
    Saw wife and babe to the churchyard borne;
And he sailed away, he sailed away, —
    For that is the sailor's way to mourn.
And ever, 't is said, as he sailed and sailed,
Heart grew reckless and fortune failed,
Till old age drifted him back to shore,
To his hut and his lobster-pots once more.

The house is empty, the board is bare;
 His dish he scours, his jacket he mends;
And now 't is the dory that needs repair;
 He fishes; his lobster-traps he tends;
And, rowing at nightfall many a mile,
Brings floodwood home to his winter pile;
Then his fire 's to kindle, and supper to cook;
The storm his music, his thoughts his book.

He sleeps, he wakes; and this is his life.
 Nor kindred nor friend in all the earth;
Nor laughter of child, nor gossip of wife;
 Not even a cat to his silent hearth!
Only the sand-hills, wrinkled and hoar,
Bask in the sunset, round his door,
Where now I can see him sit, as gray
And weather-beaten and lonely as they.

OLD MAN GRAM

In little Gram Court lives old man Gram,
 The patriarch of the place;
  Where often you 'll see his face,
Eager and greedy, peering about,
As he goes bustling in and out,
  At a wriggling, rickety pace,
  Brisk octogenarian's pace.
He rattles his stick at my heels, and brags
As he comes shuffling along the flags,
Brags of his riches and brags of his rags,
  Much work and little play.
" You see 'where I am," says old man Gram,
  " You see where I am to-day!

" I came to town at twelve years old,
  With a shilling in this 'ere pocket," —
  You should see him chuckle and knock it!
" The town to me was a big stout chest,
  With fortunes locked in the till, but I guessed

A silver key would unlock it,
My little key would unlock it!
I found in a rag-shop kept by a Jew
A place to sleep and a job to do,
And managed to make my shilling two;
And that's always been my way.
Now see where I am," cries old man Gram,
"Now see where I am to-day!"

In his den a-top of the butcher's shop,
He lies in his lair of husks,
And sups on gruels and rusks,
And a bone now and then, to pick and gnaw,
With hardly a tooth in his tough old jaw,
But a couple of curious tusks,
Ah, picturesque, terrible tusks!
Though half Gram Court he calls his own,
Here, hoarding his rents, he has lived alone,
Until, like a hungry wolf, he has grown
Gaunt and shaggy and gray.
"You see where I am," growled old man Gram,
As I looked in to-day.

"I might have a wife to make my broth, —
Which would be convenient, rather!
And younkers to call me father;
But a wife would be after my chink, you see,
And — bantlings for them that like!" snarls he;
"I never would have the bother;
They're an awful expense and bother!
I went to propose at fifty-four,
But stopped as I raised my hand to the door;
'To think of a dozen brats or more!'
Says I, and I turned away.
Now see where I am," brags old man Gram,
"Only see where I am to-day!

"I had once a niece, who came to town
As poor as any church mouse;
She wanted to keep my house!

'Tut! I have no house to keep! go back!'
I gave her a dollar and told her to pack;
   At which she made such a touse —
   You never did see such a touse!
Whole rows of houses were mine, she said;
I had more bank shares than hairs in my head,
And gold like so much iron or lead —
   All which I could n't gainsay.
Men see where I am," grins old man Gram;
   "They see where I am to-day.

"But if there is anything I detest,
   And for which I have no occasion,
   Sir, it 's a poor relation!
They 're always plenty, and always in need;
Take one, and soon you will have to feed
   Just about half the nation;
   They 'll swarm from all over the nation!
And I have a rule, though it 's nothing new:
'T is a lesson I learned from my friend, the Jew:
Whatever I fancy, whatever I do,
   I always ask, Will it pay?
Now see where I am," boasts old man Gram,
   "Just see where I am to-day!"

The little boys dread his coming tread,
   They are pale as he passes by;
   And the sauciest curs are shy, —
His stick is so thick, and he looks so grim;
Not even a beggar will beg of him,
   You should hear him mention why!
   There 's a very good reason why.
The poor he hates, and he has n't a friend,
And none but a fool will give or lend;
"For, only begin, there 'll be no end;
   That 's what I always say.
Now see where I am," crows old man Gram,
   "Just see where I am to-day!"

His miserly gain is the harvest-grain,
All the rest is chaff and stubble ;
And the life beyond is a bubble :
We are as the beasts : and he thinks, on the whole,
It 's quite as well that he has no soul,
For that might give him trouble,
Might give him a deal of trouble !
The long and short of the old man's creed
Is to live for himself and to feed his greed :
The world is a very good world indeed,
If only a chap might stay ;
" Only stay where I am," whines old man Gram,
" Stay just where I am to-day ! "

THE ISLE OF LAMBS

In sunlight slept the gilded cliff,
The ocean beat below,
The gray gulls flapped along the wave,
The seas broke, huge and slow.

The drenched rocks rose like buffaloes,
With matted sea-weed manes ;
Each shaggy hide shook off the tide
In dripping crystal rains.

Up rose Monk Rock's bald scalp and locks :
The heavy, drownèd hair
Below the crown hung sad and brown,
The crown was bleached and bare.

And out from shore, a league or more,
Entranced in purple calms,
Where summer seemed eternal, dreamed
The lovely Isle of Lambs.

I said : " Those rocks like scattered flocks
Lie basking in the sun,
And fancy sees a golden fleece
Enfolding every one."

An old man sat upon the cliff;
His hair like silver flame
Flared in the breeze : " Not so," he said,
" Our island got its name.

But as each year our sheep we shear,
The younglings of the flock
Are chosen, and banished to that small
Green world of grass and rock.

" There, pastured on the virgin turf,
And watered faithfully
By rain and dew, the summer through,
Encircled by the sea,

" They sport, they lie beneath the sky,
Fenced in by shining waves,
Or shelter seek, when winds are bleak,
Among the cliffs and caves."

Still as I questioned him, he said :
" This quiet farm I till."
A house he showed high up the road,
Half hidden by the hill.

" 'T is now threescore long years and more,
Long years of lonely toil,
Since Ruth and I came here, to try
Our fortunes on the soil.

" Not yet for me God's sun had risen,
His face I could not see ;
But she, my light, my moon by night,
Reflected Him to me.

" So when she died my world was dark :
No hope, but grim Despair,
Despair and Hate, his gloomy mate,
Walked with me everywhere.

" They laid their burden on my soul;
 They would not let me pray;
Hate and Despair, a dismal pair,
 Were with me night and day.

" They said : ' Behold the fisher-boy!
 He laughs a lengthened peal.
For bait he takes a worm, or breaks
 The cockle with his heel;

" ' Nor heeds the whitening barnacles,
 As crushingly he tramps
By the sea's edge, along the ledge
 Encrusted with their camps.'

" Then I beheld the living fish
 Their small companions slay,
And barnacles, in rocky wells,
 That snatched a viewless prey.

" The barnacles, fine fishermen,
 Their tiny scoop-nets swung;
Each breathing shell within the well
 Shot forth a shadowy tongue.

" Then said Despair : ' So all things fare;
 Alike the great and small.'
Then muttered Hate : ' Yea, God is great!
 He preyeth upon all!'

" So shearing-time came round again;
 And when my sheep were shorn,
Beneath the cliff I rigged my skiff,
 One pleasant summer morn.

" The stars were gone; I saw the Dawn
 Her crown of glory lay
With misty smile on yonder isle,
 And something seemed to say :

" ' Who spread those pastures for thy flock ?
    Who sends the herb and dew ?
Who curved round all this crystal wall ?
    He is thy Shepherd, too ! '

" Windrows of kelp lay on the beach,
    Sent hither by the storm ;
The sea's rich spoil, our meagre soil
    To nourish and to warm.

" Against the course of winds and foam,
    Shoreward, from steadfast deeps,
With mighty flow the undertow
    Its rolling burden sweeps.

" And something whispered in my heart :
    ' Beneath the waves of wrong,
The surface flow of wrong and woe,
    Are currents deep and strong,

" ' Unseen, that still to those who wait
    Bring blessedness and help.'
But, dark and stern, I would not learn
    The lesson of the kelp.

" The lambs were bound, and one by one
    I took them from the sand,
Till, all afloat in my good boat,
    I pushed out from the land.

" I took the oar, I pushed from shore ;
    And then I smiled to see
One poor, scared thing upstart and spring,
    His fettered limbs to free.

" ' You foolish lamb ! ' I chided him,
    ' Have faith in me and wait.
You do but gain a needless pain
    By striving with your fate.

" ' I know your grief, the end I know.
  Those hazy slopes, that rise
From out the sea, to you shall be
  A summer paradise.'

" The light oars dipped, they rose and dripped,
  The ripples ran beneath,
In many a whirl of pink and pearl,
  In many a sparkling wreath.

" With long, smooth swell arose and fell
  The slow, uncertain seas,
Till something stole into my soul
  Of their soft light and peace.

" A flush of hope, a breath of joy,
  To know that still for me
The dawn's bright hues could so suffuse
  That pure translucency.

" But, when the voyage was almost done,
  The discontented lamb,
With one glad bleat, shook free his feet,
  Leaped from the skiff, and swam.

" Far off the tall, forbidding wall
  Of rocky coast was seen ;
The sea was cold, the billows rolled
  A restless host between.

" Billows before and all around —
  A billowy world to swim ;
Only the boat was there afloat
  On the wide waves with him.

" He turned, dismayed ; but looked in vain
  His following mates to see ;
All, snug and warm and safe from harm,
  Were in the skiff with me.

"Ah! then he knew his shepherd's voice!
   With cries of quick distress,
Straight to my beckoning hand he came,
   In utter helplessness.

"With piteous cries, with pleading eyes,
   Upon my friendly palm
He stretched his chin; I drew him in,
   A chilled and dripping lamb.

"'This poor, repentant beast,' I said,
   'Is wiser far than I;
Against God's will rebellious still,
   I beat the waves and cry.

"'O Love look down! I sink! I drown!
   Is there no hand to reach
A pleading soul?' My boat, meanwhile,
   Drew near the rocky beach.

"How calm the waves! How clear the sea!
   Mysterious and slow,
In that deep glass, the long eel-grass
   Went waving to and fro.

"Safely to shore my freight I bore;
   Their morning voyage was done.
I loosed their bands upon the sands
   And freed them, one by one.

"They climbed the fresh and dewy slopes,
   They wandered everywhere;
With many a sweet and gladsome bleat,
   They blessed the island air.

"The beach-birds ran among the rocks,
   And, like an infant's hand,
A little star-fish stretched its five
   Pink fingers on the sand.

" Invisible, on some high crest,
   One solitary bird
Trilled clear and strong his morning song,
   The sweetest ever heard.

" The sky, all light and love, looked down
   Upon the curtained sea;
The dimpled deep in rosy sleep
   Lay breathing tranquilly.

" Upon the island's topmost rock
   I basked in holy calms;
My proud heart there I bowed in prayer,
   My joy broke forth in psalms.

" O stranger! you are young, and I
   Am in the shadowy vale;
Fourscore and ten the years have been
   Of him who tells this tale.

" And do you marvel at the peace
   That goes with hoary hairs,
This heritage of blessed age
   Which my glad spirit bears?

" The secret is not far to seek,
   If you can tell me why
One lamb thenceforth, of all my flock,
   Was precious in my eye;

" And wherefore he, more faithfully
   And fondly than the rest,
Learned to obey my voice and lay
   His head upon my breast."

That old man rose, he passed away
   In sunshine soft and still,
To his abode, high up the road,
   Behind the sunlit hill.

Then half I thought, such peace he brought,
    So clothed in light was he,
That on that coast a heavenly ghost
    Had met and talked with me.

THE BOY I LOVE

My boy, do you know the boy I love?
    I fancy I see him now;
His forehead bare in the sweet spring air,
With the wind of hope in his waving hair,
    The sunrise on his brow.

He is something near your height, may be;
    And just about your years;
Timid as you; but his will is strong,
And his love of right and his hate of wrong
    Are mightier than his fears.

He has the courage of simple truth.
    The trial that he must bear,
The peril, the ghost that frights him most,
He faces boldly, and like a ghost
    It vanishes in air.

As wildfowl take, by river and lake,
    The sunshine and the rain,
With cheerful, constant hardihood
He meets the bad luck and the good,
    The pleasure and the pain.

Come friends in need?   With heart and deed
    He gives himself to them.
He has the grace which reverence lends, —
Reverence, the crowning flower that bends
    The upright lily-stem.

Though deep and strong his sense of wrong,
    Fiery his blood and young,

His spirit is gentle, his heart is great,
He is swift to pardon and slow to hate,
    And master of his tongue.

Fond of his sports? No merrier lad's
    Sweet laughter ever rang!
But he is so generous and so frank,
His wildest wit or his maddest prank
    Can never cause a pang.

His own sweet ease, all things that please,
    He loves, like any boy;
But fosters a prudent fortitude;
Nor will he squander a future good
    To buy a fleeting joy.

Face brown or fair? I little care,
    Whatever the hue may be,
Or whether his eyes are dark or light;
If his tongue be true and his honor bright,
    He is still the boy for me.

Where does he dwell? I cannot tell;
    Nor do I know his name.
Or poor, or rich? I don't mind which;
Or learning Latin, or digging ditch;
    I love him all the same.

With high, brave heart perform your part,
    Be noble and kind as he,
Then, some fair morning, when you pass,
Fresh from glad dreams, before your glass,
    His likeness you may see.

You are puzzled? What! you think there is not
    A boy like him, — surmise
That he is only a bright ideal?
But you have power to make him real,
    And clothe him to our eyes.

You have rightly guessed : in each pure breast
Is his abiding-place.
Then let your own true life portray
His beauty, and blossom day by day
With something of his grace.

ANCESTORS

ON READING A FAMILY HISTORY

OPEN lies the book before me : in a realm obscure as dreams
I can trace the pale blue mazes of innumerable streams,
That from regions lost in distance, vales of shadow far apart,
Meet to blend their mystic forces in the torrents of my heart.

Pensively I turn the pages, pausing, curious and aghast :
What commingled, unknown currents, mighty passions of the past,
In this narrow, pulsing moment through my fragile being pour,
From the mystery behind me, to the mystery before !

I put by the book : in vision rise the gray ancestral ghosts,
Reaching back into the ages, vague, interminable hosts,
From the home of modern culture to the cave uncouth and dim,
Where — what 's he that gropes ? a savage, naked, gibbering, and grim !

I was moulded in that far-off time of ignorance and wrong,
When the world was to the crafty, to the ravenous and strong ;
Tempered in the fires of struggle, of aggression and resistance :
In the prowler and the slayer I have had a preëxistence !

Wild forefathers, I salute you ! Though your times were fierce and
     rude,
From their rugged husk of evil comes the kernel of our good.
Sweet the righteousness that follows, great the forces that foreran :
'T is the marvel still of marvels that there 's such a thing as man !

Now I see I have exacted too much justice of my race,
Of my own heart too much wisdom, of my brothers too much grace ;
Craft and greed our primal dower, wrath and hate our heritage !
Scarcely gleams as yet the crescent of the full-orbed golden age.

Man's great passions are coeval with the vital breath he draws,
Older than all codes of custom, all religions and all laws;
Before prudence was, or justice, they were proved and justified:
We may shame them or redeem them, their dominion will abide.

Still the darker age will linger in the slowly brightening present,
Still the old moon's fading phantom in the bosom of the crescent;
The white crown of reason covers the old kingdom of unrest,
And I feel at times the stirring of the savage in my breast.

Wrong and insult find me weaponed for a more heroic strife;
In the sheath of mercy quivers the barbarian's ready knife!
But I blame no more the givers for the rudeness of the dower:
'T was the roughness of the thistle that insured the future flower.

Somehow hidden in the slayer was the singer yet to be,
In the fiercest of my fathers lived the prophecy of me;
But the turbid rivers flowing to my heart were filtered through
Tranquil veins of honest toilers to a more cerulean hue.

O my fathers, in whose bosoms slowly dawned the later light,
In whom grew the thirst for knowledge, in whom burned the love of
     right,
All my heart goes out to know you!   With a yearning near to pain,
I once more take up the volume, but I turn the leaves in vain.

Not a voice, of all your voices, comes to me from out the vast;
Not a thought, of all your thinking, into living form has passed:
As I peer into the darkness, not a being of my name
Stands revealed against the shadows in the beacon-glare of fame.

Yet your presence, O my parents, in my inmost self I find,
Your persistent spectres haunting the dim chambers of the mind:
Old convulsions of the planet in the new earth leave their trace,
And the child's heart is an index to the story of his race.

Each with his unuttered secret down the common road you went,
Winged with hope and exultation, bowed with toil and discontent:
Fear and triumph and bereavement, birth and death and love and strife,
Wove the evanescent vesture of your many-colored life.

Your long-silent generations first in me have found a tongue,
And I bear the mystic burden of a thousand lives unsung :
Hence this love for all that 's human, the strange sympathies I feel,
Subtle memories and emotions which I stammer to reveal.

Now I also, in my season, walk beneath the sun and moon,
Face the hoary storms of winter, breathe the luxury of June :
Here to gaze awhile and wonder, here to weep and laugh and kiss ;
Then to join the pale procession sweeping down the dark abyss.

To each little life its moment !   We are sparkles of the sea :
Still the interminable billows heave and gleam, — and where are we ?
Still forever rising, following, mingling with the mighty roar,
Wave on wave the generations break upon the eternal shore.

Here I joy and sing and suffer, in this moment fleeting fast,
Then become myself a phantom of the far-receding past,
When our modern shall be ancient, and the narrow times expand,
Down through ever-broadening eras, to a future vast and grand.

Clouds of ancestors, ascending from this sublunary coast,
Here am I, enrolled already in your ever-mustering host !
Here and now the rivers blended in my blood once more divide,
In the fair lad leaping yonder, in these darlings by my side.

Children's children, I salute you !   From this hour and from this land,
To your far-off generations I uplift the signal hand !
Well contented, I resign you to the vision which I see, —
O fraternity of nations !   O republics yet to be !

Yours the full-blown flower of freedom, which in struggle we have
        sown ;
Yours the spiritual science, that shall overarch our own.
You, in turn, will look with wonder, from a more enlightened time,
Upon us, your rude forefathers, in an age of war and crime !

Half our virtues will seem vices by your broader, higher right,
And the brightness of the present will be shadow in that light ;
For, behold, our boasted culture is a morning cloud, unfurled
In the dawning of the ages and the twilight of the world !

TWOSCORE AND TEN

ACROSS the sleepy, sun-barred atmosphere
  Of the pew-checkered, square old meeting-house,
Through the high window, I could see and hear
  The far crows cawing in the forest boughs.

The earnest preacher talked of Youth and Age:
  " Life is a book, whose lines are flitting fast;
Each word a moment, every year a page,
  Till, leaf by leaf, we quickly turn the last."

Even while he spoke, the sunshine's witness crept
  By many a fair and many a grizzled head,
Some drooping heavily, as if they slept,
  Over the unspelled minutes as they sped.

A boy of twelve, with fancies fresh and strong,
  Who found the text no cushion of repose,
Who deemed the shortest sermon far too long,
  My thoughts were in the tree-tops with the crows;

Or farther still I soared, upon the back
  Of white clouds sailing in the shoreless blue,
Till he recalled me from their dazzling track
  To the old meeting-house and high-backed pew.

" To eager childhood, as it turns the leaf,
  How long and bright the unread page appears!
But to the aged, looking back, how brief,
  How brief the tale of half a hundred years!"

Over the drowsy pews the preacher's word
  Resounded, as he paused to wipe his brows:
I seem to hear it now, as then I heard,
  Reëchoing in the hollow meeting-house.

" Our youth is gone, and thick and thicker come
  The hoary years, like tempest-driven snows;
Flies fast, flies fast, life's wasting pendulum,
  And ever faster as it shorter grows."

My mates sat wondering wearily the while
    How long before his *Lastly* would come in,
Or glancing at the girls across the aisle,
    Or in some distant corner playing pin.

But in that moment to my inward eyes
    A sudden window opened, and I caught
Through dazzling rifts a glimpse of other skies,
    The dizzy deeps, the blue abyss of thought.

Beside me sat my father, grave and gray,
    And old, so old, at twoscore years and ten!
I said, "I will remember him this day,
    When *I* am fifty, if I live till then.

"I will remember all I see and hear,
    My very thoughts, and how life seems tc me,
This Sunday morning in my thirteenth year; —
    How will it seem when I am old as he?

"What is the work that I shall find to do?
    Shall I be worthy of his honored name?
Poor and obscure? or will my dream come true,
    My secret dream of happiness and fame?"

Ah me, the years betwixt that hour and this!
    The ancient meeting-house has passed away,
And in its place a modern edifice
    Invites the well-dressed worshipper to-day.

With it have passed the well-remembered faces:
    The old are gone, the boys are gray-haired men;
They too are scattered, strangers fill their places;
    And here am I at twoscore years and ten!

How strangely, wandering here beside the sea,
    The voice of crows in yonder forest boughs,
A cloud, a Sabbath bell, bring back to me
    That morning in the gaunt old meeting-house!

An oasis amid the desert years,
    That golden Sunday smiles as then it smiled :
I see the venerated head ; through tears
    I see myself, that far-off wondering child!

The pews, the preacher, and the whitewashed wall,
    An imaged book, with careless children turning
Its awful pages, — I remember all ;
    My very thoughts, the questioning and yearning ;

The haunting faith, the shadowy superstition,
    That I was somehow chosen, the special care
Of Powers that led me through life's changeful vision,
    Spirits and Influences of earth and air.

In curious pity of myself, grown wise,
    I think what then I was and dared to hope,
And how my poor achievements satirize
    The boy's brave dream and happy horoscope.

To see the future flushed with morning fire,
    Rosy with banners, bright with beckoning spears,
Fresh fields inviting courage and desire, —
    This is the glory of our youthful years.

To feel the pettiness of prizes won,
    With all our vast ambition ; to behold
So much attempted and so little done, —
    This is the bitterness of growing old.

Yet why repine ?   Though soon we care no more
    For triumphs which, till won, appear so sweet,
They serve their use, as toys held out before
    Beguiled our infancy to try its feet.

Not in rewards, but in the strength to strive,
    The blessing lies, and new experience gained ;
In daily duties done, hope kept alive,
    That Love and Thought are housed and entertained.

So not in vain the struggle, though the prize
    Awaiting me was other than it seemed.
My feet have missed the paths of Paradise,
    Yet life is even more blessed than I deemed.

Riches I never sought, and have not found,
    And Fame has passed me with averted eye;
In creeks and bays my quiet voyage is bound,
    While the great world without goes surging by.

No withering envy of another's lot,
    Nor nightmare of contention, plagues my rest:
For me alike what is and what is not,
    Both what I have and what I lack, are best.

A flower more sacred than far-seen success
    Perfumes my solitary path; I find
Sweet compensation in my humbleness,
    And reap the harvest of a tranquil mind.

I keep some portion of my early dream;
    Brokenly bright, like moonbeams on a river,
It lights my life, a far elusive gleam,
    Moves as I move, and leads me on forever.

Our earliest longings prophesy the man,
    Our fullest wisdom still enfolds the child;
And in my life I trace that larger plan
    Whereby at last all things are reconciled.

The storm-clad years, the years that howl and hasten,
    The world, where simple faith soon grows estranged,
Toil, passion, loss, all things that mould and chasten,
    Still leave the inmost part of us unchanged.

O boy of long ago, whose name I bear,
    Small self, half-hidden by the antique pew,
Across the years I see you, sitting there,
    Wondering and gazing out into the blue;

And marvel at this sober, gray-haired man
  I am or seem! How changed my days, how tame
The wild, swift hopes with which my youth began!
  Yet in my inmost self I am the same.

The dreamy soul, too sensitive and shy,
  The brooding tenderness for bird and flower,
The old, old wonder at the earth and sky,
  And sense of guidance by an Unseen Power, —

These keep perpetual childhood in my heart.
  The peaks of age, that looked so bare and cold,
Those peaks and I are still as far apart
  As in the years when fifty seemed so old.

Age, that appeared far off a bourn at rest,
  Recedes as I advance; the fount of joy
Rises perennial in my grateful breast;
  And still at fifty I am but a boy.

BOOK V

THE LOST EARL AND OTHER POEMS

WITH NEWLY GATHERED LEAVES

I ask my soul why, day and night,
I pore and ponder and indite.

Vainly, my life long, I have sought
To find some utterance for my thought,
By lip or pen, by word or token,
To speak what in me lies unspoken;
My tongue gives freely all the rest,
But locks the sweetest and the best.

I lived remote, I labored long,
In tale and rhyme, romance and song,
To sow that seed of heavenly wheat
That tortures me with inward heat.
In vain projected, it returns,
And in my bosom beats and burns.

The uttered word falls cold and dead,
The living word is still unsaid.
And should it be my fate forever
To fail, in ceaseless fond endeavor,
To sow the soul's exhaustless seed,
And reach to deeps that still recede,
I yet, by eldest law, must choose
The blissful thraldom of the Muse,
Bend all to her imperious will,
And still her last commands fulfil.

THE LOST EARL AND OTHER POEMS

THE LOST EARL

WITH his lariat coiled on the horn of his saddle,
  Face bearded and bronzed, in the broad-shadowed hat;
High boot-tops, and fringed leather leggings astraddle
  His bronco's brown sides; pistol-belt, and all that;
His shout ringing out, a bluff, resonant basso,
  Above the herd's bellowing; hand that can hurl
At a gallop the long-looped and wide-swinging lasso, —
  There rides — can you fancy? — the son of an earl.

With the best and the worst a familiar companion;
  Who often in winter, at twenty below,
While guarding his cattle within the deep cañon,
  Camps down in his blankets, rolled up on the snow;
Bold rider and roper, to aid in a round-up,
  Head off a stampede, run the ringleaders down:
In him — does he pause to remember? — are bound up
  The hopes of a race of old knightly renown.

The world's pampered minion, he yet, in requital
  Of all its proud favors, could fling them aside
As a swimmer his raiment, shed riches and title,
  And plunge into life, breast the turbulent tide!
Some caprice, you infer, or a sudden declension
  Of fortune, the cause? Rather say, the revolt
Of a strong native soul against soulless convention,
  And privilege shared by the roué and dolt.

He chafed at the gilded constraints of his station,
  The bright ball-and-chain of the name that he bore;

Grew sick of the smiles of discreet adulation,
    That worshipped, not worth, but the honors men wore.
With falsities stifled, with flatteries sated,
    He loathed, as some player, his wearisome part,
The homage of lips where he righteously hated,
    The rank that forbade him the choice of his heart.

(For that choice, it is told, fell to one far below him
    In station, who yet was so loyal and true
In the love which he won, she could love and forego him,
    And even his nobleness nobly outdo;
Who scorned to climb up to a class that would scorn to
    Receive her its peer; and refusing to dim
The coronet's brightness her brow was not born to,
    Lived maidenly faithful to love and to him.)

Was it then, in despair at the pitiful wrangle
    His preference raised, he resolved to be free,
To escape from his toils, break the tyrannous tangle
    Of custom and caste, of descent and degree?
In this lot which he chose, has he sometimes repented
    The impulse that urged him? In scenes such as these,
Hard lodgment, hard fare, has he never lamented
    The days of relinquished enjoyment and ease?

Was that impulse a fault? Would he speak, would he tell us
    His sober conclusion! For good or for ill,
There are tides of the spirit which sometimes impel us,
    Sub-currents, more potent than reason and will,
That out of our sordid conditions uplift us,
    And make our poor common humanity great.
We toy with the helm, but they draw us, they drift us,
    They shape the deep courses of life and of fate.

But then comes regret, when the ebb leaves us stranded
    In doubt and disaster: was such his reward?
How much we might gain would the fellow be candid,
    This volunteer ranchman who might be a lord!
Could we think with his thoughts as he rides in the shadow
    That falls from the foothills when, suddenly chill,

Far over the mesas of lone Colorado
  The fast-creeping twilight spreads solemn and still.

From the rose-tinted, snow-covered peaks, the bright sources
  Of torrents and rivers, the glow pales away ;
Through cañons and gulches the wild watercourses
  Rush hurried and hoarse : just the time, you would say,
For our exile to fall into sombre reflection, —
  The scion of earls, from the uppermost branch
Of the civilized tree, in its cultured perfection,
  Set here in the desolate life of the ranch !

Amid wastes of gray sagebrush, of grama and bunch-grass ;
  The comrade of cowboys, with souls scarce above
The level of driven dumb creatures that munch grass ;
  Self-banished from paths of preferment and love,
An unreturned prodigal, mumbling his husk :
  At least so your sapient soul has divined,
As he gallops far off and forlorn through the dusk.
  But little men know of a man's hidden mind.

In his jacket he carries a thumbed pocket Homer,
  To con at odd spells as he watches his herd ;
And at times, in his cottage (but that's a misnomer ;
  A hut with one room !) you may hear, on my word,
These cool summer twilights (in moments not taken
  For washing his dishes or darning his socks),
On strings deftly thrummed a strange music awaken,
  Mazurka of Chopin's, sonata of Bach's.

As over the wide-shouldered Rockies the gleam
  Of day yet illumines the vastness and distance
Of snow-hooded summits, so shines the still beam
  Of high thought, high resolve, on his lonely existence.
(And a maiden, they say, of her own sweet accord,
  Who to-night may be sailing the moonlighted sea,
To the ranchman brings what she denied to the lord.
  Idle rumor, no doubt. But, however it be) —

Our knight of the lasso, long-lineaged Norman,
  Now guiding his herd to good pasture and drink,

Now buying and selling, stock-owner and foreman,
  Feels life fresh and strong; well content, as I think,
That the world of traditional leisure and sport
  Without him should amble its indolent round.
Though lost to his title, to kindred and court,
  Here first in rude labor his manhood is found.

His conclusion is this, or I sadly mistake it:
  " To each his own part; rugged action for me!
Be men, and not masks; fill your sphere or forsake it.
  Use power and wealth; but 't is time to be free
When the trappings of life prove a burden and fetter.
  The walls of my forefather's castle are stanch,
But a cabin, with liberty, shelters me better.
  Be lord of your realm, be it earldom or ranch ! "

HOW THE KING LOST HIS CROWN

THE King's men, when they had slain the boar,
Strung him aloft on the fisher's oar,
And, two behind and two before,
In triumph bore him along the shore.
    " An oar ! " says the King: " 't is a trifle ! — why
    Did the fisher frown and the good wife sigh ? "
    " A trifle, sire ! " was the Fool's reply ;
    " Then frown or laugh who will ! for I,
    Who laugh at all and am only a clown,
      Will never more laugh at trifles ! "

A runner next day leaped down the sand,
And launched a skiff from the fisher's strand ;
For he cried, — " An army invades the land !
The passes are seized on either hand !
    And I must carry my message straight
    Across the lake to the castle gate ! "
    The castle he neared, but the waves were great,
    The fanged rocks foamed like jaws of Fate ;
    And lacking an oar the boat went down.
      The Furies laugh at trifles !

The swimmer against the waves began
To strive, as a valiant swimmer can.
" Methinks," said the Fool, " 't were no bad plan
If succor were sent to the drowning man! "
 To succor a perilled pawn instead,
 The monarch, moving his rook ahead, —
 Bowed over the chessmen, white and red, —
 Gave " Check! " — then looked on the lake and said,
 " The boat is lost, the man will drown! "
  O King! beware of trifles!

To the lords and mirthful dames the bard
Was trolling his latest song; the guard
Were casting dice in the castle yard;
And the captains all were drinking hard.
 Then came the chief of the halberdiers,
 And told to the King's astounded ears:
 " An army on every side appears!
 An army with banners and bows and spears!
 They have gained the wall and surprised the town! "
  Our fates are woven of trifles!

The red usurper reached the throne;
The tidings over the realm were blown;
And, flying to alien lands alone
With a trusty few, the King made moan.
 But long and loudly laughed the Clown:
 " We broke the oar and the boat went down,
 And so the messenger chanced to drown:
 The messenger lost, we lost the town;
 And the loss of the town has cost a crown;
  And all these things are trifles! "

MY CAREER

My mother, they said, was a soldier's child;
 My father played in the band.
She was pretty and gay, he was handsome and wild,
 And she gave him her foolish hand.

He owed so much that he could n't pay,
He borrowed some more and they ran away;
But my poor mother, whom he outran,
Put up at an almshouse, where began
    (I think I never just knew the year)
      My career —
    My extraordinary career!

He ran so well she lost his track
    In the little delay I made;
He ran so far he never came back,
    And there, of course, we stayed;
And, while the decrepit old pauper wives
Tossed me about, she brightened the knives,
And set the table, and swept the floor,
And scrubbed as she never had scrubbed before;
    But still watched over, with many a tear,
      My career —
    The beginning of my career.

In lap, or cradle, or on all-fours,
    I thrived, and made my way,
And tumbled about the poor-house doors,
    Till a lady came, one day,
A wealthy widow, who begged for me.
"I want your beautiful boy," says she,
"To fill the place of one I have lost.
I will love him and rear him, and spare no cost
    To form his mind, and give him, my dear,
      A career —
    Maybe a distinguished career!"

My mother took on at a terrible rate,
    And called it a sin and a shame;
She would keep her darling in spite of fate;
    But consented, all the same.
To the widow's she went, and left me there,
Then fled in despair, I never knew where,
A childless mother, to mourn and roam;
While I had luxury, friends, and a home,

With everything that could aid and cheer
My career —
My fortunate career!

My friends were as kind as friends could be,
And gave me teachers and books ;
But I never could see their use to me,
With fine clothes and good looks,
Money to spend, and a fortune still
Awaiting me in the widow's will.
So, very possibly, I looked down
On the poor, industrious youths in town,
And followed as proud as a prince or peer,
My career —
Quite early, a gay career!

I could drive and dress and dance and dine,
With exquisite grace and dash ;
My taste was fine in horses and wine,
And I sported a sweet moustache.
The widow, no doubt, sometimes complained
Of the rather high tone that I maintained,
My talents wasted and youth misspent,
And wept at the way her money went ;
For, though it was pleasant, I own 't was dear :
My career
Was a pretty high-toned career!

"I have lost a bet ! I must pay this debt ! "
I coaxed ; she could n't refuse.
A genteel fellow sometimes will get
Into scrapes, and where 's the use
Of having a fussy old woman about,
Who can't, or won't, help a fellow out ?
I rushed from her presence a hundred times,
And threatened to plunge into horrid crimes,
To end as a robber or buccaneer
My career —
My desperate career!

It was long to wait for a grand estate,
    But I was in luck at last.
I was tall and straight, I was twenty-eight,
    And, though a trifle fast,
A party the girls were mad to catch!
Considered a most amazing match
By smiling mammas and bowing papas,
And a deucedly delicate thing it was,
    With sirens on every side, to steer
        My career —
    Safely my free career!

For why should I marry, and have the care
    Of children and a wife?
'T was burden enough, by George! to bear
    My own light butterfly life —
A thing I never could understand!
With fashion and wealth, gay friends at hand,
No thought for another, there weighed on me
At times such weariness and ennui
    As few would have fancied could come near
        My career —
    My enviable career!

Yet I should state that I chose a mate,
    For a very good cause, indeed.
It was rather late; I was forty-eight;
    My moustache had gone to seed;
And, worst of all, one day I found
My fortune was high and dry aground!
So I looked about, resolved to win
Some widow, as rich as my first had been,
    From the rubbish of beggarly debts to clear
        My career —
    My really superb career!

Too lucky by half, I may say it now,
    Was I when I went to woo.
I never could get along, somehow,
    With Widow Number Two.

A woman of taste, she could n't but be
In love with an elegant man like me ;
But she was a shrew, and she soon took fright,
Drew her prim lips and her purse-strings tight,
 And eyed with an eye quite too severe
  My career —
 Jealous of my career !

She scrimped me up and she screwed me down,
 In a most ridiculous way.
For a man of renown, the beau of the town,
 'T was extremely little pay.
There never was husband fond as I —
Particularly when she came to die ;
But in her will she was cruel still,
And cut me off, by a codicil,
 With hardly enough to maintain a mere
  Mean career !
 A pittance for *my* career !

Of the schemes I tried when drifting about
 There 's little enough to tell.
As a mixer of fancy drinks, no doubt,
 I might have succeeded well.
I had no other art or trade ;
And the fine, rich friends I asked for aid
Grew cold, scarce deigning at times to use
A word of pity or poor excuse ;
 But viewing with secret glee, I fear,
  My career —
 My steady down-hill career !

My buttoned coat had a hungry look ;
 I sponged from bar to bar ;
Whoever would trust or treat, I took
 A glass or a bad cigar.
Homeless, alone, I walked the street ;
The old faces now that I chanced to meet
Passed by, with a smile at my altered style,
My tight cravat, and my battered tile ;

And jubilant youngsters turned to jeer
My career —
My often zigzag career!

No need to relate what buffets of fate
I afterward underwent.
I am feeble of gait; I am sixty-eight;
My back and my knees are bent.
To the passers-by I have held my hat;
But, Heaven be thanked, there's an end of that!
To the poor-house I have come home, at last,
To the poor-house where my first years passed,
Old and infirm, to finish here
My career —
My rather played-out career!

CAPTAIN SEABORN

I

OUR ship went down, and not a boat
Outrode the storm's intensity;
But I alone was left afloat
Upon the blue immensity:
My raft and I together lashed,
The wild seas racing under us,
Till reefs uprose, and breakers dashed
About us, blind and thunderous.

Still, like Mazeppa to his horse,
I clung, while, half submerging me,
On foaming shoals with fearful force
The winds and waves were urging me.
I swooned: I woke: my dim eyes glanced
Upon a hideous rabblement
Of islanders that round me pranced
With frantic yells and babblement.

Half-drowned they dragged me from the sea
Up the white beach, and, seating me

Against a skull-encircled tree,
  Made ghastly signs of eating me.
The frizzled women crouched to look
  My body over curiously;
The tattooed braves above me shook
  Their battle-axes furiously.

Forth from my sailor's pouch, to buy
  My life of those fell savages,
I drew such slight effects as I
  Had saved from the sea's ravages.
With thimble, coins, carved ivory ball,
  I flattered and invited them;
A rusted jack-knife, most of all,
  Astonished and delighted them.

Then fruits they brought and mats they spread
  With singular celerity:
Not death I gained, but gifts instead,
  And cannibal prosperity.
I lived with them and learned their speech;
  I curbed their fierce brutality,
And strove with simple truths to reach
  Their dim spirituality.

The arts of peace, the love of right,
  I tried to teach; economy
Of health; what makes the day and night —
  Some notion of astronomy;
Treatment of neighbors at a feast —
  More genial ways of toasting them;
To love their fellow-men, at least
  A little, without roasting them.

No white sail found those coral bays,
  Wide rings of reefs defending them;
And so I lived my savage days,
  With little hope of ending them.
Three frightful years! Though loved by some,
  A priest-led faction hated me,

Until it seemed that martyrdom,
   For all my pains, awaited me.

Fearful of change, and not content
   With foiling and defeating me,
My enemies once more were bent
   On finishing and eating me.
In no wise wishing to assist
   At any such festivities,
(All the more reason to resist
   Their cannibal proclivities!)

With scant provisions snatched in haste
   My small canoe encumbering,
Into the round sea's rolling waste,
   While all the isle was slumbering,
One midnight, when the low late moon
   Across the shoals was shimmering,
I paddled, from the still lagoon
   And channel darkly glimmering.

Five days adrift! the indolent
   Warm waves about me weltering:
The suns were fierce, my food was spent,
   And I was starved and sweltering:
When ho! a ship! How strange to meet
   Fair manners and urbanity!
How strange my native speech, how sweet
   The accents of humanity!

II

Thus all my efforts to redeem
   That sinister society
Were left behind, a nightmare dream
   Of horror and anxiety.
My changeful life was full and fleet;
   But long the hope attended me,
To see that land again, and greet
   The chiefs who once befriended me.

So, as I sailed those seas once more,
   When many years had passed away,
My ship dropped anchor off the shore
   Where I had been a castaway.
Amid the reefs we rowed to land,
   And, eager as a lover is
To seek his mistress, to the strand
   I strode, to make discoveries.

Less changed than my own life appeared
   The wondrous island scenery;
Near by, the groves of cocoa reared
   Their fans of waving greenery;
There the old, shaggy, cane-thatched town;
   And, habited still sparingly,
The islanders came straggling down,
   And heard my questions staringly.

With signs of woe their arms they flung
   When I, in broken sentences
Of their well-nigh forgotten tongue,
   Inquired for old acquaintances.
" Dead! dead! " my friendly chiefs and they
   Who from the isle had driven me.
But when I spoke my sobriquet,
   The name the tribe had given me,

'T was strange! the sudden eagerness
   And zeal with which they greeted it.
" Son-of-the-Great-Sea-Mother? yes! " —
   They joyfully repeated it.
" He 's there! " — They pointed.   Bound to know
   What this amazing blunder meant,
Forthwith I followed to a low,
   Rude door, in utter wonderment.

Their temple! lined with sacred stones
   And heathen curiosities;
Dried birds and fishes, reptiles' bones,
   And various monstrosities;

Relics and charms, strung round the place,
　　Trophies of fights and scrimmages ;
And, propped behind the central space,
　　The rudest of carved images, —

Which I myself with shells and knife
　　Had shaped, in my captivity !
A task to keep my heart and life
　　From purposeless passivity.
The mouth too wide, too short the nose,
　　How well I recollected it !
Now here, a grinning idol, those
　　Sad wretches had erected it ;

Tricked and bedizened in a style
　　Preposterous and laughable !
I gazed ; the guardian priest the while
　　Eyeing me, grimly affable.
Swarthy and sleek, with hideous smirk
　　Admitting me to see it, he
Called it grand magic, handiwork
　　And image of their deity !

" Out of the ocean, in his sleep,"
　　('T was hard to listen seriously !)
" He came to us, and in the deep
　　Vanished again mysteriously.
He taught our people " (thus the priest's
　　Narration is translatable)
" To discontinue at their feasts
　　Some customs he found hatable ;

" Not to hunt men, although we were,
　　As now, a strong and bold people ;
Nor beat our women ; nor inter
　　Alive our sick and old people ;
To have more clothes and fewer wives,
　　With houses more commodious ;
To speak true words, and make our lives
　　In other ways less odious.

" These changes we found politic,
    Though backward in assuming them.
So now we leave our old and sick
    To starve, before inhuming them.
While yet some rich men on the coast
    Practice the old polygamy,
The poor have one wife, or, at most,
    Restrict themselves to bigamy.

" And though some warriors of renown
    Continue anthropophagous,
'T is rare that human flesh goes down
    The low caste man's œsophagus.
Woman we seldom beat, while she
    Is faithful and obedient;
We only hunt an enemy,
    And lie when it 's expedient.

" Old men remember, still a few,
    How he appeared and talked with them;
Though not till he was gone they knew
    A deity had walked with them.
This image in his hands became
    The very form and face of him;
So now we call it by his name,
    And worship it in place of him;

" And in our sorceries draw from it
    Responses and admonishment."
All which I heard with infinite
    Misgiving and astonishment,
That fable thus should swallow fact,
    And truth to myth degenerate,
And I by wooden proxy act
    The god, for tribes to venerate !

I said, " The being you adore,
    Who came and went in mystery,
Was but a sailor washed ashore ! "
    And told the simple history.

" My words and work your prophets foiled,
　　They treated me despitefully,
And I escaped." The priest recoiled,
　　And glared upon me frightfully.

"And as for this dumb log " — I felt
　　Such absolute disgust with it,
I twirled my walking-stick and dealt
　　An inconsiderate thrust with it.
"Taboo ! taboo !" Too late the call :
　　The clumsy idol fell at once
Against the mummies on the wall,
　　The rattling skins and skeletons.

The priest, in horror at my speech,
　　Had glared, aghast and stammering ;
But now he raised his warning screech,
　　And half the tribe came clamoring.
My comrades hurried me away,
　　While, close behind us clattering,
The mob pursued us to the bay,
　　And clubs and stones fell pattering.

Embarking, we in haste let fall
　　The gifts which I had brought for them,
But more than this, alas for all
　　My hopes ! I could do naught for them ;
Nor could I venture more among
　　The clans of that vicinity,
Because I had with impious tongue
　　Denied my own divinity.

THE KANSAS FARMER

WE talked or read, or idly sat beholding,
　　Betwixt the wire-strung poles and April sky,
From dawn till dusk, the endlessly unfolding,
　　Swift panorama of the land sweep by.

The twilight closed upon a lonesome prairie, —
  A paling sunset pierced by one faint star,
Above a house low-browed and solitary,
  Seen from the windows of our passing car.

For miles there was no other habitation.
  Out from a neighboring marsh a heron took flight,
Rose, gray and silent as an exhalation,
  And grew a speck far in the fading light.

Framed by the doorway in the frowning gable,
  The figure of a man stood dark and still;
No roof beside, but just a turf-walled stable,
  Half-thatched with grass, half-sunken in the hill.

A solemn mule couched on his bony haunches;
  A lank sow leaned and rubbed against her sty;
No tree, but one bare locust, in whose branches
  Turkeys were roosting, black against the sky.

The man stood gazing, gaunt of frame and gloomy;
  So melancholy and so motionless,
A sharp compassionating thrill shot through me,
  With thinking of his utter loneliness.

Far from the cheerful light of human faces,
  The glow of friendly converse, how could he
Endure a lot as bare of all the graces
  As the surrounding hills of house or tree?

He gazed as if with sad surmise and longing, —
  As thick as sparks above the rushing train,
His kindled thoughts and aspirations thronging
  Toward some great good which he could never gain.

He saw each day that mighty, thundering shuttle
  Across the continent hurled to and fro;
But of the life, the invisible and subtle
  Wide web it wove, how little could he know!

The train flew on, and, snugly housed within it,
  We saw the lonely exile left behind ;
But not till that brief vision of a minute
  Was photographed forever in the mind.

The train sped on with loud, relentless clanging ;
  But gentler fancies in my heart awoke,
As I recalled, in the wan twilight hanging
  Above his roof, a wreath of cottage smoke.

Symbol of household cheer the whole world over !
  Perfect contentment brims no mortal breast ;
The dweller with the prairie-dog and gopher,
  No doubt, has his due portion with the rest.

His evening meal upon the coals was cooking ;
  A babe, I fain would think, made glad the house ;
A wife, I 'm sure ; but he was anxious, looking
  To see his boys come driving home the cows.

No thought had he to join the world's great battle,
  Or follow in the ranks of wealth and pride.
His home, his farm, his own small herd of cattle,
  These are his world ; he knows no world beside.

Though few of life's fair consolations enter
  The door, to us so desolate and dim,
That cabin on the prairie is the centre
  Of the round earth and rolling heavens to him.

He, too, — so fancy runs, — has his ambition :
  To build a barn, renew that two years' loan,
Improve each day a little his condition,
  And leave his children's better than his own.

To petty cares, the lack of tools and fences,
  To rains, droughts, weeds, the price of pork and corn,
He gives his years ; yet finds its recompenses
  Even in the life we picture so forlorn.

Man, to the last a child, who still amuses
    Himself all day with trifles great and small,
Cherishes most the few poor toys he uses,
    But, given too many, learns to scorn them all.

Sweeter than ease, sometimes, is rude privation;
    Less tedious than long leisure to live through
Are days full packed with healthful occupation ;
    Too many friends as irksome as too few.

How little for our daily need suffices,
    Could each but know, contented with his share !
The frugal dish, that luxury despises,
    Is to the humble sweet and wholesome fare.

With hope, a constant, cloud-illuming crescent,
    With love, and work for head or hands, these three,
Alike the mightiest king or lowliest peasant
    Finds life worth living, each in his degree.

Culture and gold are good, but not by building
    More stately porches may we look to win
Peace to our dwelling; nor by gayly gilding
    The fountain can we raise the flood within.

We ply the fount with toil and rest and revel,
    One casts in empires, and one bagatelles ;
Still happiness in men will seek its level,
    As water from one source in many wells.

A MOTHER'S TRAGEDY

HE fell in a wayside brawl, not far from his mother's door.
We picked him up, two or three of us ; one ran on before,
To give her a decent warning, while we turned into the place,
Lugging him, horribly limp, with his hat laid over his face.

We heard a sharp voice in the doorway: "Don't fear but I shall be
    strong !
What is one sorrow the more to a heart that is seared with wrong ?

My son? something dreadful! They've killed him!" And tearless,
    terrible eyes
Looked down on us and our burden : no wringing of hands, nor cries :

But, going before, she cleared the lounge that we laid him on ;
Uncovered with her own hand the face upstaring and wan,
The small, dark wound in the temple, and slow, dull trickling red ;
Then writhed in a spasm of horror and agony over the dead.

The doctors came and looked grave ; there was nothing more to be
    done ;
And there the old mother sat by the side of her murdered son,
Rigid, erect, and under her neatly combed white hair
Her gleaming features fixed in a frozen and fierce despair.

The neighbors gathered round, where she sat tearless and grim ;
Full of compassion for her, but hardly sorry for him ;
Full of compassion for her, but wondering if, on the whole,
'T were better to wish her joy, or weakly attempt to console.

She seemed to fathom their thoughts : " Yes, little cause," she said,
" Did ever he give while living, that I should mourn for him dead !
And life is so full of misfortunes that death seems far from the
    worst.
Yet he is the babe of my bosom, the child I have borne and nursed.

" The same?   Oh, merciful powers ! 't was well that I could n't see
On the innocent forehead I kissed the horror that was to be !
Not see these clotted locks in the silky hair I curled —
The happiest mother and prettiest baby in all the world.

" He sickened, too, that summer, just after his father died ;
And well do I recollect how I clung to him then, and cried,
And called on the cruel fates, and promised to forgive
All their unkindness to me, if only my child might live.

" ' Spare him ! ' I said, ' whatever my widowed life must bear ;
Spare him ! ' And the cruel fates, in mockery of my prayer —
Or was it Heaven, to punish my obduracy and pride ? —
Seemed in mercy to grant what mercy would have denied.

"There are sons who honor their mothers; and is there an earthly
    joy
Like hers who watches the growth in grace of her one dear boy?
But look at us now, and tell me if ever I was one
That dreamt she was such a mother and he would be such a son!

"I bore with his childish passions, and petted his whims, until
They grew to be snarling faults of ingratitude and self-will.
I tried to curb and restrain them, but they were too fierce and strong,
And they turned and tore the hand that had fostered them too long.

"I hid in my heart, and pardoned, whatever wrong he had done;
And strangers said: 'What a treasure you have in your only son!'
And oh! he was fair to behold! And I marveled how he could be
Always so kind to others, and never kind to me.

"Upon those who gave him least, he could smile like an angel of light;
Upon me, who gave him most, he vented his anger and spite.
Was it his, or mine, the fault? And whose, at last, was the blame,
When the fire in his blood broke out in open riot and shame?

"He was as he was: perverse — a nature that understood
Nothing of self-denial, of duty or gratitude;
No aim but the hour's enjoyment, no higher ambition on earth
Than just to be ranked good fellow with fellows of shallow worth.

"With a greed that had no eyes to see beyond the day,
Me and my slender savings he looked upon as his prey;
In the sieve of self-indulgence pouring his powers and gains;
Never counting the cost in future losses and pains.

"He was as he was: if your boy is born with a crippled limb,
Or blind, or deaf, do you think of laying the blame on him?
And one is infirm of reason, and one is deformed of soul,
And one, a Goliath of passion, a pigmy in self-control.

"He was as he was, from his birth — no will or wish of his own;
Or the will was flesh of his flesh, the wish was bone of his bone.
It is easy to say, we are free to follow evil or good;
Whatever we follow or leave, the choice is in our blood.

"Oh, yes! he should have cared for good men's counsel and praise,
And heeded the pleading love that strove with him all his days.
But the force that obeys the magnet is not in stone, but in steel;
And the secret is in ourselves of the influences we feel.

"He was as he was!   He was born so!   No need to question why
He was cursed with faults that neither his father had nor I.
Traits good in themselves sometimes appear in strange excess,
And generous heats flame out in folly and recklessness.

"You sooner might track the wind, or an underground stream to its
     source,
Than some inherited taint through its hidden and fitful course,
The vice that has lurked so long in generations past,
To burst its decent bounds and rage in our sons at last.

"He was as he was; accuse him, excuse him, what you will;
And I, who have loved him most, and pitied, accuse him still.
For, though we may bear and forbear, and pardon, and suffer long,
The right is forever right, and the wrong is eternally wrong.

"And I am his mother; and all that is left of my boy lies there!
The frolic of youth, and the frenzy, alternate sport and despair;
Desire that would have dissolved — a mere lump in his cup — the
     earth!
Gone out like a flame that is quenched, like a fire that is dead on the
     hearth.

"I can neither rejoice nor grieve — my heart is like stone in my
     breast.
He was naught but a burden and thorn, and I know that what is, is
     best.
Yet I shall be lost without him.   The very trouble and care
That pass with him out of my life will leave it empty and bare.

"I would hope; I would pray for him!   *Is* there another and happier
     sphere,
Where the soul may arise from the cloud of evil that clung to it here?
Or has he rushed into that world all aflame with the passions of this?
I would hope; I would know!   I cannot look into the dark abyss!

"Maybe not all are immortal; the souls of sinners may die,
Burn briefly in Heaven, and vanish, like meteors dropped in our sky.
I shall follow him soon, I shall follow; and oh! that our spirits may live,
If only to know each other, to know and embrace and forgive!"

The neighbors gathered near, and departed, one by one;
And there the old mother sat by the side of her murdered son,
With ever the icy despair, the look out of eyes that had shed
So many tears for the living, they had none to weep for the dead.

AFTER THE SALE

THE wagon, with high fantastic load
    Of household goods, is at the gate;
The shadows darken down the road;
    Why does the old man wait?
Bureau, bedstead, rocking-chair,
Upturned table with heels in air, —
Whatever the grudging fates would spare, —
Lie huddled and heaped and tumbled there,
    A melancholy freight!

"Of all his riches," the teamster said,
    "Now only this precious pile remains!
A blanket and bed for his old gray head,
    For all his life-long pains.
Hard case, I own! but they say that Pride
Must have a fall." His ropes he tied
In the chill March wind. "Hurry up!" he cried,
    And gathered in the reins.

The old wife bows her stricken face
    On the doorstone, weary and worn and gray.
The old man lingers about the place,
    Taking a last survey;
Looks in once more at the great barn door,
On the empty mow and the vacant floor:
All the gains of his life have gone before,
    And why should he care to stay?

Only a stool with a broken leg
    Is left, and a bucket without a bail.
The harness is gone from hook and peg,
    Even the whip from its nail :
Dreary shadows hang from the wall.
No friendly whinny from shed or stall,
Nor unmilked heifer's welcoming call ;
The poultry and pigs have vanished, all
    Swept out by the sheriff's sale.

Back to the dooryard well he goes
    For a parting look, a farewell drink.
How drippingly that bucket rose
    And poised for him on the brink,
In the summers gone, and plashed his feet,
When the men came in from the harvest heat!
How blessedly cool the draught, how sweet,
    'T is misery now to think.

What scenes of peaceful, prosperous life
    Once filled the yard, so desolate now!
When he often would say to his pleased, proud wife,
    That the farm appeared, somehow,
More thrifty and cheery than other men's,
With its cattle in pasture and swine in pens,
Bleating of lambs and cackle of hens,
    And well-stored crib and mow.

The early years of their proud success,
    The years of failure and mutual blame,
Are past, with the toil that was happiness,
    And the strife that was sorrow and shame.
She came to him hopeful and strong and fair —
Now who is the sad wraith sitting there,
With her burden of grief, and her old thin hair,
    Bowed over her feeble frame?

" Do you remember? This well," he said,
    " Was sunk that summer when Jane was born.

She used to stand in the old house-shed
    And blow the dinner-horn,
In after years, — or climb a rail
Of the dooryard fence for a cheery hail, —
Then run to the curb for a brimming pail,
    When I came up from the corn."

Why think of her now? against whose name
    His lips and heart long since were sealed;
Whose memory in their lives became
    A sorrow that never has healed.
Her step is on the creaking stair,
Her girlish image is everywhere!
He hears her laughter, he sees her hair
Blow back in the wind, as she comes to bear
    His luncheon to the field.

" 'T was a terrible wrong!" The old wife spoke,
    Swaying her gaunt frame to and fro.
" I 'll say it now!" Her strained voice broke
    Into a wail of woe.
" It haunts me awake, it haunts me asleep!
And silence has been so hard to keep —
So long! — but there is a grief too deep
    For ever a man to know!"

A quaver of anguish shook his tone,
    His look was pierced with a keen remorse:
" The blame, I suppose, was all my own;
    And I have no heart, of course!
Great Heaven! nor any grief to hide!"
Lifting his gloomy hat aside,
He looked up, haggard and hollow-eyed,
Like one whose burning soul had dried
    His tears at their very source.

"No, no! I don't mean that," she wept.
    "I 've felt you suffering many a day,
And often at night when you thought I slept,
    And when I have heard you pray,

Until it seemed that my heart would burst.
And as for the blame, you know, at first,
I claimed you were right, and did my worst
    To force her to obey.

" For the dream of our lives had been to make
    Our Jane a lady fit for a lord ;
Our schemes were all for our children's sake,
    And it seemed a cruel reward
To see her with careless scorn refuse —
For all the arguments we could use —
The men you most approved, and choose
    The one you most abhorred.

" But when she had chosen and all was done,
    You need n't have been so hard and stern,
We might have forgiven the poor dear one,
    And welcomed her return.
You never could know what she was to me,
You never will know how I yearn to see
My child again — how homesickly
    I yearn, and yearn, and yearn !

" She chose for herself, and who can tell ?
    She braved your will, it 's true, and yet
She may, for all that, have chosen well.
    And how can we forget ?
We chose for Alice, and unawares
Rushed with her into a rich man's snares,
Who tangled us up in his loose affairs,
    And dragged us down with debt."

" Well, well ! " — with a heavy sigh — " Let 's go !
    I have n't been always wise.   Ah, Jane !
Some things might not be done just so,
    If they were to do again.
But Alice is dead and the farm is gone ;
Our hopes, and all that we built them on,
Friends, wealth, are scattered hither and yon,
    And only ourselves remain.

" These boughs will blossom and fruits will fall
      The same!   When I changed the orchard lot,
And fenced it all with good stone wall,
      And planned the garden plot,
And built the arbor and planted trees,
And made a home for our pride and ease,
We little thought these were all to please
      Strangers who knew us not!

" Others will reap where we have sown;
      But others never can understand
What watchful care these fields have known,
      Or how I loved the land.
Here maids will marry and babes be born,
The sun will shine on the wheat and corn,
Crops be gathered and sheep be shorn,
      But by a stranger's hand.

" Come, wife! "   With bitterest vain regret,
      Remembering all good things that were,
The old man yet can half forget
      His woes, in pity of her.
She entered, a young man's happy bride,
She crowned his home with hope and pride,
And now goes forth by an old man's side,
      A weary wanderer.

With slow, disconsolate, broken talk,
      They look their last and pass the gate;
The wagon is gone and they must walk;
      A mile, and it's growing late.
She bears a parcel, he lifts a pack.
But what do they see there, up the track,
Against the sunset, looming black?
'T is strange! the wagon is coming back
      With its melancholy freight!

And what is the driver shrieking out?
      Now Heaven for a moment keep them sane!

" Turn about ! turn about ! " they hear him shout,
    As he flourishes whip and rein —
" You 've a home and a good friend yet, you 'll find ! "
A coach is following close behind ;
A face — a voice — Oh, Heaven be kind !
Oh, lips that tremble and tears that blind !
    Oh, breaking hearts, it 's Jane !

THREE WORLDS

I

IN youth the world, a newly blown
    Prismatic bubble,
Shows the enchanted soul her own
    Enchanting double.

The light and dew of heavenly dreams
    Filled my young vision,
And life rose clothed in orient beams,
    Bright apparition !

Then love in each fair bosom beat,
    A pure emotion ;
And friendship was a long and sweet
    Ideal devotion.

Woman was truth ; and age was then
    Holy as hoary.
Strangely about the brows of men
    There shone a glory,

A radiance shed by my rapt sight
    And reverent spirit ;
How changed the life, how paled the light,
    As I drew near it !

'T was my own ardent youth (alas,
    How unsuspected !)
Whose image in the bubble's glass
    I saw reflected.

O magic youth, that could suffuse
  The bright creation
With its own dreams and rainbow hues
  Of aspiration!

II

The wondrous years no more were mine,
  When fervent Fancy
Remade the world by her divine,
  Sweet necromancy.

But still, as paled that earlier flame,
  My zeal grew warmer
To serve my kind; and I became
  A world-reformer.

For every problem then I saw
  Some new solution,
Could I remodel human law
  And institution!

To wed in work the heart and mind,
  Make life a mission
Of wise good-will to all mankind,
  Was my ambition.

Bondage and ignorance should cease;
  Reason and culture
Should banish war, the dove of peace
  Succeed the vulture.

But patiently as I reshaped
  The old equation,
I found some factor still escaped
  My calculation.

No philosophic scheme, nor act
  Of legislature,
Can yoke the storm and cataract
  Of human nature.

The moral crusade may proceed
    By means immoral;
And too much zeal for peace may lead
    To many a quarrel.

A thankless task has he who tries
    To chip and model
The world to just the form and size
    Of his own noddle.

Is it because of hopes long tossed
    Or heart grown harder?
Now I have also something lost
    Of that last ardor.

No dungeon door will cease to creak,
    Nor chain be broken,
For any word I hoped to speak,
    But leave unspoken.

My noon is past, as many things,
    Alas, remind me!
Slowly about my shadow swings,
    Lengthening behind me.

The unaccomplished task laid down
    I leave to others;
The voice, the victory, and the crown,
    To you, my brothers!

Not doubting, though my lips be dumb,
    But trusting wholly
In that fair time which yet shall come, —
    Shall come, though slowly.

Not in our hurrying years, but late,
    Through generations,
The race shall rise which I await
    With perfect patience.

Youth's brave illusion, manhood's hope,
    Vision of sages,
Are augury and horoscope
    Of future ages.

A harp-like sound is in my ear,
    A far-off humming:
I see the golden cloud, I hear
    The chariots coming!

III

Nearer and sweeter than I thought,
    One world has waited,
Though not the world my fancy wrought,
    Or hope created:

A world of common light and air,
    Of earth and azure;
Of love girt round by fear, and care
    Dearer than pleasure;

Of simple wants and few, good-will
    To friend and neighbor;
And each day's cup each day must fill
    With thought and labor;

Furtherance and help, with ample scope
    For tears and laughter;
Of child-like faith, and earnest hope,
    In the hereafter;

Patience in pain; in every ill,
    Cross, and privation,
If not contentment, patience still,
    And resignation.

My brother's wrong I may not right,
    But I can share it;
My own I 'll study less to fight,
    And more to bear it.

The nettle-sting of others' deeds
  I 'll strive to pardon,
And look to find the lurking weeds
  In my own garden.

I 'll till my little plot of ground,
  And pay my taxes,
And let the headlong globe go round
  Upon its axis.

Aspire who may to seize the helm
  And guide creation,
If I can rule my little realm
  With moderation, —

My own small kingdom, act and thought
  And chaste affection,
Trained powers, and passions duly brought
  Into subjection,

The world of home, of wife and child, —
  Good-by, ambition !
I 'll live serenely reconciled
  To my condition.

With years a richer life begins,
  The spirit mellows :
Ripe age gives tone to violins,
  Wine, and good fellows.

I 'll marry action to repose,
  Busily idle,
As through great scenes a traveller goes
  With slackened bridle.

To loftier aims let me aspire,
  To higher beauty ;
Freedom to follow my desire
  Be one with duty.

About our common mother earth
  Flow seas of ether;
Heaven holds her in her starry girth,
  The clouds enwreath her.

Forever mystery, love, the soul's
  Boundless ideal,
Like a diviner ether rolls
  About the real.

And second youth can still suffuse
  The bright creation
With its own dreams and rainbow hues
  Of aspiration.

THE SEEKING

I

By ways of dreaming and doing,
  Man seeks the bourn of the blest;
Youth yearns for the Fortunate Islands,
  Age pines for the haven of rest.

And we say to ourselves, "Oh! surely,
  Beneath some bluer skies,
Just over our bleak horizon,
  The land of our longing lies."

Each seeks some favored pathway,
  Secure to him alone;
But every pathway thither
  With broken hearts is strown.

II

The Giver of Sleep breathed also,
  Into our clay, the breath
And fire of unrest, to save us
  From indolent life in death.

Fair is the opening rosebud,
  And fair the full-blown rose;
And sweet, after rest, is action,
  And, after action, repose.

But indolence, like the cow-bird,
  That's hatched in an alien nest,
Crowds out the native virtues,
  And soon usurps the breast.

Better the endless endeavor,
  The strong deed rushing on,
And Happiness that, ere we know her
  And name her, smiles and is gone!

III

We wait for the welling of waters
  That never pass the brink;
We pour our lives in the fountain,
  But cannot stay to drink.

"To-morrow," says Youthful Ardor,
  Twining the vine and the rose,
"I will couch in these braided bowers,
  As blithe as the breeze that blows."

"To-morrow," says earnest Manhood,
  Yet adding land to land,
"I will walk in the alleys of leisure,
  And rest from the work of my hand."

"To-morrow," says Age, still training
  The vine to the trembling wall,
Till the Dark sweeps down upon us,
  And the Shadow that swallows all.

IV

Ebb-tide chased by the flood-tide,
  Night by the dawn pursued,
And ever contentment hounded
  By fresh inquietude!

Not what we have done avails us,
  But what we do and are;
We turn from the deed that is setting,
  And steer for the rising star.

We may wreck our hearts in the voyage;
  But never shall sail or oar,
Nor wind of enchantment, waft us
  Nearer the longed-for shore.

In vain each past attainment;
  No sooner the port appears
Than the spirit, ever aspiring,
  Spreads sail for untried spheres.

Whatever region entices,
  Whatever siren sings,
Still onward beckons the phantom
  Of unaccomplished things.

HYMN OF THE AIR

NOURISHER and encloser of all life
Am I.   Before man was, or beast, or tree,
I in my wingèd chariot moved upon
The desolate, weltering waste that was the world,
And bade it fructify.   And life appeared;
Innumerable transitory forms
Limned and erased in each successive age,
Their early outlines lost, or later known
Traced in the rocky tablets of the globe.
Strange, wingless birds that tracked the baking sands;
Ophidian and amphibian, and the huge
Iguanodon, and mighty beasts that tore
Tall forests, pasturing on their succulent boughs;
These and their kind, emerging from the dim,
Slow-wakening, solitary, uncouth orb,
Stalked forth, — rude types of creatures yet to be; —
Rock-gnawing lichens that forerun the feet

Of violets; fungi watery and gross;
Mosses that build and belt the corpulent bog;
And tree-like ferns enormous from the moist
And steaming earth towered densely; them I fed
On carbon from my over-brimming cup,
Storing it in their veins for future man.

Nourisher and encloser of all life:
All things that creep or fly, and they that dwell
Within the dim inhabitable deep,
And herb and shrub, and all fair waving forms
Of verdure, but for my sustaining might,
My presence and sustaining might withdrawn,
Would fail in universal void : breath, flame,
And sense, and strength of foot, and power of flight.
The condor, circling high above his crags,
Circling securely in my azure realm,
Earthward with all his plumes would drop like lead.
And sound would cease, with voice of bird and beast;
The cataract in its plunge would make no noise;
The tumbling billow on the foamless beach
Would lapse in silence; even the waves would sink,
And all the bright seas to a ghastly film
Subside and shrivel, heaved by ghosts of tides.
Nor cloud would be, nor ever morning red,
Nor rains, nor rivers, nor the blessed dew.

About the seas I flow, an ampler sea,
Diaphanous and shoreless; earth my floor,
The mountain-chains my reefs; my surface waves,
Ethereal, tumbling high beneath the stars,
More silvery soft than aught but light itself,
And beautiful, could finite eyes behold,
But only spirits behold, whose radiant forms
Bathe in my almost spiritual flood.
Stupendous tides, to whose huge volume those
That ridge the broad-backed sea with sweeping swells
Are but as ripples, roll beneath the moon
Eternally, unchafed by any strand,
In unimaginable loneliness,

And silence broken by no sound save where
With fiery plash the raining meteors fall.

Far down, curved duly with the curving sphere,
The white clouds curdle, pierced by quiet crags;
With rifts that show the large plan of the world,
Oceans and continents and ice-capped poles,
Rivers and towns and crawling beasts and men.
Forever, high above those realms of change,
I take the sunshine on my crest, and bare
My pure, cold bosom to the moon and stars;
While at my feet the pictured seasons pass
In beauty, or amidst battling elements,
When clouds charge clouds and lightnings cross their swords,
And my wild skirts are fringed with flying storms.

I am the fountain of all winds that blow;
Parent of zephyrs and flower-scented gales,
Sweet as the breath of lovers when they kiss
Under vine-shadows on soft summer eves.

Ministers of a vast beneficence,
Forever on fleet errands to and fro
My breezes fly; beneath their glancing wings
Making the glad waves leap and clap their hands;
Wafting through sun and shadow round the curve
Innumerable fleets; fanning parched climes,
And purifying over-peopled towns;
Bearing in airy urns to thirsty lands
The copious exhalations of the sea,
To frozen realms the heat of torrid suns.

Yet trust me not, for I am changeable:
Oh! trust me not, for in my glassiest calms
Terror and fury couch, and tempest breeds.
My blue-roofed cavern is the nursing-place
Of rains and snows and hurricanes, the lair
Of young tornadoes and the whirlwind's whelps.

I am invisible, yet terrible.
All moods are mine. The fleets I waft, I smite.

In their mad whirling dance my dread cyclones,
Turbaned with thunder-clouds, in roaring robes
Gathering the uptorn seas and desert sands,
Darken and devastate the affrighted globe.

Eternal battlefield of cold and heat ;
Forever-swaying balance, reservoir
Of indestructible tumultuous force ;
Wafter of ships ; mother of fierce monsoons ;
Dispenser of the heavenly rain and dew ;
Purger of lands, physician of sick climes ;
Floating in peace the rosy evening cloud,
Or curled white cirrus of midsummer noons ;
Gentle or stern, in calm or tempest, I
Fulfil my manifold appointed use.

In my divine alembic I transmute
Death and the poisonous vapors of the world
Into fresh life and beauty.   Tribes of men,
Interminable processions, insect, brute,
The multitudinous tranquil race of plants,
All things that perish, in my chemic glass
Distil and change, exhale and disappear ;
The beauteous flower, and she more beautiful
Who lifts it from the stalk with loving hand ;
Tyrants and slaves, the eagle and the gnat,
Leviathan and python, lion and lamb :
I waste and mingle, I diffuse and blow
About the world their wandering elements,
To pour them forth anew in living forms.

Enfolder and disposer of all life
Am I : and yet not I.   Oh ! faithless man,
How canst thou feel my power and mystery,
And know the invisible force that clasps thee round,
And have in me thy being, and yet doubt
The Spirit whose similitude I am,
The Power that framed the world, and me, and thee ?

THE POET

A YOUTH there was, and his dwelling amid great wonders stood;
There laughed the verdurous valley, there gloomed the serious wood;
And round about were the voices of winds and of rushing streams;
And his days were drugged with illusions, his nights were drunken with
    dreams.

The years flew by, like the wild fowl, one by one, over the glen,
Till a man he was grown, gazed after by men and the daughters of
    men;
A bard in the midst of a people that trafficked and schemed and
    wrought,
They red with the sunlight of action, he pale with the moonlight of
    thought.

And many looked after and loved him, but wayward and rapt went he;
And blessed were his days, but ever he longed for better to be;
And fair and sweet were the maidens, but only the face of the gray,
Thin wraith, the bodiless moonshine, beside his pillow lay.

The strings of his lute never trembled to human joys and woes,
But told of the clouds and the flowers, and the love that no man knows:
He turned his song, as a Claude-glass, to image the shapes and gleams
That float in the Limbus of fancy, that drift in the Hades of dreams.

But once and again to his bedside a Vision of visions had come,
When the world was mantled in darkness, and all its voices were dumb,
Save only, afar in the forest, a moan and a glimmer of locks,
Where the lost brook wailed as it wandered, and beat its white breast on
    the rocks.

Then the chill dim space of his chamber unfolded and bloomed as a
    flower,
Filling with glory and fragrance the lonely and desolate hour;
Over his closed cold eyelids a breath moved, vital and warm,
And a soul came out of the fragrance, and out of the glory a form.

And in the still air of the heaven they made all around and above
Were eyes of ravishing brightness, a face of ineffable love;

From a forehead of snow flamed backward the hair's soft golden fire ;
And a voice, or the soul of a voice, said, " I am your heart's desire.

" Into life by the love of the sculptor a marble maiden was warmed ;
And out of your wish I was fashioned, and out of your faith I was
    formed.
The word I utter is only a pearl of your innermost thought ;
My wisdom, the deep-hidden treasure that up from your breast I have
    brought.

I am twin-born of your being : to every mortal is given
His angel, unseen, bending near him, as Earth is leaned over by
    Heaven ;
Both one, as the stem and the flower of the water-lily are one,
Below in the ooze and the shimmer, above in the azure and sun.

" I dwell in the life of the spirit, yet ever am close at your side ;
And I say to you, out of the stillness of light wherein I abide, —
O man ! in the midst of illusions, be ever alert to hear
The lisp of your Psyche, the whisper that breathes in the ear of your
    ear.

" O poet ! with doubt and denial vex not your mind overmuch :
They dull the delicate forces, the chords that respond to my touch.
The bounds of your metaphysics enclose but a sterile clod :
Waste not your thought upon thinking, nor dogmatize about God.

" And dwell no longer in dreamland, the realm of fable and fay ;
Await not the feast of To-morrow, but break the bread of To-day.
Pine not for the nymph Perfection, nor follow the glance of Pride ;
But beckon the helpful maiden, call Comfort to your side.

" Embody your pale ideals, and give to the dreams of youth,
With the form of art, which is beauty, the soul of art, which is truth.
And still, in the midst of illusions, be ever alert to hear
The word of your Psyche, the whisper that breathes in the ear of your
    ear.

" The angels are still descending that to the patriarch came ;
Just over each upturned forehead plays the celestial flame.

Above your doubts and repinings, the heavens are opened wide
To flood your life with the fulness of light wherein I abide.

"Within the trembling dewdrop, that toward the morning turns,
The world in little is mirrored, a whole creation burns;
And every heart that is lifted, and every soul that aspires,
Is a spark of the Infinite Spirit, a focus of heavenly fires."

The vision departed, and over the world's dim boundary rolled
The shining billow of daybreak, the surges of crimson and gold.
The wheels of traffic resounded, the blows of the builders rang,
Sweet maidens smiled in the doorways, and children shouted and sang.

The cry of the sibilant saw-mill rose vehement and loud,
The white mill-waters curdled, and fell like a falling cloud;
While afar on the misty lowland went flying the iron steed,
White-plumed, a phantom of beauty, swift-wheeled, a marvel of speed!

The Poet went forth, beholding the earth created new;
He bathed his brow in its freshness, he washed his heart in its dew;
He heard the chorus of farm-yards, the jubilee of the birds,
The far-away tinkle, the lowing of pasture-going herds.

He saw the lake all a-shiver with pictures of shores and trees,
Soft etchings of cloud and shadow, the mezzotint of the breeze;
And thinly ascending and curling, in clefts of the dark-green hills,
The smokes of embowered dwellings, like upward-winding rills.

He heard blithe sounds of labor blend with the brooks that ran,
The mighty rhythm of nature rhyme in the works of man;
And whether he roamed the woodland, or traversed the busy street,
He moved in a world of wonders, with miracles at his feet.

And he vowed, "I will rend as a garment the dream I have dreamed so
        long,
Put living men in my measures, this light and this land in my song;
For never was fabled country so fair as this I behold:
I dwell in a realm of enchantment, I live in an age of gold!"

AT MOUNT DESERT [1]

BAR HARBOR

I

PANOPLIED with crags and trees,
    And begirt
By blue islands in soft seas,
    Which invert
Idle yachts on glassy days, —
Who shall paint your purple bays,
Who can frame you in a phrase,
    Mount Desert ?

Beetling ledges and sublime
    Ocean swells ;
Caverns green with weeds and slime,
    Blue with shells ;
Isle of rest for weary lives,
Woodland walks and dusty drives,
Seaside villas and big hives
    Of hotels.

Rocks where dreamers half the day
    Sit inert ;
Where girls gossip and crochet,
Play lawn-tennis, and, they say,
    Sometimes flirt ;

[1] In this rhyme of Mount Desert the more common pronunciation of the name is adopted, with the anomalous accent on the final syllable, which appears to be a survival from the French, not very desirable ; while it is to be regretted that the full significance of the name given by the Voyageur Champlain to these " Islands of the Desolate Mountains " — *Isles des Monts Deserts* — could not have been preserved.

The bird which flits through the ninth stanza is the black guillemot, a Northern waterfowl, bearing sufficient resemblance to a pigeon to suggest its local name ; its nearly black plumage has a greenish tinge, with a conspicuous white spot on the wing. Its soft, plaintive whistle faintly suggests the note of the wood pewee. It frequents in great numbers some of the islands and crags of the far coast of Maine, where it breeds.

The harebell is scattered profusely almost everywhere along the cliffs ; its clusters are especially abundant and beautiful about Sol's Cliff, a ruggedly picturesque crag not far from Bar Harbor.

Place to read, or sketch, or row;
Town of hops and shops and show:
By these tokens tourists know
    Mount Desert.

Every morning sees a mile,
    Less or more,
Of strange vehicles defile
    By your door:
Choose one, mount, and bowl along
On a buckboard light and strong,
Lilting, tilting on its long
    Limber floor.

Or the dismal fog shuts down,
    Chill and gray;
Over harbor, coast and town,
Dismal, drizzling, it sweeps down,
    Day by day,
In interminable drifts,
Till some morning, lo, it lifts!
And again through ragged rifts
    Gleams the bay.

Sheeny vapors ride the air
    And the sea,
Touching, trailing, here and there,
Till each mountain seems to wear
    A toupee;
Or a scimiter of lace
Shears a headland from its base,
And leaves hanging there in space
    Rock and tree.

II

Quit the world of news and dress,
    Cards and calls!
To the vaulted wilderness,
    Which inwalls

Mossy chasms and tangled nooks!
Where the fleeing wood-nymph looks
From the veils of flashing brooks
    And swift falls.

Loose your snowy-pinioned skiff,
    Launch in space!
Or explore with me this cliff,
    From its face,
Which the wind and surges fret,
Past the plumèd parapet,
Where no touch of man has yet
    Left a trace.

As you scale the splintered jag
    Toward the sky,—
As you pass the jutting jag,
The sea-pigeons on the crag
    Downward fly;
From the swells not far remote,
Where the pied flock sits afloat,
Comes their softly whistled note,
    Like a sigh.

Slim against the fringy line
    Of the firs,
The outleaning birches shine;
There the tresses of the pine;
    The wind stirs
The green-tufted tamarack;
And the cedars, bristling black,
In the mountain's craggy back
    Strike their spurs.

You may search the woods in vain,
    Everywhere,
For the lonely thrush, whose strain
    Fills the air.
Here the shy bunchberries house,
Where blue-tinted balsam boughs
Weave a covert for the grouse
    And the hare.

III

The white-throated sparrow sings
    In the trees.
Tint of mosses, glint of wings,
Oh, the thousand lovely things
    That one sees!
Loveliest, frailest, of them all
Are these wild flowers, blue and small,
Wavering on the bleak sea-wall
    In the breeze.

Find a foothold in the ledge,
    There they spring;
On its utmost dizzy edge,
    There they cling;
Where there's room for tuft to grow
In the crevices below,
While waves dash and tempests blow,
    There they swing!

Little Ariels that perform
    Their pure part
In rude scenes of strife and storm,
    They upstart
From gray cleft and scanty mould.
So late flowers of love unfold,
Sweet relentings, in some old,
    Rugged heart.

Region where the harebell blows,
    Wave-begirt!
Let the season's round of shows,
    Which divert
Careless eyes in yonder town,
Justify your fair renown;
But these flowers shall be your crown,
    Mount Desert!

By what magic, out of air,
    Do they spin, —
Out of sunlight, dew, and air,

The slight bonnets that they wear,
        Blue and thin?
Children of the rock and sky!
Little people, you and I
Surely by some mystic tie
        Are akin.

Huddled here in pleasant flocks
        On the verge,
Nodding hoods and fluttering locks,
Half-way down the rifted rocks
        That emerge
From the billows tumbling white,
Do you feel a fine delight
In the breezes and the bright
        Bursting surge?

Larger cousins of these meek,
        Tiny elves!
Belles of Mount Desert, who seek
Your sweet namesakes on the bleak
        Crannied shelves;
Following far the lovely lures, —
Dainty relatives of yours,
Little charming miniatures
        Of yourselves! —

Cull them here betwixt the brink
        And the foam!
Choose a cluster by the brink,
Lift them gently from their chink,
        Bear them home, —
Every flower a fairy vase
Brimmed with light of breezy bays
In each bell the summer day's
        Azure dome!

To the city's footworn flags
        They will bring
Winds and voices of these crags,
        Where they cling,

Leaping surf and leaning trees,
Cool, bright hours of joyous ease,
And green islands in the sea's
    Shining ring.

THE BELL–BUOY AT MOUNT DESERT

SOUTHWEST HARBOR

I

AT the gateway of the bay,
    On the currents that come and go,
    The bell-buoy heaves and swings.
Forever seeming to say :
    " Woe ! woe ! " to the mariner, " woe !
Beware of the reefs below ! "
To and fro, to and fro,
    The bell-buoy rocks and rings.

In calm or storm, through all
    The changes of night and day,
    Blithe sun or blinding spray,
        With the wail of the winds that blow,
        With the moan of the ebb and flow,
While the billows swell and fall,
Goes forth that warning call —
    Night and day, night and day,
Peals forth the mournful knell
Of that iron sentinel,
Of the wave-swung, warning bell,
    At the gateway of the bay.

Where the granite-snouted ledges
    Lurk in their pimpled hides,
        Scraggy with whelks and bosses,
        And shaggy with black sea-mosses,
Just showing the tawny edges
    Of their backs in the burying tides,
Shouldering off the foam ;

Where they lie in wait to gore
With their terrible tusks the sides
Of the fair ship flying home;
There the bowing bell-buoy rides,
With a dull reverberant roar
Evermore, evermore
Crying: "Woe!" to the mariner, "woe!
Beware of the rocks below!
Beware of the treacherous shore!"

II

At evening, from your boat,
You may see the sombre bell
In its black and massy frame,
Peered through by the sunset flame;
A solemn silhouette,
In a skeleton turret, set
On the balanced and anchored float,
A-swing with the crimson swell.

When the soft, slumberous haze
Of drowsy midsummer days
Pours around inlets and bays
A glassy ethereal gleam;
And over far isles and sails
Drop violet veils beyond veils,
Till headland and cliff but seem
The unreal shapes of a dream;
When hardly the loon and gull,
In the lap of the languid lull,
Appear to waver and dip:
Then the buoy sways, heavy and slow,
And the bell tolls, sad and low,
Like the bell of a sunken ship,
That heaves with the heaving hull,
Wave-rocked on the reefs below.

At times to the dreamy eye,
In the glamour of glistening weather
That girdles the sea and sky,

While ocean and island lie
   Like a lion and lamb together :
When the billow that bursts its sheaf
Of silver over the reef
   Falls light and white as a feather,
Curled all the length of the reef ;
Then the bell, like a darker plume,
Nods over the downy spume
   In the veiled voluptuous weather.

At times so gently stirred,
   It seems like a waving bough
To invite the wandering bird.
At intervals still is heard
   That sullen note — as now ! —
Clanging its mournful and lone
Perpetual monotone.

III

A dismal, dolorous sound,
   You would say, heard anywhere,
   Be the weather foul or fair !
Not so to the homeward-bound
Late crew from the fishing-ground,
   Some muffled and murky night ;
Or the steamer heaving her lead
And groping in doubt and dread,
   Through drizzle and fog, by the light
Of her lantern eyes, which shed
A misty glare at her head ;
   Reaching out quivering rays,
   Antennæ-like, in the haze,
To find her dubious way.
   To the pilot's practised ear
      In such dark and anxious times,
That peal, as I have heard say,
   Signaling, sudden and clear,
   The course which he shall steer,
   Is a cheerier sound to hear
      Than sweetest belfry chimes.

But when, on this border-realm
Of created things, once more
The powers of chaos outpour
Their legions, and overwhelm
    With darkness and dire uproar,
    In their mad foray, this fair
    Frontier of created things ;
When they scatter the fishing-fleet
And stun the shore with the beat
    And buffet of billowy wings,
And trample of thunderous feet —
What life, out there in the surges,
    Flings frantic arms in air
As it tosses and sinks and emerges —
    Beckons with wild despair,
        And tongues that doleful peal ?
Now loud in the leaping surges,
    Now stifled with wind and wave.
No simple device of good
Stout metal and bolted wood,
        But surely a thing that can feel,
    And strong in its struggle to save
        The shoreward driving keel !
Boom ! boom ! boom !
Out of the horror of gloom
A sound of dolor and doom
        To the helmsman at the wheel.

IV

The seasons come and go,
    And still in storm or calm,
    On the ocean's palpitant palm,
        The bell-buoy rocks and rolls.
The summers come and go,
And, mantled in whirling snow,
Ice-capped, amid foam and floe,
        The bell-buoy tumbles and tolls.
To and fro, loud or low,
    Ever that sound of fear !
    You listen and seem to hear

A voice, as of some wild seer,
  A cry and a warning to souls
  Over life's treacherous shoals.

THE CABIN

READ AT THE CLAFLIN GARDEN PARTY GIVEN TO MRS. H. B. STOWE, IN
CELEBRATION OF HER SEVENTIETH BIRTHDAY, JUNE 14, 1882

GENIUS, 't is said, knows not itself,
  But works unconscious wholly.
Even so she wrought, who built in thought
  The Cabin of the Lowly.

A wife with common wifely cares,
  What mighty dreams enwrapt her!
What fancies burned, until she turned
  To write some flaming chapter!

Her life was like some quiet bridge,
  Impetuous tides sweep under.
So week by week the story grew,
  From wonder on to wonder.

Wisdom could not conceive the plot,
  Nor wit and fancy spin it;
The woman's part, the wife's deep heart,
  All mother's love, were in it.

Hatred of tyranny and wrong,
  Compassion sweet and holy,
Sorrow and Guilt and Terror built
  That Cabin of the Lowly.

And in the morning light, behold,
  By some divine mutation,
Its roof became a sky of flame,
  A portent to the nation!

The Slave went forth through all the earth,
  He preached to priest and rabbin;

He spoke all tongues ; in every land
   Opened that lowly Cabin.

Anon a school for kinder rule,
   For freer thoughts and manners ;
Then from its door what armies pour
   With bayonets and banners !

More potent still than fires that kill,
   Or logic that convinces,
The tale she told to high and low,
   To peasants and to princes.

That tale belongs with Freedom's songs,
   The hero's high endeavor,
And all brave deeds that serve the needs
   Of Liberty forever !

I greet her now, when South and North
   Have ceased their deadly quarrels ;
And say, or sing, while here I fling
   This leaf upon her laurels : —

She loosed the rivets of the slave ;
   She likewise lifted woman,
And proved her right to share with man
   All labors pure and human.

Women, they say, must yield, obey,
   Rear children, dance cotillions :
While this one wrote, she cast the vote
   Of unenfranchised millions !

ODE

READ AT THE DEDICATION OF THE SOLDIERS' MONUMENT AT ARLING-
TON, MASS., JUNE 17, 1887

LIKE Peace itself, as calm and fair, —
   White flower from battle-furrows grown,
   Its beauty blossomed into stone, —
Stands this still shaft in this June air !

Long may the heavens upon it shed
  The dews of eve, the beams of morn,
  And light, for ages yet unborn,
The deeds of our heroic dead!

They kept their country's faith, and fought
  The New World's promise to fulfil, —
  To hold, and leave unbroken still,
The ring of States the fathers wrought.

As cheerfully each artisan,
  In some great work, performs his part,
  Though knowing not the Master's art
And purpose, in the perfect plan; —

So they, alike the sires and sons,
  Toiled at one pattern, one divine,
  Inscrutable, and vast design,
Which through a nation's fabric runs.

They strove, at duty's high behest,
  For liberty and equal laws;
  And in so striving served a cause
Whose grander scope they dimly guessed.

We ask not of their birth, nor need
  The story of their years be sung;
  Who die for truth are always young,
And dear in their immortal deed.

Life at the best is brief, and wrong
  Is evermore to face and quell;
  They who have done their duty well,
They only, have lived well and long.

Oh! blessed are they whose troubled days
  Are nobly rounded, to our eyes,
  By some large act of sacrifice,
Beyond all earthly blame or praise.

No more shall cold detraction come
    To search their lives, nor fortune fret;
    The book is closed, and on it set
The sacred seal of martyrdom.

Friends, living comrades, gather round!
    And wave, ye winds, oh! gently wave
    The flag they loved and died to save,
Above our consecrated ground.

To them this fair memorial stone
    We raise, to be henceforth a sign
    Of patriot's zeal, and Freedom's shrine;
And Fame adopts them for her own.

AFTER THE CONCERT

JOSEF HOFMANN, PIANIST AND COMPOSER, AGED 10

THE tempest of applause he met
    As meekly as a bending bud!
A boy of humble birth, and yet
    A prince of more than royal blood.

For him no bauble handed down,
    No sceptre despot ever bore,
But Music's heavenly realm, the crown
    Which youthful Handel won and wore!

How laughed the *Allegro's* gay disdain, —
    What rippling pearly melodies
Showered on us their enchanted rain, —
    When his small fingers swept the keys!

They leaped, they flew, they flashed through all
    The jubilant chords; or dropped, in play,
As carelessly as petals fall
    From cherry-boughs in breezy May.

He tossed us Schumann's sparkling airs;
  Struck Rubinstein's sweet storms of tone:
We followed, up the starry stairs,
  The shining feet of Mendelssohn.

He wove, around an untried theme,
  So varied and so blithe a strain,
It wrapt us in a radiant dream
  Of little Wolfgang come again.

The very roof with plaudits shook;
  And still, above their bursting flood,
The thunder and the gusts he took
  As simply as a swaying bud.

Ah, could he know, the wondrous boy!
  When he had vanished from our gaze,
What tearful yearnings veiled our joy,
  What prayers were mingled with our praise!

We longed to shield him from the gales
  Of coming time; to lay his head
In lulling arms, and tell him tales,
  And fold him in his quiet bed.

Waste not too soon, O burning star!
  Your bright young life; but nurse its beam,
That it may rise and light afar
  The world's unresting, troubled stream.

Heaven fend, from that too ardent heart,
  The griefs of great and gifted men,
The sordid miseries of Mozart,
  The woes of mighty Beethoven.

Heir to a throne unstained by wrong,
  Possess your sphere, unvexed by strife;
Conquer new realms, rule well and long,
  Nor lose the deeper things of life.

The unsullied ray that guides the soul
    Is more than glory's blinding flame;
And helpful manhood, sound and whole,
    Than all the works of art and fame.

January, 1888.

QUATRAINS AND EPIGRAMS

ABRAHAM LINCOLN

HEROIC soul, in homely garb half hid,
    Sincere, sagacious, melancholy, quaint,
What he endured, no less than what he did,
    Has reared his monument and crowned him saint.

TEMPTATION

HOW sweet, till past, then hideous evermore!
    Like that false fay the legend tells us of,
That seemed a lovely woman, viewed before,
    But, from behind, all hollow, like a trough.

PHAETON

HOT youth, in haste your high career to run,
Heed the wise counsel Phœbus gave his son,
And spare the whip! brace the firm reins with nerve,
Nor ever from the middle pathway swerve.

MATERIALIST

HE took a tawny handful from the strand:
" What we can grasp," he said, " we understand,
    And nothing more:" when, lo! the laughing sand
Slid swiftly from his vainly clutching hand.

IDEALIST

THE World is but a frozen kind of gas,
A transient ice we sport on, where, alas!
Diverted by the pictures in the glass,
We heed not the Realities that pass.

SENSUALIST

"Live while we live!" he cried; but did not guess,
Fooled by the phantom, Pleasure, how much less
Enjoyment runs in rivers of excess
Than overbrims divine abstemiousness.

YEARS AND ART

Youth strikes a skill-less blow, but the metal is all aglow;
Age has the experienced hand, but the fire in the forge is low.

HOW CAN I WELCOME AGE?

How can I welcome age, or behold without dismay
The beautiful days go by and the great years glide away?
Lightly I hold the world, but I look upon children and wife,
And though I dread not death, they make me in love with life.

AN ODIOUS COMPARISON

When to my haughty spirit I rehearse
        My verse,
Faulty enough it seems; yet sometimes when
I measure it by that of other men,
        Why, then —
I see how easily it might be worse.

DIDACTIC POET

Poet! you do your genius wrong
    By always reaching
For some deep lesson, spoil your song
    By too much teaching.

Let brighter beauty, rising love,
    Just hint your moral,
As whitening surges break above
    The reef of coral.

IMPROVISATORE

Fused in the fires of passion, in the fervor of fancy wrought,
In reason's ice-brook temper the flaming sword of your thought.

XAVIER DE MAISTRE'S EPITAPH ON HIMSELF

FROM THE FRENCH

HERE lies, beneath this cold gray stone,
　　Xavier, whom all things filled with wonder;
Who sought to know whence the winds blow,
　　And how and why Jove rolls the thunder.

He many a book of magic prized,
　　And read from morn till evening's fall,
And drank death's wave at last, surprised
　　That he knew nothing after all!

BON VOYAGE!

FOR THE FAREWELL BANQUET TO F. H. U., BEFORE HIS DEPARTURE FOR GLASGOW

WHEN to the land of Scott and Burns,
　　Bannocks and haggis, classic dishes!
Our friend departs, he takes our hearts
　　Along with him, in all good wishes.

May these attend, a viewless throng,
　　To guard the ship that bears him over!
No fog delay, nor storm, but may
　　Kind fortune be his constant lover.

If tempests smite the wild seas white,
　　And Titan billows reel and totter,
Let never plank go down with Frank,
　　Nor Underwood be under water!

WIDOW BROWN'S CHRISTMAS

HIS window is over the factory flume;
And Elkanah there, in his counting-room,
　　Sits hugging a littered table.
His beard is white as the foam, and his cheek
Is weather-beaten and withered and bleak
　　As the old brown factory gable.

Christmas is near; and he, it is clear,
Is squaring accounts with the parting year;
Setting forth, in column and row,
Whatever a penny of gain can show —
Mortgages, dividends, and rents,
City bonds and gover'ments;
A factory here and a tannery there,
Good bank stock and railroad share; —
As fast as his busy brain can count,
    Or his busy pen indite 'em,
Figuring profit and gross amount,
    And adding item to item.
Thinks he: "It 's a good round sum I make;
Don't seem much like I was goin' to break!"
    And he looked again as he poised his pen
    To fillip the drop of ink off.
But just as he gave the pen a shake,
He said "Ho! ho!" at a strange mistake
    He found himself on the brink of:
He said "Ha! ha!" and his lips drew in
With a hard, dry, leathery kind of grin,
    As much like the smile of a crocodile
    As anything you can think of.

"I declare! there 's Widder Brown
In the cottage over in Tannery Town!
The family had the house rent free
As long as her husband worked for me.
A good, smart, faithful chap was Jim —
Wish I had forty as good as him!
But he died one day, and left her there;
And I put the place in the parson's care —
For the only man in the town I dare
    To trust is Parson Emery,
To see that the house don't run away,
And collect the rent she agreed to pay.
I 'll write a letter this very day,
    To jog the good man's memory."

The letter was straightway penned and sent;
And it preached hard times to a dreary extent:

"For money is tight at ten per cent. ;
Often no sooner got than spent;
The poor man finds it a heavy stent
    To earn his mess of pottage ;
And so," concluded the argument,
"You may, if you please, remit the rent
    Jim's widder owes for the cottage."

In two days' time the answer came.
"The parson is prompt.   But — what in the name! "
He cried as he opened and read the same :
    How extremely odd it sounded!
"Dear, noble, generous, honored friend " —
Were terms he could n't well comprehend ;
And when he had struggled on to the end,
    He was utterly astounded.

He gasped and gurgled, and then burst out:
"What 'n thunder 's the ol' fool ravin' about ?
He 's crazy, without a shadder o' doubt !
    A-writin' to me as if I was a saint !
Wa'al, mabby I be, and then mabby I ain't.
An' what 's his argyment ? why, to be sure,
That I am a marciful man to the poor,
    An' feel for the sufferin' brother,
An' stay the widder whose staff is gone ;
An' so he continners a-layin' it on,
    An' he ain't sarcastical, nuther !

"Blamed ol' blunderhead ! could n't he see
'T the poor I was marciful tu meant me ?
But here he goes on, in a gushin' mood,
To tell o' the woman's gratitude,
Because I 've been so exceedingly good
    As to pity her sad condition,
An' give him the blessed authority tu
Remit — remit — the rent that is due.
Why don't he remit, then ? wish I knew !
'Stid o' that, here 's more of his hullabalew,
    To thank me for the remission !

"Remission — remit — oh, drat the dunce!"
   And he rushed for a dictionary;
It having occurred to him all at once
   That the meanings sometimes vary
Of even the simplest words we write;
And that a prosy old parson might
Use one, and a man of business quite
   Another, vocabulary.
Finger and eye ran down the page:
"R, a — R, e" — he was flushed with rage:
"Remember — Remind — Remit!" — at last
The terrible talon had it fast,
With the definition against it set:
"Send back," he read; but, lower yet,
"To release, to forgive, as a sin or a debt!"
Ah, through that mesh in the treacherous net
   Had slipped the widow's pittance!
'T was so! 't was strange! 't was very absurd,
That thus from a phrase, or a single word,
With equal reason could be inferred
   Collection of debt or quittance!
Words have their forks, like highways, whence
To left and right run the roads of sense;
And, taking the wrong derivative,
The heedless old parson had come to give
   Remission instead of remittance.

Elkanah glared for a moment, and then,
With a snort at the book, and a scoff at the men
Who invented the language, seized his pen,
Tore one letter, and wrote again,
   Protruding his chin, while the hard dry grin
   Grew terribly savage and sinister;
Till, too impatient to brook delay,
He quite forgot it was Christmas-day,
Swung on his ulster, and swooped away
   Toward Tannery Town and the Widow Brown
   And the good old blundering minister.

As out by the forenoon train he went,
   He had ample time to consider:

"To be soft-soaped to sich an extent —
    Cracked up like a spavined hoss that 's meant
        To be sold to the highest bidder —
    It 's pooty dumbed rough on a plain old gent
    That never was known to give a cent,
    Say nothin' o' seventy dollars' rent,
        To anybody's widder!
An' I ain't one o' the kind that cares
To be boosted up in a woman's prayers
        Fer a favor I never did her.

"Yet she might pray fer me all her days,
    An' I would n't object to the parson's praise,
        That he spreads so thick in his letter;
    But though he believes it himself, and though
    Other folks may think it 's all jes' so,
        The plague is, I know better!
He 'll wonder what sort of a beast I be,
When I tell him square out how it seemed to me,
What a blamed, ridickelous, fool's idee,
        That I should forgive a debtor!"

Quick moist flushes, strange hot streaks,
Shot down to his shins and up to his cheeks.
He loosened his collar, and wondered what
In time made 'em keep the cars so hot.
Still, as he thought of the interview
He was going to seek, the warmer he grew.
And he said to himself, with a leer, "Must be
I 'm fond of parsons' s'ciety!
Fer what else under the canopy
I 'm makin' the trip fer, I can't see;
Sence a letter or tu would as soon undu
        The snarl he 's got me inter,
Save railroad fare, an' the wear an' tear
        Of a journey in midwinter.

"It 's an awk'ard mess, I du declare!
The widder she 'll cry, an' the parson he 'll stare,
An' like enough somebody else will swear —

Wish I was back in my office chair!
Fer why should I go twelve mile or so
       An' lose my time an' my dinner,
To prove to their face, beyond a doubt,
'T I ain't no saint, as they make out,
       But a hardened sort of a sinner?"

Some such thoughts perplexed his brain,
As up to the station rolled the train,
With slackening speed and brakes screwed down,
And the brakeman bawled out, "Tannery Town!"
"Wa'al, here I be!" With a gathering frown
And firm-set teeth, old Elkanah straight
Took his way to the parson's gate;
No longer inclined to turn about,
       In a flurry of confusion,
But grimly resolved to carry out
       His original resolution.
Though, after all, he approached the spot,
Outwardly cold and inwardly hot,
As a brave man goes to be hanged or shot,
Or whatever else he thinks is not
       The thing for his constitution.
And when this answer he received,
"Parson ain't to hum" — will it be believed?
He felt like the very same man reprieved
       At the moment of execution.

Wa'al, no, he would n't go in and wait;
He stood in the snow at the parsonage gate:
No train back till half-past one,
And the village bells had just begun
To ring for noon: for a minute or two
He stood, uncertain what to do,
Looking doubtfully up and down
The dreary streets of Tannery Town,
And thought of his money and Mrs. Brown:
       Then this is what he did do —
He turned his feet up the snowy street,
       And went to call on the widow.

'T was Christmas time, as I said before;
And when, arrived at the cottage door,
　　He reached for the old bell handle,
He paused a moment, amazed and grim,
For he heard such a racket as seemed to him,
In the home of the late lamented Jim,
　　Sufficient cause for scandal.

A short, sharp ring: then a hurried noise
Of whispering, scampering girls and boys;
And the door was opened a little space,
Through which peered out, with a bashful grace,
　　A surprisingly pretty-looking,
Timidly smiling, bright young blonde;
And Elkanah caught, from the room beyond,
　　A savory sniff, a wonderful whiff,
　　Of most delicious cooking.

He sees a table, with neat cloth spread,
Steaming dishes, and cream-white bread;
Cranberry sauce, and thick squash pies;
And the curly brown pates and wondering eyes
　　Of the imps that had made the clatter;
Then the mother just bringing in, to crown
Her banquet, a beautiful, golden-brown,
　　Great roasted goose on a platter.

A crabbed old man, to whom the sight
Of happy children gave small delight;
A hungry man, who had come so far
To a feast his presence could only mar;
　　An iron-fisted miser,
Who would seldom afford himself a fat,
Delectable Christmas goose like that,
Or indulge in anything half so good —
Confronting the widow, there he stood,
　　Just showing one grim incisor;
And it certainly seemed that his presence would —
　　To say the least — surprise her.

For he said to himself, "Her means are spent,
An' she has n't a penny to pay her rent!
    While this is the way she gorges
Her ravenous tribe on the fat of the land.
I 'll let her know that I understand
    Whose money pays fer the orgies!"

But, seeing the old man standing there,
The widow, seemingly unaware
    Of his brow's severe contraction;
Perceiving only his thin white hair,
And his almost venerable air,
Wiped her fingers, and placed a chair,
    With a charmingly natural action;
Welcoming him with never a trace
Of guile in her smiling and grateful face;
Accounting this visit the crowning grace
    Of his noble benefaction.

"Oh, sir!" she began, "I am glad you are here" —
With a quivering lip and a starting tear —
"To see what happiness" (this was gall
    To the stingy old wretch) "you have given us all!
Since you were so good" — "Not I," he cried;
"I never was good!" But she replied,
    With gentle, sweet insistence:
"It seems but a trifle to you, no doubt;
Such kindness as yours" — Here he burst out,
"I tell ye, woman, ye 're talkin' about
    A thing that has no existence."

"Ah, you may say that, since you have shown
A goodness you are too good to own!
But I could never, with what I know,
Permit another to wrong you so."
Then up spoke one of the younger crew:
"Ye may bet yer dollars on that! it 's true;
For only yesterday, I tell you,
    Was n't she in high dudgeon,
Just hearing you called by Deacon Shaw

The keenest old skinflint ever he saw!
He said he would sooner have hoped to draw
Sap from a hatchet or blood from a straw,
Than money that was n't allowed by law,
　　From such an old curmudgeon.

"Well, what have I said?"　"Hush, Jamie, hush!"
　Cries the mother, in consternation;
　While Elkanah starts, with an angry flush
　　And a vigorous exclamation.
"Did he say that? — say that of me?
He 's tighter himself than the bark of a tree."
"He has more heart than he lets folks see:
A little like you in that," says she.
"Ho! ho! wa'al, wa'al! that 's a queer idee!
　That 's a curi's ca'calation!"

"But he, when at last he understood
　What a friend you had been, how exceedingly good,
　To my poor orphans," she went on,
"And me — for the sake of him that is gone —
He was humbled; he took it quite to heart;
Declared you had acted a noble part,
　　And expressed sincere repentance
　For having misjudged you so till now.
　But your example" — "Example! I vow,
Mis' Brown," snarls Elkanah; but somehow
　He could n't complete the sentence.

"Your Christian example!" the widow cries,
"Who wants proof of it? there it lies" —
　With a glance of pride at the great squash pies,
　　And the goose superbly basted.
"The deacon was here at half-past one;
And at half-past two the proof had begun:
The goose was brought by the deacon's son,
And then it seemed as if every one
　Must do as the deacon and you had done."
"Yes, sir," says Jamie; "and was n't it fun!
It was ring, ring, ring! it was run, run, run!

Squashes that weighed pretty nigh a ton!
 Such apples you never tasted!"
"It came to us in our sorest need,"
The widow resumed; "and all are agreed
'T was a harvest of which you sowed the seed.
You see your charity was, indeed,
 An example that was n't wasted."

"My charity!" Elkanah groaned. "Well, well!"
"'T was more of a blessing than I can tell;"—
She choked a little and wiped a tear—
"For we have been dreadfully poor this year.
'T is a hard, hard struggle to provide
For my five little ones since he died.
Faithfully, every day, I meant
To save a little to pay my rent;
I stinted and planned, but still I found,
As often as Saturday night came round,
I had spared, when they were patched and fed,
Hardly enough for Sunday's bread.
Such constant weariness, want, and care
Seemed often more than a life could bear.
Then came, oh! sir, your gracious gift,
Which all of a sudden seemed to lift
The burden that weighed me to the ground;
And all these other good friends came round;
And so, in our joy and thankfulness,
It seemed to me I could do no less
Than make a feast," she said with a smile.
"Be patient! be quiet!" For all the while
 The hungry children clamored,
And climbed the chairs, and peeped at the pies,
And ogled the goose with wistful eyes.
"'T is a favor," said she, "I should greatly prize,
If you would sit by, and not despise
The bounty which Heaven through you supplies."
"Hem! wa'al! ye take me by surprise.
 Don't know," the old man stammered.

She smilingly reached for his coat and hat,
And the goose was fragrant, the goose was fat!

" I think you will stay." " Wa'al, as to that,
    I don't dine out very often;
I called to explain — but never mind.
Fact is, Mis' Brown, I have n't dined;
And if you insist — sence you air so kind " —
He was rather surprised himself to find
    His heart beginning to soften.

" Don't care 'f I du." And down he sat.
The goose was fragrant, the goose was fat !
    The old man did the carving;
The sauce was dished, the gravy poured,
And the plates all round that little board
Were filled in a manner that did n't afford
    The slightest hint of starving.

Not in all that dreary year
Had her cottage known such cheer.
With hope, and her happy children near,
    The widow smiled contented.
Even old Elkanah ceased to be
Greatly scandalized to see
Cheerful faces and childish glee
    In the home of the late lamented.

Nature's ways are wise and kind :
Clouds pass, dawn breaks, and ever behind
Each dark sea hollow swells a wave ;
And fresh grass grows on the new-made grave ;
And softly over the broken heart,
    And its sorrowful recollections,
The leaves of another hope will start,
    And tender new affections.

The widow talked and told her plans :
What a dutiful child was Nance !
The parson had got her boys a chance
To blow the organ the coming year :
" So there will be twenty dollars clear !

The girls will help me more and more;
I 'll sew; and often, as heretofore,
Earn bread for the morrow while they sleep;
And so I have hopes that I yet may keep
    My little flock together —
With Heaven so kind and friends so good —
Send them to school, and provide them food
    And shelter from the weather.

" But oh! what a change for them and me;
How different now it all would be,
If my dear husband " — Mrs. Brown
Here, for some reason, quite broke down;
And even old Elkanah's sight grew weak.
You might have observed in his withered cheek
    Some unaccustomed twitches,
And in his voice, when he tried to speak,
    Some very unusual hitches;
For, seeing how long she yet must strain
Her utmost energies, just to gain
Bread for her babes — perhaps in vain —
He had some twinges of shame and pain,
And a curious feeling I can't explain,
    At the thought of his hoarded riches.

" Hem! wa'al, Mis' Brown! it 's a pooty tough case! "
He made a motion as if to place
His hand in his pocket, but drew it back.
" Though I must say, you 've got a knack!
You 're gettin' along, an' I 'm dreffle glad!
No more, no, thank'ee, ma'am! I hain't had
Sich a dinner as this, I don't know when! "
Down went the uncertain hand again.
    " Your children are well, an' growin';
Few years, your boys 'll be rich men —
    Mabby they will, no knowin'."
He merely pushed back his empty plate,
Then tugged at his watch. " Ha! is it so late?
I 'd no idee on't! train won't wait;
    Guess I 'll haf to be goin'! "

"Must you, indeed!   How the time has flown!"
The lonely old man had never known
So grateful a soul, a look and tone
     So gentle and so caressing;
And while she handed his hat and coat,
Arranged the collar about his throat,
Smoothed the creases, and brushed his arm,
He felt a strange, bewildering charm,
The very touch of her hand shed such
     Unconscious love and blessing!

"I thought there was something he came to say,
To explain!" cries Jamie.   "Ah, yes! by the way!"
     Says Elkanah, slightly flurried;
"A leetle mistake — but that's all right!
The parson, he did n't take in, not quite,
My full intent regardin' the rent:
     Don't be the least mite worried
'Bout that fer sartin another year. —
Bless me! I b'lieve it's the train I hear!
     Good-day!"   And off he hurried.

He seemed surrounded and pursued
By spirits of joy and gratitude!
And he said to himself, "I must conclude,
Although the ol' parson wa'n't very shrewd,
     'T was a lucky mistake o' his'n!"
And he felt some most surprising things,
Strange perturbations and flutterings,
As of something within him spreading wings —
     The angel within, new-risen!

"I'm beat if there ain't the parson now!"
With eager stride and radiant brow
The minister crossed a steep by-street,
Through ridges of snow leg-deep, to greet
The friend of the widow and fatherless,
Who growled to himself, "Good thing, I guess,
Fer some of the fatherless folks we know,
Me and him did n't meet an hour ago —
     Good thing all round, should n't wonder!"

The parson came panting up the hill,
Hands out, with a greeting of warm good-will ;
All smiles ; serenely unconscious still
    Of his most amazing blunder.

A soul as simple as rills that run
Joyous and clear in the summer sun !
Not one who had chosen his work, but one
    The Lord Himself had chosen;
A child of faith, and a shepherd indeed ;
Not one of those whose formal creed
Has the tinkling sound and the hollow look
Of ice left over a shrunken brook —
Shrunken away from the living day,
    Leaving its surface frozen.

Under the leafless village elms
The parson waylays and overwhelms
    With more felicitation
Of the late epistolary sort
The impatient old man, who cuts him short
    With a quaint gesticulation.

"No more o' that, please understand !
    I 've seen Jim's widder." This time the hand
Dives into the pocket, and brings out
A bright bank-note : " Guess the' ain't no doubt
But what we 'd oughter give her a lift ;
An' here 's a trifle, a Christmas gift,
    I was pooty nigh fergittin'.
Remit her rent the comin' year ;
And I 'd like to remit to her now this 'ere.
By the way ! " drawls he, with a sidelong leer,
" Did j' ever notice — it 's kind o' queer —
    There 's tew ways o' remittin' ? "

NEWLY GATHERED LEAVES

EVENING AT NAPLES

I

THE day went down, beneath an amber sky,
  On all the wonders of that magic land :
There, an old crater's burnt-out Cyclops eye :
  Here, Virgil paced in thought the curving strand.

On shores and cities glowed the late, low sun ;
  On plumed Vesuvius mirrored in the wave ;
And faintly flushed the wan-ribbed skeleton,
  Pompeii standing in her open grave.

On plume and peak the parting sunset flame
  Lingered, diffused, an upward-fading gleam.
Capri, remote on the rimmed sea, became
  A roseate mist and melted into dream.

The soft sirocco, from hot Afric sands
  Blowing all day across the Midland Deep,
Sank with the sun upon the empurpled lands,
  With all its Libyan languors lulled asleep.

II

I stood at evening on a terraced height
  And viewed the wondrous world, city and sea,
Sails softly wafted on pale bands of light,
  Or to still moorings drifting dreamily.

The goat-bells' tinkling ceased upon the air ;
  The human tide's interminable roar
Rose, a dull murmur, to my terrace stair,
  The sullen thunder of a lone, low shore.

Garden and villa and curved parapet
  Darkened around me ; myriad-roofed, far down
The mountain-slopes, where coast and mountain met,
  Gloomy and vast and slumberous, spread the town.

III

As night drew on, unnumbered gleams appeared;
  Where lanterned ships on lanterned shadows lay;
By distant coasts; and where Vesuvius reared
  His tawny torch above the clouded Bay;

The lighthouse bursting into sudden blaze,
  Flashing its spear of beams across the sea;
The broad Riviera's constellated rays;
  And all the city's starred immensity.

By day unseen, the crater's spectral light
  Increased and reddened, far aloof and lone;
The vulture cloud abroad on the still night
  Spread balanced wings, perched on the flickering cone.

Unseen by day, that dull portentous glow,
  A pulsing core of fire that climbed and fell,
Illumed the murk, — mysterious, veiled, and slow, —
  Dim flashes from the throbbing throat of hell.

The upheaved cloud, with windless folds wide flung,
  Huge as the mountain's double, piled in space,
Poised peak on peak miraculously hung,
  Burying the stars in its inverted base.

IV

Anon from the snow-muffled Apennines,
  Fitful at first, a rushing wind came forth
And whirled about me, clashing boughs and vines,
  Keen as a gust from my own native North.

Over the city roofs and courts it played;
  With wafts of most delicious coolness blessed
The stifled streets; and, swelling seaward, swayed
  The pillared cloud on the volcano's crest.

As if a bodiless power with wings of air
  Closed with the phantom, scattered and dislimned
The towering shape, and swept the Orient bare,
  With all its ancient lustrous orbs undimmed:

Ranging the heavens forever, the Hyades,
   Like starry waterfowl in arrowy flight;
The Bull's bright horns, the Pleiads' golden bees;
   And there, most glorious of the hosts of night, —

Emerging from the crater's flying reek
   Back from that gorge of Chaos wildly blown,
One conquering knee above the red-lipped peak, —
   Orion with his sword and blazing zone!

CUBA

'T is the island of the orange, of the yucca and the palm,
Where the white-armed, laughing beaches lave in coves of foam-edged
      calm,
And the shy flamingo rises like a wingèd oriflamme.

'T is the home of endless summer, by cool trade-winds overblown;
'T is the Eden of the Ocean lying lovely and alone,
But trailed over by the serpent, and with sin and ruin sown.

'T is the island of the mango, the banana and the cane;
'T is the land of beauty blighted by the spoiler's cruel reign;
'T is the haunt of vultures flocking to the devastated plain.

'T is the isle of birds and blossoms, sea-girt realm of bloom and song;
Land of yet unconquered freemen who have striven and suffered long;
Land awaiting its redemption from four centuries of wrong!
   May, 1898.

A LITTLE CHILD

Unconscious childhood's tiny grasp
   Draws us from business, books, and art;
Mightier than all the world, the clasp
   Of one small hand upon the heart!

Of late, with lids that mimicked death,
   In fever flames our darling lay;
While we who watched her fluttering breath
   Could only wait, and hope, and pray.

Pale gliding shapes and whispered words
  Haunted the hushed and shadowy room,
Till the first twitter of the birds
  Awoke, and daybreak edged the gloom.

On vacant chairs and silent walls,
  Where lonely watchers of the night
Grow old, how strange, how spectral, falls
  The mockery of the morning light!

As in a trance of fear we moved:
  Peril to one we cannot save,
Peril and pain to one beloved,
  Make trembling cowards of the brave.

The dawn rose, pitilessly bright;
  The sunshine wore an alien hue;
There was not any more delight
  In song of bird or spark of dew.

How idle seemed the task that claimed
  A cold, accustomed service still!
Each worldly wish was quelled and shamed;
  Alike were tidings good and ill..

The golden fields and azure skies
  Were veiled in sorrowful eclipse,
Till beamed again those darkened eyes,
  Till smiled once more those childish lips.

Another night: all night she slept.
  She woke: O joy! was ever dawn
So heavenly sweet as that which swept
  With drizzling showers the trees and lawn!

The hillside frowned, by lowering brows
  Of gloomy thickets overhung;
But in the dripping chestnut boughs
  A cheerful robin perched and sung.

Dear omen of her blest release
   From pain and the Great Dread past by!
Peace filled our souls, the light of peace
   Was over all the earth and sky.

Oh, happiest day of all the year!
   Each moment had its joyous thrill:
Whatever came brought hope and cheer;
   Alike were tidings good and ill.

Now never more, O heart, be sad,
   When cloud and tempest drench the pane,
But keep the day with thoughts as glad
   As robins singing in the rain!

OWNERSHIP

ALONG the endlessly blockaded street
   Our car moved, with a hundred starts and stops.
Two children, kneeling on the cushioned seat,
   Looked out upon the gay, wide-windowed shops.

A boy and girl, both delicately fair:
   He, with bright ringlets rippling down his back;
She, with a wondrous fleece of flaxen hair;
   A sleek old nurse beside them, shining black.

They watched the shops, and played a pretty game
   Of owning things, with eager rivalry:
Whatever each was first to choose and name
   Was his or hers, as it might chance to be.

"That is my rocking-horse!" declared the boy.
   And she: "The whip is mine! the yellow reins!"
So they contended, claiming every toy,
   And boasting their imaginary gains.

"That is my lamp!" "I'll have the lamp-shade!" "No!
   The shade goes with the lamp!" "You selfish thing!

You took my horse's reins! You cheat!" And so
   They fell at last to downright quarrelling.

"Don't call me selfish!" "But you are!" "You dare" —
   She tweaked his curls, he doubled his small fists,
And in a moment they were pulling hair,
   And pounding like a pair of pugilists.

The unconcerned old negress all the while
   Showed her white teeth and laughed with cynic lip,
As I suppose dark angels sometimes smile
   At men's mad strife for transient ownership.

A BIRTHDAY WISH

TO A YOUNG VIOLINIST

WHEN you take up your violin, how soon
The lax, discordant strings are touched in tune
To the sweet sequence of enchanting sounds;
Heaven's golden ladder of melodious rounds!

So, on this birthday, take up life anew,
Dear girl! and with resolves so firm and true,
Master its chords, that all the year shall be
Attuned to soul-uplifting harmony!

OUT IN THE WORLD

THE inevitable day
   Of their parting sweetly rose:
Day of dread to them that stay,
   Day of hope to him who goes.

When the rumbling coach-and-four
   Round the shady porch appears,
They dismiss him from the door
   With their blessings and their tears.

Something bright his eyelash hides:
  On the coach's topmost seat
Bravely smiling forth he rides,
  In the Maytime fresh and sweet.

Joy with him has fled away;
  And a strange funereal gloom
Falls upon the vacant day,
  Fills his empty, silent room.

Youth is thoughtless, not unkind:
  Ah, dear boy, if he but knew
What deep solace they will find
  In his letters, all too few!

They await each hour that brings
  Tidings of his fair career,
With what anxious questionings,
  With what faith, and with what fear!

Faith, that ever in the sight
  Of protecting seraphim
He will follow truth and right,
  Letting fortune follow him.

Will he, in a world where wrong
  Sways the many, right the few,
Tread with instincts pure and strong,
  Shun the false and choose the true?

He the while, with hope elate,
  As if life were always May,
Journeys onward, to what fate
  He divines no more than they.

Is it health and happiness?
  Is it soul-consuming care?
Is it honor and success?
  Is it failure and despair?

Enterprise and wit and skill,
  Haughty, tender, brave and just,
Shall his future not fulfil
  His bright promise, their great trust?

Vain the question: well, may be,
  That beyond the azure brim
Of each day no man can see
  What the wide world holds for him.

Learn this truth and leave the rest:
  Each, whatever his estate,
In his own unconscious breast
  Bears the talisman of fate.

Who has strength, with self-control,
  Love and faith and rectitude,
Fortune fails not, for his soul
  Is the lodestar of all good.

IN A CORRIDOR

SCENE. — *The National Capitol*

WE two alone in the corridor,
  As I live! and meeting face to face!
  Will *he* turn back? or must *I* give place?
Or, here on the marble floor,
Shall we settle our little score?

Head high, with its long lank Indian hair,
  Nose straight before and eyes askew,
  He stalks right on, and sweeps me through
With a cold, unconscious stare,
As if I were made of air!

He had always just that insolent way,
  With his Southern blood and his cavalier scorn.
  Joe Belter, old boy, look here!   You 've sworn
To shoot me at sight, they say,
Here I am!   Now shoot away!

In self-defence you will fight?   That's cool,
  After all the terrible threats I 've heard.
  I thought Joe Belter a man of his word;
You were never a coward or fool
When we were together at school.

You sneer — Have I anything else to say?
  Well, yes!   'T was curious, but, somehow,
  I could n't but think, as you passed just now,
Of the look you gave old Pray —
Do you remember the day?

For the silly lampoon we had posted, I
  Had been just expelled.   Up towered a head:
  "If *he* goes, *I* go too!" you said;
And swept him, as you marched by,
With just that look of the eye.

We went, as free as the winds that blew,
  To the woods, and lived in our hut by the lake,
  Till you were recalled, and I for your sake.
Then, only to be with you,
Was the sweetest pleasure I knew!

You may scoff at it now; but I tell you, Joe,
  I could never forget some things that have been.
  How first did our wretched feud begin?
For, I vow, I hardly know,
It happened so long ago!

The worst that ever made fools contend:
  The long revenge of a love reversed!
  No foe so bitter as he who, first
Having loved too much, in the end
Has turned against his friend.

I ruined your railroad scheme?   And so
  You threatened my life!   Of course I knew
  I might have been Governor but for you;
And I merely returned the blow
Of a couple of years ago.

So the game goes on.   But in spite of all,
   There are things, as I said, that I can't forget;
   And when, after all these years, we met
The other night at the ball,
And throughout that glittering hall, —

In the great gay world assembled there, —
   No strangers passed each other by
   So strange to each other as you and I,
And I saw the gray in your hair,
And your look of age and care;

Then all of a sudden it all took flight, —
   The buzzing crowd, the wavering dance,
   The flowers, the jewels, the butterfly fans,
The beauty and blaze of light, —
And we were alone in the night!

Alone by the moonlit lake once more,
   Stretched side by side on the soft warm sand;
   The ripples ran glistening up the strand,
A wind from the woodland bore
Fresh odors along the shore.

A whippoorwill sang near by in the wood,
   And his voice, so lonely, so wild and shrill,
   With answering voices seemed to fill
The forest, — far-off, subdued,
In the heart of the solitude.

We talked of the years to come, and then
   Of our love over all, like the moon on the lake,
   Whose pathway of light no storm should break,
As we vowed again and again,
When we should be men among men.

We talked till our hearts were filled with tears.
   Then a cloud blew up, and the lake grew black —
   And a peal of the orchestra brass brought back
The intervening years,
And the blaze of the chandeliers:

The unclean hand in the dainty glove,
　　Hate in the heart and a smile on the face,
　　And heat, and glitter, and glare, in place
Of the perfect faith and love,
And the stars through the boughs above!

Then I said, "Whatever revenge he may take,
　　I will let it pass, and remember still
　　That moon and the voice of the whippoorwill,
And forgive him all for the sake
Of those lonely hours by the lake."

Resentment is swift, and pride is strong,
　　But the same old love lies under all.
　　Our leaves are fading, and soon must fall,
And I grieve to think how long
We have treasured wrath and wrong.

What, tears? you too! — I did not know
　　That your boy was dead! And you are alone?
　　Ah, life has sorrows enough of its own
Without the aid of a foe!
Give me your fist, old Joe!

THE WINNOWER

SOMEWHERE, nowhere, — in some vague realm or clime, —
　　I saw a mighty-statured Phantom stand;
His feet were on this threshing-floor of Time,
　　A fan was in his hand.

He smote with it, and all things streamed and whirled
　　Before the blast of its tempestuous beat;
The ancient institutions of the world
　　Became as chaff and wheat.

Fear pierced my soul, but soon a thrilling joy
　　Flowered from that root, and my numbed lips grew brave.
O dread Conserver that must yet destroy!
　　Destroyer that will save!

Strong Winnower of the things of death and life,
    I know you now, I cried. Smite with your fan!
Winnow the earth of enmity and strife!
    Winnow the heart of man!

A thousand sophistries perplex the ray
    Of the world's dawning freedom: Seraph, smite!
Winnow the clouds that dim the newborn day!
    Winnow the morning light!

There's naught so true in science and in creeds,
    And naught so good in governments and states,
But something truer evermore succeeds,
    And better still awaits.

With bristling hosts and battlemented walls
    Kings menace kings, and nations groan therefor:
Winnow the armaments and arsenals,
    The iron husks of war!

Toil without end, to fill a few white hands
    Of idle lords, gaunt millions still endure:
Winnow the unsunned hoards and unshared lands,
    Estranging rich and poor!

Riches bear rule till Labor turns in hate,
    And tyrant Wealth confronts the despot, Work:
Winnow the world's oppressors, small and great!
    Winnow the Tsar and Turk!

Pale anarchists conspire, mad to possess,
    Or to pull down, what sober thrift has built:
Winnow alike the haunts of Lawlessness,
    The gilded halls of Guilt!

Our politics are false and infidel,
    Our trusted chiefs bend to the baser cause:
Smite with your fan! O Winnower, winnow well
    The makers of our laws!

All barriers built by avarice, pride, and wrong,
　　Dividing men, — unbuild them with the breath
And buffet of your mighty fan, O strong
　　Angel of change and death!

Winnow this anxious life of pain and care!
　　But gently, winnow gently! Hear our cries!
To love at least be merciful! Oh, spare
　　Our tender human ties! —

But cries are vain; nor cries nor prayers avail
　　To hasten or delay the Winnower's hand;
Nothing so huge and firm, so fine or frail,
　　But it at last is fanned, —

Empires, beliefs, the things of art and fame,
　　The broad-based pyramids, the poet's page;
To his eternal patience 't is the same,
　　A moment or an age.

Before his fan the mountains form and flee,
　　Continents pass; and in its rhythmic beat
The flying stars and whirling nebulæ
　　Are but as chaff and wheat.

Does naught, of all that Time and Nature yield,
　　Does naught, at last, but thought and spirit remain?
Nature and Time the changeful harvest field,
　　Souls the immortal grain!

INDEX

INDEX OF TITLES

Titles in small capitals indicate the principal divisions of the work; those in italics, minor divisions.

INDEX OF FIRST LINES

The Romantic Tradition in American Literature

An Arno Press Collection

Alcott, A. Bronson, editor. **Conversations with Children on the Gospels.** Boston, 1836/1837. Two volumes in one.

Bartol, C[yrus] A. **Discourses on the Christian Spirit and Life.** 2nd edition. Boston, 1850.

Boker, George H[enry]. **Poems of the War.** Boston, 1864.

Brooks, Charles T. **Poems, Original and Translated.** Selected and edited by W. P. Andrews. Boston, 1885.

Brownell, Henry Howard. **War-Lyrics** and Other Poems. Boston, 1866.

Brownson, O[restes] A. **Essays and Reviews Chiefly on Theology, Politics, and Socialism.** New York, 1852.

Channing, [William] Ellery (The Younger). **Poems.** Boston, 1843.

Channing, [William] Ellery (The Younger). **Poems of Sixty-Five Years.** Edited by F. B. Sanborn. Philadelphia and Concord, 1902.

Chivers, Thomas Holley. **Eonchs of Ruby:** A Gift of Love. New York, 1851.

Chivers, Thomas Holley. **Virginalia;** or, Songs of My Summer Nights. (Reprinted from *Research Classics*, No. 2, 1942). Philadelphia, 1853.

Cooke, Philip Pendleton. **Froissart Ballads,** and Other Poems. Philadelphia, 1847.

Cranch, Christopher Pearse. **The Bird and the Bell,** with Other Poems. Boston, 1875.

[Dall], Caroline W. Healey, editor. **Margaret and Her Friends.** Boston, 1895.

[D'Arusmont], Frances Wright. **A Few Days in Athens.** Boston, 1850.

Everett, Edward. **Orations and Speeches,** on Various Occasions. Boston, 1836.

Holland, J[osiah] G[ilbert]. **The Marble Prophecy,** and Other Poems. New York, 1872.

Huntington, William Reed. **Sonnets and a Dream.** Jamaica, N. Y., 1899.

Jackson, Helen [Hunt]. **Poems.** Boston, 1892.

Miller, Joaquin (Cincinnatus Hiner Miller). **The Complete Poetical Works of Joaquin Miller.** San Francisco, 1897.

Parker, Theodore. **A Discourse of Matters Pertaining to Religion.** Boston, 1842.

Pinkney, Edward C. **Poems.** Baltimore, 1838.

Reed, Sampson. **Observations on the Growth of the Mind.** *Including,* **Genius** (Reprinted from *Aesthetic Papers,* Boston, 1849). 5th edition. Boston, 1859.

Sill, Edward Rowland. **The Poetical Works of Edward Rowland Sill.** Boston and New York, 1906.

Simms, William Gilmore. **Poems:** Descriptive, Dramatic, Legendary and Contemplative. New York, 1853. Two volumes in one.

Simms, William Gilmore, editor. **War Poetry of the South.** New York, 1866.

Stickney, Trumbull. **The Poems of Trumbull Stickney.** Boston and New York, 1905.

Timrod, Henry. **The Poems of Henry Timrod.** Edited by Paul H. Hayne. New York, 1873.

Trowbridge, John Townsend. **The Poetical Works of John Townsend Trowbridge.** Boston and New York, 1903.

Very, Jones. **Essays and Poems.** [Edited by R. W. Emerson]. Boston, 1839.

Very, Jones. **Poems and Essays.** Boston and New York, 1886.

White, Richard Grant, editor. **Poetry:** Lyrical, Narrative, and Satirical of the Civil War. New York, 1866.

Wilde, Richard Henry. **Hesperia:** A Poem. Edited by His Son (William Wilde). Boston, 1867.

Willis, Nathaniel Parker. **The Poems, Sacred, Passionate, and Humorous, of Nathaniel Parker Willis.** New York, 1868.